GENDER, ECONOMIES AND ENTITLEMENTS IN AFRICA

Elizabeth Annan-Yao
Zenebe N. Bashaw
Christine G. Ishengoma
Godisang Mookodi
Grace Ongile
Charmaine Pereira
Manthiba Phalane
Richard Ssewakiryanga
Sylvia Tamale
Chris Okechukwu Uroh

CODESRIA Gender Series 2

CODESRIA

COUNCIL FOR THE DEVELOPMENT OF
SOCIAL SCIENCE RESEARCH IN AFRICA

ISBN: 2-86978-139-3

Typeset by Djibril Fall

Cover image designed by Andre Nel, UNISA Press

Distributed in Africa by CODESRIA

Distributed elsewhere by
African Books Collective, Oxford, UK
Web site: www.africanbookscollective.com

CODESRIA would like to express its gratitude to the Swedish International
Development Cooperation Agency (SIDA/SAREC), the International Development
Research Centre (IDRC), Ford Foundation, MacArthur Foundation, Carnegie
Corporation, the Norwegian Ministry of Foreign Affairs, the Danish Agency for
International Development (DANIDA), the French Ministry of Cooperation, the United
Nations Development Programme (UNDP), the Netherlands Ministry of Foreign
Affairs, Rockefeller Foundation, FINIDA, NORAD, CIDA, IIEP/ADEA, OECD, IFS,
OXFAM America, UN/UNICEF and the Government of Senegal for supporting its
research, training and publication programmes

Contents

Contributors

Elizabeth Annan-Yao is currently Professor of Sociology at the University of Cocody-Abidjan, Deputy Director of Research at the Institute of Ethno-Sociology of the same university, and co-edits the *African Sociological Review*. She is specialized in Population and Development with emphasis on Migrations, Reproductive Health and Education.

Zenebe N. Bashaw is at the Institute of Development Research (IDR) in Addis Ababa Ethiopia.

Christine G. Ishengoma is currently a Lecturer in the Department of Agricultural Education and Extension in the Sokoine University of Agriculture, Tanzania. She is also the Director of a Tanzanian NGO, the Women Poverty alleviation. Her areas of interest for research are Gender Issues, Food Security, Community Nutrition, Processing and Adding value Crops, Poverty Reduction Issues, Economic and Marketing.

Godisang Mookodi is a Lecturer in the Department of Sociology in the University of Botswana. Her areas of research, teaching and publication include: gender relations and identities, development and economic change, domestic units (households and family structure). Her contribution to gender discourse in African Social Sciences, policy and practice is aimed at fostering a recognition of the important interface between macro-societal processes and individual agency within different societal contexts.

Grace Ongile holds a PhD Degree in Economics. Currently she is a Senior Programme Officer at the African Capacity Building Foundation (ACBF), Harare, Zimbabwe. She has been a coordinator of a research program, International Trade and Gender in East Africa.

Charmaine Pereira is an independent scholar based in Abuja, Nigeria. Her research interests include feminism and women's struggles, the state and civil society, and sexual harassment in Nigerian universities. She has taught at universities in Britain and Nigeria, and is currently the National Co-ordinator of the Network for Women's Studies in Nigeria.

Manthiba Phalane teaches at the University of Venda for Science and Technology, Northern Provence, South Africa.

Richard Ssewakiryanga currently works as a Government Consultant with the Government of Uganda. He is a social scientist with postgraduate training in gender studies and social anthropology from Makerere University in Uganda. He has also pursued a number of research fellowships at Northwestern University (USA), University of Sussex (UK), and Legon University (Ghana). His research work has focused mainly on gender and development issues, poverty and policy processes and cultural studies.

Sylvia Tamale is a feminist activist and senior lecturer at Makerere University's Law Faculty in Uganda. She has published widely on a variety of topics, including her groundbreaking book, *When Hens Begin to Crow: Gender and Parliamentary Politics in Uganda* (Westview Press, 1999).

Chris Okechukwu Uroh was a lecturer in the Department of Philosophy at the University of Ibadan, Nigeria. Before his sudden death in 2003, he published widely and edited a book with Samir Amin entitled *Africa and the Challenge of Development*.

Preface

Over the years since its founding in 1973, gender research and training activities have assumed a progressively important role and place in the work of the Council for the Development of Social Science Research in Africa (CODESRIA). Within the framework of the Council's strategic plans for the period 2002–2007, a decision was made to carry the existing institutional commitment one step further by launching a *CODESRIA Gender Series* that would also serve the goal of creatively extending the frontiers of the institution's publications programme. The hope was that through the *Series*, not only would the Council take a lead role in showcasing the best in African gender research but also provide a platform for the emergence of new talents to flower. The thematic variety and analytic quality of contemporary debates and research in Africa around gender issues is testimony to the mileage that has been successfully covered since the early days when African feminists struggled hard to make their voices heard. Today, few are the social scientists who are not aware of the basic issues in gender research and the community of those who apply the gender approach is growing. But as several of the participants at the CODESRIA-sponsored April 2002 Cairo international symposium on new directions in African gender research also observed, the challenges that remain in engendering the social sciences and the policy process are numerous, and addressing them requires the mustering of the capacities and convening powers of institutions like CODESRIA. The Council stands ready to play its part in meeting these challenges and the new *Gender Series* is designed as a modest contribution which in full bloom will capture current debates and deepen the African contribution to reflections on the theme of gender, feminism and society.

As indicated earlier, CODESRIA's commitment to the goal of engendering the social sciences and humanities in Africa dates back a long time. Some of the early research which the Council supported was instrumental in the development of new perspectives in African gender research while an investment has also been made in recent years in the provision of opportunities for training younger scholars in gender methodologies. In this connection, the CODESRIA Gender Institute has run every year since its inception in 1998, covering a variety of themes and gaining in respect and recognition among female and male scholars alike. The path-breaking 1992 international conference which the Council hosted on the theme of engendering the social sciences stimulated a series of initiatives and debates, and also generated some of CODESRIA's best-selling publications. The emergence of an active and networked community of gender researchers in Africa in which CODESRIA has played a frontline role underscores the point that a positive wind of change has blown across the social research community, and there is no turning back the clock of the struggle for gender equality. This notwithstanding, the term 'feminist' still generates fear among some male (and female) researchers, and as Fatou Sow observed in her keynote address at the CODESRIA 10th General Assembly, it is still not completely given that women can fully enjoy their rights without let or hindrance (*'les femmes ont le droit d'avoir les droits'*).

Through its gender-related scientific activities and the launching of its *Gender Series*, CODESRIA acknowledges the need to challenge the masculinities under-pinning the structures of repression that target women. It is to be hoped that the *Series* will be kept alive and nourished with insightful research and debates that challenge conventional wisdom, structures and ideologies that are narrowly in-formed by caricatures of gender realities. While much research has been done in this regard by feminist scholars elsewhere, in Africa, sustained research remains to be initiated in ways that are sensitive to the predicaments of women at differ-ent levels of society within and across national and regional boundaries. CODESRIA is committed to encouraging research along these lines. However, the rigour with which such research is conducted is of utmost importance, if gender studies and feminist scholarship are not to fall prey to the same myopia that accounts for the insensitivities of mainstream male-centred perspectives or the irrelevancies of western approaches masquerading as a universalism that takes no cognisance of the African historical context or which is ill-adapted to African concerns.

Most of the papers that have been selected to launch the *CODESRIA Gender Series* were initially presented at the April 2002 Cairo symposium which was or-ganised around five main objectives, namely, to: (a) provide a space/platform for an exchange of ideas as well as a sharing of visions on gender-related themes and issues from pan-African perspectives; (b) prioritise areas of gender research that have a potentiality to transform social relations; (c) encourage gender-based knowl-edge production which is informed by African realities and give a 'voice' to younger African scholars; (d) identify ways and means of improving advocacy and con-solidating linkages between knowledge production and activism for the advance-ment of women interests; and, (e) work towards a cross fertilisation of ideas, methodologies and epistemologies, as well as consider ideas for the creation of comparative research networks on issues affecting women and their livelihoods. The first four publications chosen to launch the *CODESRIA Gender Series* bear testimony to the diversity of interests in the field of gender research, diversities which are necessary for a healthy debate that advances knowledge. The Council hopes that readers will be sufficiently stimulated as to consider contributing manuscripts for consideration for publication in the *Series*.

Adebayo Olukoshi   Francis B. Nyamnjoh
Executive Secretary   Head of Publications

1

Analysis of Gender Relations in the Family, Formal Education and Health

Elizabeth Annan-Yao

Introduction

Gender is a socially constructed term depicting the system of relations between women and men. It designates behaviours, attitudes, roles, status and other processes that govern relationships among the sexes in a given socio-cultural, socio-economic and/or socio-political context. This means that *gender relations* vary not only from one community to another, but also according to different social classes in a given society.

Gender relations in patrilineal communities differ greatly from those in matrilineal communities. In the former, women tend to be totally submissive to men be they fathers, brothers, husbands or uncles. They also have limited decision-making powers and freedom of speech, especially in public. Consequently, women have no political attributions, cannot inherit property and easily yield to forced marriages. In counterpoint, although women are submissive to men in matrilineal communities, they have some decision-making powers and liberty of expression, and can generally choose their own husband. They can be Queen-Mothers in the political domain and can even inherit property from their maternal uncles and mothers.

Gender relations equally change according to one's social class. As a result, economically and/or politically empowered women, usually on top of the social ladder, play roles that make them less submissive to men. They can be directors of private firms, successful traders, occupy key governmental administrative positions, ministers, parliamentarians, mayors and so on. Nevertheless, since society usually considers these roles to be masculine, women in these positions experience difficulties in being accepted and have to struggle to maintain credibility.

Generally however, gender relations are always patriarchal in nature and therefore necessarily male dominated, particularly in Africa. So, whether in a matrilineal or patrilineal community, the upper or lower classes, men always insist on the subordinate status of women. This results in various manifestations of gender inequalities including gender stereotypes, biases, harmful practices and other forms of discrimination against women, with negative impacts on development. Consequently, promoting gender equality has become recognised as a necessary tool for development.

This chapter will present a situation analysis of gender relations in the family, formal education, and health with a view to identifying challenges that women and girls face in these institutions. It will then examine perspectives and directions in gender relations while proposing strategies to redress gender inequalities in the above mentioned social processes.

Situational Analysis of Gender Relations

The Family

A close examination of girls' and women's situation in the family reveals a lot of discrimination in this institution. The girl-child, in particular, experiences discrimination right from the womb. Often, women discovered by traditional practitioners to be pregnant with baby girls are subjected to certain behavioural and food taboos in the family (Yao 1998). In some traditional African societies, girls are denied even the simple right to existence in the minds of their fathers who are the family heads! In the highly Islamic and patriarchal communities of Niger, Burkina Faso, Cameroon and so on, son-preference is dominant and detrimental to girls in the family. When men are asked the number of children they have, they only count the sons, totally neglecting any daughters born to them.[1] To these men, girls are not important because they belong to the female gender. They are therefore undervalued in comparison with their brothers who are given the right to existence by their fathers. Women in these types of societies accept these attitudes thereby perpetuating gender discrimination.

As the main educators of children of both sexes in the traditional African families, women socialise boys and girls to accept conditions of exploitation of females by males through the values they transmit. Boys then grow up with a superiority complex while girls are made to accept and internalise an inferior position in society. Although this form of socialisation results in gender inequalities, it is considered by the family to be perfectly normal. Consequently, girls accept the dominating role attributed to men (and boys) by society, become submissive to men and aim to fulfil social roles as wives and mothers, sometimes at incredibly rather early ages. Their education is therefore centred on their social and biological reproductive roles.

As social reproducers, girls are automatically educated to become the future caretakers of the family. Consequently, they are taught to appropriate the multiple roles their mothers play in the family. These roles range from food production and preparation to the portage of water and fuel over long distances, as well as household chores like house-cleaning, laundry, taking care of household members and so on. This excessive workload which society imposes on girls, who work along with their mothers in the private sphere, deprives them of any potential they may have to participate in public life and explains their inhibition from playing leadership roles in society later on in life.

Instructions regarding girls' biological reproductive role focus on accepting marriage, pregnancy, birth and lactation as the very essence of female existence. When this role is successfully accomplished women and girls acquire prestige and high social status in their communities. These teachings serve to maintain the subordinate status of females. They also encourage polygyny, early marriage and early pregnancy: elements that accentuate gender inequalities and create reproductive health problems.

In some countries, particularly in closed, patrilineal communities, girls are considered transitory members of their families because the ultimate aim of their parents is to marry them off obligatorily into other families. Male family members exploit the transient nature of girls in their birth-homes to argue that they are not valuable to their birth families. This attitude hampers girls' right to protection by their families and makes them uncomfortable therein. It also creates a constraint to sound psychological development of girls and reinforces gender discrimination.

In many parts of Africa, women and girls have no inheritance rights. Even where legal provisions exist, they are not effectively applied. Consequently, married women for example, cannot inherit land or any property from their deceased husbands. Widows are thus left destitute or are passed on to their surviving brothers-in-law. This perpetuates the levirate tradition, a blatant type of gender discrimination imposed on vulnerable women with little choice or options.

From these foregoing, it is clear that, through the family, girls are socialised to perpetuate socially and culturally sanctioned gender rules made and imposed by men. Girls are born into discrimination and it follows them throughout their lives, depriving them of their basic rights as full citizens. Even their citizenship is questioned: if girls are not full members of their family how can they be full citizens of their country? Being usually cloistered in the private sphere of life, their self-development is severely hampered as they lack access to information on their different rights. They therefore grow into womanhood nourishing an inferiority complex and being unaware of what goes on in the public domain. In addition, they are prevented from participating fully in the developmental processes of their countries because they can hardly bring themselves out as main actors in the public sphere. Formal education could perhaps be a way out for girls to move from the private to the public sphere of life.

Formal Education

Through formal education, knowledge is transmitted while trained and skilled human resources produced. In the transmission of knowledge, schools teach individuals how to do things as well as the roles they must play in society and how to conform to social values. Formal educational systems are thus value-ridden and participate in shaping learners into female and male genders. In this way, schools can perpetuate gender discriminations embedded in the family and rooting from it.

In Africa, there are great disparities in male and female educational levels. A close examination of the Net Primary Enrolment Ratios (NPER) in various countries reveals blatant gender disparities as well as great differences between countries, as Table 1 clearly indicates.

Generally, girls lag far behind boys in primary school enrolment, with male-female differences ranging from 8 points in Mauritania to as much as 33 points in Benin. Interestingly, the NPER of countries in the Sahel contrast sharply with those of the other countries. In the former, girls' NPER is worse than elsewhere. For example, 19 percent enrolment for girls and 30 percent for boys in Niger; or 25 percent for girls and 38 percent for boys in Mali are far below Togo's 69 percent and 93 percent respectively for girls and boys. This is mainly due to negative cultural attitudes that limit females' access to education, in particular, the perception that women and girls' roles in society is confined to the home. Additionally, girls' schooling is seen to deprive mothers of valuable domestic help and labour making mothers reluctant to release their girls for school.

Even when girls manage to enrol initially, several other factors inhibit them from continuing in school or attaining the highest possible educational qualification. These include socio-cultural constraints like early marriages, teenage pregnancies and some initiation rites. Sometimes girls' education is not considered cost-effective in the belief that they are unintelligent. Furthermore because of poverty in families, more girls quit school to engage in economic activities to contribute to the survival of their families. Shrinking governments' resources due to the generalised economic crisis and accompanying Structural Adjustment Programmes that led to reduced government expenditure on education also account for low completion rates (World Bank 1999).

Consequently, only a small percentage of pupils enrolled in first year primary reach the fifth year primary as indicated by the following figures: Mali: 17 percent, Congo Democratic Republic: 25 percent, Guinea: 35 percent (UNICEF). Desegregated data show that the dropout rates are much higher for girls than for boys. In Central African Republic, for example, of all the children who completed their primary education in 1987, only 30 percent were girls (Annan-Yao,

Table 1: Net Primary Enrolment Rates in Selected Countries – 1996

Country Net Primary Enrolment Rates	Boys (%)	Girls (%)
Benin	80	47
Burkina Faso	37	24
Central Africa Republic (1990)	64	42
Chad	59	33
Congo Democratic Republic (1990)	61	48
Côte d'Ivoire	63	47
Gambia	72	57
Guinea	50	33
Mali	38	25
Mauritania	61	53
Niger	30	19
Senegal	65	55
Togo	93	69

Source: UNESCO, *Education for All: Status and Trends 2000*, Paris, p.69.

1998). In Senegal, girls' dropout rate in 1997/98 was 10.42 percent as against 3.19 percent for boys in grade 6. Gender disparities at this point are also flagrant. Table 2 below gives the percentages of the 1995 cohort of boys and girls reaching grade 5 in some selected countries.

Mali has the greatest gender gap (22 points) followed by Togo with 19 points (Table 2). The other countries have gender differences below 10 points. It can generally be stated that primary school completion rates are higher for boys than for girls in most African countries. As mentioned above, traditions and customs like early marriage, premature pregnancies, whether in or outside marriage, make girls drop out of the school system at this level. Pregnancies outside marriage often happen to girls in urban settings because of lack of adult guidance. They also come with disastrous consequences like induced abortions, maternal morbidity and maternal mortality.

Table 2: Percentage of 1995 Cohort Reaching Grade 5

Country	Boys (%)	Girls (%)
Benin	64	57
Chad	62	53
Côte d'Ivoire	77	71
Mali	92	70
Senegal	89	85
Togo	79	60

Source: UNESCO, 2000(a), p.69.

At Secondary School level, gender disparities in enrolment rates are also significant as Table 3 highlights.

Table 3: Girls Secondary School Enrolment Rates as Percentage of Boys' in 1995

Country	Percentage
Benin	41
Burkina Faso	50
Cameroon	69
Cape Verde	93
Central African Republic	35
Chad	23
Congo Democratic Republic	45
Côte d'Ivoire	52
Gambia	36
Ghana	64
Guinea	33
Guinea Bissau	44
Mali	55
Niger	56
Nigeria	85
Senegal	52
Togo	35

Source: UNICEF, *La Situation des Enfants dans le Monde 1998, New York*, Genève, p.128.

Figures displayed in table 3 are significantly high for Cape Verde and Nigeria where for every 100 boys enrolled in secondary school, respectively 93 and 85 girls also get enrolled. The rest of the countries have rates ranging from 69 percent in Cameroon to as low as 23 percent in Chad. Eight countries are still struggling with girls' secondary enrolment rates below the 50 percent mark. Whether high or low, these percentages clearly prove male domination in this area as well.

Similarly, Tertiary Level, enrolment rates for boys and girls demonstrate great gender disparities. According to UNESCO sources, in 1995, all the sub-Saharan African countries registered more male students than females in this sector. Table 4 gives a clearer picture of the tertiary situation in some selected countries.

Table 4: Tertiary Enrolment Ratios in Selected Countries in 1995 (%)

Country	Male (%)	Female (%)
Côte d'Ivoire	6.7	2.1
Togo	5.6	0.8
Benin	4.2	0.9
Burkina Faso	**1.6**	**0.5**

Source: UNESCO, Statistical Review of Education in the World, 1995.

All the figures indicate that girls' enrolment rates are far less than those of boys in the subregion and so, school dropout rates are much higher for girls than for boys. This poor status of girls' education has very serious implications for the development of the sub region and the future of the continent as a whole. Females constitute over 50 percent of Africa's human resources. If they are left behind in education then Africa will not be able to attain socio-economic development that ultimately leads to sustainable development.'

Currently, the benefits of girls' education to society are generally acknowledged. Female education lowers fertility; enables women to better execute programmes of development; gradually changes mentalities by promoting gender equity (Annan-Yao, 1998a: 32-33); contributes to the realisation of Human Rights as it incites the participation of women in society and encourages mothers to aspire for the best education for their children.

Health
African societies tend to differentiate between girls and boys in health matters because of socio-cultural beliefs and this adversely affects girls' health and nutritional status. This generally happens in patriarchal communities where

'son preference' is prevalent and where girls are not considered as members of their birth-family because they are usually married off and have to leave home.

In the Western and Central African regions for example, overall mortality rates for under fives are amongst the highest in the world: 184 percent compared to the global average of 88 percent (UNICEF). All indications are that girls' mortality rates are higher than those of boys. A study undertaken by the African Centre for Women in 1997 reveals that negative cultural attitudes towards girls result in less health care and nutrition for girls and explains why under five mortality rates are higher for girls (ECA 1997). Some of the countries highlighted by the study include Cameroon, Togo, and Mauritania where 'girls tend to be more undernourished than boys the same age and are taken for medical treatment and vaccinations less frequently – especially if there is a fee for the service' (ECA 1997: 44). Underdevelopment also contributes to the high mortality rates: low GNP's (average of 319 for the region); low literacy rates (average of 44 percent for females and 66 percent for males) mean that facilities and resources are suboptimal for the countries' child care, health and development needs.

Similarly, heavy workloads and poor feeding for girls increase their poor health and nutritional status. Rural girls are generally obligated to help their mothers in household chores of fetching wood and water, cooking, cleaning up, tending to family members and so on. This generally implies long and tedious working hours for girls. Moreover, in certain traditional societies (Baoule and Malinke of Côte d'Ivoire for example), girls eat with their mothers only after the men and boys have finished their meal, which means that they hardly get a balanced diet. Hard work and inappropriate diet impact on girls' health, placing them at a disadvantage compared to boys.

When girls become teenagers, they are also exposed to gender-specific reproductive health problems like early pregnancy due to early marriage and premature sexuality, unwanted pregnancy, abortion, sexual exploitation and commercial sex, and consequences of STD and HIV/ AIDS. Pregnancy, childbirth and abortion-related mortality and morbidity (fistulae, sterility) are high in the region, with adolescent girls accounting for a huge part of these figures. A joint UNECA/ UNICEF study (1994) shows that in Central African Republic, Congo, Guinea, Guinea-Bissau, Niger and Sierra Leone, over 20 percent of pregnancies are by girls under the age of 20. It is estimated that in sub-Saharan Africa, adolescent girls account for 25 percent of the current high maternal mortality rates (MMR). In 1990, this rate averaged 980 maternal deaths for 100,000 live births. Table 5 displays the overall MMR for most countries of West and Central Africa.

The figures in Table 5 are alarming because the region's maternal mortality rates (MMR) remain the highest in the world. The world's average MMR is 430; Latin America's is 190; Southern Asia's is 610 and the industrialised countries have only 13 maternal deaths for every 100,000 live births. In spite of government policies in Reproductive Health emphasising maternal morbidity reduction and family planning activities, these figures remain high because of the socio-cultural factors mentioned above as well as the inordinate power that men have over women in all fields, including sexuality.

Table 5: Maternal Mortality Rates for 100,000 Live Births – 1990

Country	Rates
Benin	990
Burkina Faso	930
Cameroon	550
Cape Verde	
Central African Republic	700
Chad	1500
Congo	890
Congo Democratic Republic	870
Côte d'Ivoire	810
Gabon	500
Gambia	1100
Ghana	740
Guinea	1600
Guinea Bissau	910
Guinea (Equatorial)	820
Liberia	560
Mali	1200
Mauritania	930
Niger	1200
Nigeria	1000
Senegal	1200
Sierra Leone	1800
Togo	640

Source: UNICEF, *La Situation des Enfants dans le Monde 1998,* New York, Genève, pp.128-131.

HIV prevalence in the big cities of Africa is estimated between 10 percent and 12 percent. Abidjan's 10–15 percent rate (Desgrees Du Lou 1998) is clearly an exception. Even there, females have higher infection rates than males. For example, while sero-prevalence among pregnant women in Dakar is only 1 percent, it is 15 percent in the city of Abidjan (SIDA 1999). In fact women and girls are particularly vulnerable to HIV/AIDS for biological reasons. However, girls are infected much earlier and have higher prevalence rates than boys in the 15 to 19 years' age group (ILO 1999). Because HIV is primarily transmitted heterosexually in Africa, this implies that girls are exposed to sexual intercourse much earlier than boys. This happens through early (and forced) marriages, and sexual intercourse (usually forced) with older men in exchange for gifts. Consequently, HIV transmission in Africa is driven by the unequal gender relationships that give men rights over women in reproductive health matters. Moreover, difficult socio-economic conditions which girls face in recent years tend to push them into prostitution for survival and expose them to HIV/AIDS more than their male counterparts.

Improved transport services and migrations (whether for employment or forced because of armed conflicts, natural disasters etc.) have exacerbated the spread of AIDS in the region, increasing the exposure of rural areas to the disease. Different government sources also inform about high concentration of AIDS around the borders between Côte d'Ivoire and Liberia, Guinea and Sierra Leone, Guinea and Liberia, which all constitute zones currently affected by war. In these cases, gender inequality and attendant social and economic biases against women heighten their vulnerability to HIV/AIDS.

In traditional societies, ancestral customs maintain practices that are considered harmful and illegal by modern standards. Reasons given for these customs range from preservation of girls' virginity (in order to honour their family and that of their husband) to prevention of immorality (which can happen through premature sexuality if girls are not married off early enough). All these constitute what has become known as harmful traditional practices and are now both a health and a human rights issue. Just as the Convention on the Rights of the Child (CRC) condemn them as torture and child abuse, the 46th World Health Assembly in 1992 adopted a resolution calling for the elimination of these practices. In this respect, Female Genital Mutilation (FGM), early marriage and forced feeding of girls will have to be treated in the light of their bad implications on girls' and women's health as well as the need for females to be protected against such practices.

There is a great deal of variations in these practices depending on the countries, ethnic groups, communities and religions involved. FGM for example, is practised in a great number of African countries though information on prevalence is not available for all States. According to World Health Organisation (WHO) sources, 2 million girls are exposed to sexual mutilation every year. From the point of view of traditionalists, girls are protected through these practices.

However, modern society views Female Genital Mutilation (FGM), early marriage (and early pregnancy which emanates from the former), forced feeding of girls to fatten them and other such activities as effective ways that men use to ensure control over girls' lives and their reproductive health. This modern view poses the problem of girls' rights to enjoy good health, physical integrity and protection from child abuse if they are too young to make any decisions themselves on their reproductive rights. Table 6 gives an overview of estimated FGM prevalence in selected Western and Central Africa States.

Table 6: FGM Prevalence in Selected Countries in 1992

Country	Prevalence (estimated) Rates (%)
Benin	50
Burkina Faso	70
Central African Republic	50
Chad	60
Côte d'Ivoire	60
Ghana	30
Guinea	50
Guinea Bissau	50
Liberia	60
Mali	75
Niger	20
Nigeria	50
Senegal	20
Sierra Leone	90
Togo	50

Source: Nahid Toubia, *Female Genital Mutilation: A Call for Global Action, Women Ink,* New York,1993 p.25.

The rates vary according to countries, with a high 90 percent prevalence for Sierra Leone and low 20 percent for Niger and Senegal. It should be emphasised that not all the ethnic groups assembled in a given country practise FGM and no particular religious community condones it as a religious requirement. FGM therefore stems from culture and not religion. For example, the predominant ethnic group of Niger, the Hausa, and the most important ethnic group of Senegal, the Wolof, both Moslems in majority, do not practise FGM. This explains why there are low rates of the phenomenon in both countries where only minority groups

(Bambara & Peuls in Senegal; Peuls in Niger) engage in FGM. In Sierra Leone, all ethnic groups practise FGM except the Christian Krios in the Western region and in the Capital. Similarly, in the Bendel State of Nigeria, FGM is common not only among all ethnic groups but also in all religious communities – Christians, Moslems, Animists.

Female genital mutilation has serious implications on girls' health. Depending on the degree of mutilation, girls suffer different degrees of damage on their reproductive organs. When consequences are not fatal, they leave girls with serious physical disorders or psychological traumas. Some physical consequences include urinary tract infections, painful intercourse, fistulae and complications in childbirth. Psychological effects include the lack of sexual desire and loss of self-confidence.

In most ethnic groups of Africa, virginity and fertility not only elevate a girl's social status as an individual, but also enhances the dignity of her family. Moreover, the bridal price or dowry paid to the girl's family constitutes an investment, which solders the relationship between the families of the bride and bridegroom. Consequently, girls are traditionally married early (and enter motherhood early) to ensure that their virginity is intact for their husband. Forced, early marriage is therefore very common in sub-Saharan Africa. In rural Niger for instance, 45 percent of girls get married before age 15. The rate is 19 percent for rural Senegal, 17 percent for rural Gambia and 10 percent for rural Burkina Faso. These figures are naturally lower in the cities – Dakar: 3 percent; Ouagadougou: 5 percent; Niamey: 12 percent and Bamako: 16 percent. It is worth noting that apart from Niamey, urban Niger has a high prevalence of early marriage: 25 percent (CERPOD, INSAH, CILSS 1996).

Early marriage (which is usually forced because the girls are too young to decide for themselves) becomes a health issue when (premature) pregnancy occurs soon after marriage. It is also not uncommon to find urban girls with premature, premarital pregnancies. Girls are not physically prepared for childbearing since their linear growth is not complete and the birth canal is not yet mature. They therefore face maternal and/or infant death, fistulae, hypertensive disorders and other severe health consequences.

Forced feeding is practised mainly in the ruling circles of the Moor society in Mauritania, in some communities of Niger (Arabs, Zarma) and in some ethnic groups of Northern Mali and Northern Burkina Faso. The custom consists of forcing girl children under 10 years old to absorb a lot of rich food, especially milk, to fatten them and get them ready for early marriage. They have to be beautified and also made to appear more mature than they really are, in order to be 'marriable'. Forced feeding has ill effects on girls' health because they create physiological disorders like liver sclerosis, hypertension and so on.

Additionally, nutritional taboos also discriminate against girls by dictating specific foods that may not be eaten by girls and pregnant mothers. Many of the tabooed foods are highly nutritious and their prohibition causes health problems to girls and women (anaemia and malnutrition). Good examples are seen in the sharing of fowl and game meat where men and boys get the nutritious and fleshy parts while girls and women only receive bony and lean parts.

FGM, early marriage and early pregnancy, forced feeding, nutritional taboos are all harmful practices against girls but because they are deeply rooted in mentalities of practitioners, combating them becomes a real challenge. Some practitioners, especially the women, realise how harmful these customs are to girls' health but because of fear of ostracism, they adhere to them and socialise the girls to accept them as the social norm. Eradication of these negative customs cannot be possible unless those fighting for change understand the reasons for these beliefs and practices so that they would be enabled to know where and how to start the communication activities destined for changing these negative mentalities and behaviours. A change of mentalities will eventually lead to the acceptance of legal remedies against these negative cultural traditions by their practitioners and thus promote gender equality for overall human development.

Perspectives/Directions in Gender Relations

In principle, most African countries fully recognise the fundamental Human and Civil Rights of Women and Girls in society. As members of the Organisation for African Unity (OAU), all States of the continent adhere to the Charter on the Rights and Welfare of the African Child (CRWAC). Most of the States have ratified the Convention on the Rights of the Child (CRC) and the Convention on the Elimination of All Forms of Discrimination Against Women (CEDAW).

The CRWAC, the CRC and the CEDAW respectively protect, and condemn discrimination against, children and women in all its forms. Article 3 of CEDAW for example, stipulates that: 'All appropriate measures shall be taken… towards the eradication of prejudice and the abolition of all other practices which are based on the idea of inferiority of women'. However negative cultural attitudes are so strong, in families, especially in the rural communities, that girls have very little or no social status at all. From this perspective, girls (and even women) are still not considered full human beings with inherent rights as the CRC and the CEDAW and other Human Rights Conventions stipulate. They are minors!

Directions in this domain will require a deep understanding of these negative customs in order to facilitate the construction of appropriate advocacy tools (key IEC messages through audio and visual means) to be used for transforming mentalities and rendering them open to legal remedies. This would be one of the best ways of making traditionalists accept girls and women as full members of society, which will enable them to better participate in the developmental process.

In formal education, legal measures like Education Laws, which render education compulsory and (in some countries like Gambia and Liberia) free for all, have been instituted by governments. Positive discrimination in favour of girls' enrolment, free distribution of textbooks to girls, readmission of teenage mothers into schools after delivery and creation of Special Units for Girls' Education have been set up by various governments. Despite these efforts, persistent erroneous beliefs and ideologies as well as financial problems constrain the realisation of girls' right to education. Future directions require urgent work to change the mentalities that harbour these negative ideologies, and advocate for governments to set aside special budgets for girls' education.

Girls' social vulnerability expose them to numerous violations of their rights to good health and physical integrity. FGM, early marriage, forced feeding of girls, nutritional taboos are flagrant violations of girls' rights. In recent years, African States have tried their best to implement CRC, CEDAW and others, while improving immunisation to improve children's health. Yet, these customs are still prevalent on the continent and not all children (especially girls) benefit from immunisation. This means that perspectives and future directions should systematically increase advocacy and sensitisation of men and women in order to permanently protect girls against these harmful traditional practices as well as immunise and improve health care provision to all children, including girls. In addition, implementation of the CRC, CEDAW and other treaties has to be combined with the popularisation of these documents so as to make them accessible to a wide public in rural as well as urban areas. A better understanding of these conventions will help modify mentalities to favour the inherent rights of girls.

Strategies to Improve Gender Inequalities

In the Family

- Most States in Africa adhere to CRC and CEDAW, which is a remarkable progress in favour of the female gender. However gaps observed here are that social policies do not buttress existing legislation and so there is an urgent need for governments to harmonise the CRC and the CEDAW to national laws in order to facilitate implementation.
- Governments should also make CRC and CEDAW more common by translating them into simple formats and into local languages for all to appropriate and see the importance of gender equality for society and development.
- There is a strong need to eradicate prevailing mental and social attitudes that are prejudicial to women and girls' rights. However, States cannot rely on legislation alone. Other mechanisms need to be in place to ensure promotion of gender equality. Legislation would have sent a formal message that traditions and customs contrary to the rights of women and girls would no longer be accepted. However, since mentalities and social attitudes cannot be changed by mere legislation, constant sensitisation of

communities (both male and female members) through advocacy, communication, information and education should be urgently installed.

In Formal Education

- There is an urgent need to press for free and compulsory universal basic education for all children but especially for girls who lag behind boys in this field, even if there is now a tendency towards closing the gender gap. Particular attention needs to be paid to the countries (as in the Sahel) where girls' enrolment rates are very low.
- Adult literacy rates should also be improved to encourage change of mentalities which will in turn favour the promotion of girls' education which is a key element for targeting gender equality.
- Measures for retaining girls in the educational system for as long as possible need to be taken to reduce the high attrition rates for girls. This would include promoting policies that will improve the quality of education, and make curricula, teaching materials, school environments and teachers gender-friendly. These strategies will make education relevant for girls.
- Reproductive Health problems also need to be addressed in a specific manner. By introducing Family Life Education into late Primary Schools, girls (and boys) will be informed of the dangers of premature sexuality and other things that interrupt girls' schooling and thus widen the gender gap between boys and girls.
- States should create Girls' Education Units in Ministries of Education and ensure that National Education Policies include sections specifically geared towards girls' education while aiming to close the gender gap.
- Laws that provide opportunities for girl-students who become pregnant to be able to continue with their education before and after childbirth should be enacted to promote gender equality.
- Innovative initiatives like income generating activities and non-formal education should be encouraged for female school dropouts and girls who have never been to school in order to empower them economically and make them less dependent on men.

In Health
- There is need to improve reproductive health services and include sensitisation and advocacy against harmful traditional practices in all health centres.
- Sensitisation of the population in health matters should specifically insist on female reproductive health issues and should be particularly geared towards the male populations who are the main decision-makers in this

area so as to make them more aware of the dangers that women and girls face in this sector.

- Finally, girls who have experienced FGM, early marriage and other gender-based traumatic experiences should be organised to talk about their physical trauma to their peers and discuss their psychological trauma in public in order to discourage practitioners and girls from consenting to such harmful practices that exacerbate gender inequalities.

Note

1 Data collected from fieldwork in these countries on a UNICEF mission, January–March 2000.

References

Annan-Yao, E., 1998a, *Women Education and Population Growth in Africa,* ESP 27, Imprimerie, Souvenir, Abidjan: ADB.

Annan-Yao, E., 1998b, *Déterminants anthropologiques des recours obstétricaux dans la Commune d'Abobo,* Min. de la Santé Publique, Coopération Française, Abidjan

CERPOD, INSAH, CILSS, 1996, *Santé de la reproduction au Sahel: Les jeunes en danger,* Bamako: CERPOD.

Chinapah, V. *et al,* 2000, *Avec l'Afrique pour l'Afrique: vers l'Education de Qualité Pour Tous,* Pretoria: HSRC, UNESCO, UNICEF.

Desgrees, Du Lou, A., 1998, 'Santé de la Reproduction et SIDA en Afrique Subsaharienne,' *Population,* vol. 4, pp. 701-730

ECA African Centre for Women, 1997, *Traditional and Cultural Practices Harmful to the Girl-Child,* Occasional Paper No. 1

FNUAP, 1994, *État de la population mondiale,* New York: FNUAP.

Gillette-Faye, I., 1999, *Etude de 4 plans nationaux concernant la santé et les droits fondamentaux des femmes en matière de sexualité et de reproduction, Spotlight,* No. 18, September, GAMS, Paris: ILO.

Mensch, B. *et al,* 1999, *The Uncharted Passage: Girls Adolescence in the Developing World,* New York: Population Council.

SIDA, 1999, 'Le Suicide Collectif', *L'Autre Afrique,* No. 98, 22-30 September.

The World Bank, 1999, 'Entering the 21st Century', *World Development Report 1999/2000,* New York: Oxford University Press.

Toubia, N., 1993, *Female Genital Mutilation: A call for Global Action,* New York: Women Ink.

UNECA, UNICEF, 1994, *Atlas of the African Child,* Addis Ababa.

UNESCO, 2000a, *Education for All: Status and Trends 2000,* EFA Forum Secretariat, Paris

UNESCO, 2000a, *Education for All 2000 Assessment: Executive Summaries,* Paris: EFA Forum Secretariat.

UNICEF, 1998, *La situation des enfants dans le monde,* New York & Genève: UNICEF.

UNICEF, 1999, *La situation des enfants dans le monde*, New York & Genève.

UNICEF, *Quel espoir y a- t- il pour les enfants de l'Afrique l'Ouest et du Centre*, Abidjan: UNICEF, BRAOC.

UNICEF, 1998, *Girls at Work*, New York: UNICEF.

UNICEF, 2000, *The State of the World's Children 2000*, New York & Geneva: UNICEF.

UNICEF, 1999, *Rights of Girls*, New York: UNICEF.

UNICEF, NIPILAR, 1999, *Situation Analysis of the Girl- Child in Southern Africa*, Pretoria: UNICEF.

United Nations, 1990, *World Declaration on the Survival, Protection, and Development of Children*, New York: United Nations.

2

Gender Trauma in Africa: Enhancing Women's Links to Resources

Sylvia Tamale

Introduction

I come to Cairo with a deep sense of déjà vu! Each time I open my eyes, switch on my radio or open a book, I get this strange sense that at one point in my life I have witnessed the scenes dancing before my eyes or rebounding off my ears. In this new world of reeling technological advancement and the information superhighway, I never cease to be amazed at the way the world is fed on facts that many of us have always known. Such information is couched and presented in ways that make it appear like a 'new revelation,' an eye-opener of sorts. One latest such exposé came out of Mexico during the United Nations Development Summit a few weeks ago [March 2002]. The developed countries 'discovered' that there is a linkage between global instability and global inequality! Surprise! Under the 'Monterrey Consensus', they went on to pledge (without any overt commitments) to lift hapless countries like ours out of poverty as a solution to put an end to terrorism.

A week before that, with tremendous pomp and grandeur, the World Bank released a new report entitled, *Engendering Development* (King & Mason 2002). Released on international women's day, the report basically informed the world that there is a correlation between gender equality and economic development. In other words, the wider the gender gaps in all spheres of society, the slower the pace that society strides towards economic growth. Surprise again! We were reminded for example, that improving rural women's access to productive resources including education, land, and fertilizers in Africa could increase agricultural productivity by as much as one-fifth.

Gender inequality has persisted despite all the scholarship that has highlighted the drawbacks associated with it. In circumstances of weak state structures, corrupt leadership and civil instability, African women realize that they need to be more resourceful in order to enhance their access to and control over resources. This is not to suggest that women in Africa have not been ingenious and practical. We all know that millions of citizens on this problem-ridden continent would not be alive today were it not for the ingenuity of the African mother, grandmother, wife or sister. The point is that African women are seeking to sharpen their ingenuity further, to hone and broaden their skills in order to tackle this problem effectively.

How do we move from the continental 'gender trauma' towards real equality? What are the challenges that we face in achieving this? How many times do we have to repeat and reiterate what has become common public knowledge? Do we need more research, more reports and even more summits to drive this basic point home? How do we make our obstinate, inflexible associates acknowledge these problems and act upon them? How do we concretely take action to deal with the inequality problems that all of us present here are so familiar with?

Numerous studies have identified lack of access to and the control over resources by African women as the single most important cause of gender inequality on the continent. The socio-economic and political implications have also been repeatedly highlighted. The contradictions that African women currently face in this era of globalisation and 'African Renaissance' have inevitably developed into a particular form of political and resourceful consciousness: the most important resource that they possess currently is their labour – labour that is exploited by the patriarchal state and its patriarchs.

The spirit of an 'African Renaissance' has brought forth several home-grown continental initiatives to shape the new beginning of a transformed Africa. Perhaps the most promising would have been the New Partnership for Africa's Development (NEPAD). I say, 'would have' because sadly and unfortunately the architects of the NEPAD blueprints have repeated the mistakes of old, providing us with a formula that reads something like: 'NEPAD by the men, of the men and for the men.' This type of NEPAD is doomed to end in stillbirth.[1] As the Africa Women's Forum (AWF 2002) observed in their conference held in Nigeria last February, there is a conceptual gender gap in NEPAD. It is quite obvious that gender issues in NEPAD are reflected as an afterthought and are generally relegated to only footnote status.

This chapter seeks to bring into clear focus the link between the 'resources problem' and the wider problematic of African domesticity. This important linkage is often glossed over or even ignored. The fact that women's lives are defined by the ideology of domesticity, that their unwaged productive and reproductive labour in the domestic arena is unacknowledged, unvalued and invisible in economics statistics, largely explains their resource-less status and points to some radical ways of tackling the problem.

Domesticity in Africa

Domesticity as an ideology is historically and culturally constructed and is closely linked to patriarchy, gender/power relations and the artificial private/public distinction (Hansen 1992). Patriarchy defines women in such a way that their full and wholesome existence depends on getting married, producing children and caring for their family.[2] In Africa, it does not matter whether a woman is a successful politician, possesses three Ph.Ds and runs the most successful business in town; if she has never married and/or is childless, she is perceived to be lacking in a fundamental way. Girl children are raised and socialised into this ideology and few ever question or challenge its basic tenets. Single, childless women carry a permanent stigma like a lodestone about their necks. They are viewed by society as half-baked, even half-human. Thus, the domestic roles of mother, wife and homemaker become the key constructions of women's identity in Africa.

While patriarchy defines women in terms of domesticity, it simultaneously draws an artificial line to separate the domestic (private) arena from the public one. The public sphere represents men and is the locus of socially valued activities such as politics and business, while the private is representative of domestic activities centred around the family. The former represents society, while the latter represents culture. Women are confined (read trapped) to the domestic arena – a space where men rule over them as heads of the family – while men spend most of their time in the public realm. The rationalization is that women's reproduction roles make them biologically and 'naturally' predisposed to rearing children and taking care of the domestic sphere. Biology, instead of gender,[3] is used to explain social differences between men and women. In other words, gender differences are reduced to and justified by biological differences. Because it is perceived as their 'natural' calling, women's work is performed altruistically. Men, who are the public-actors, are supposed to represent 'their women' (as fathers, husbands or brothers) in the public sphere. Thus women depend on 'their men' to access the public realm.

In Africa, the process of separating the public-private spheres preceded colonization but was precipitated, consolidated and reinforced by colonial policies and practices. Where there had been a blurred distinction between public and private life, colonial structures and policies focused on delineating a clear distinction guided by an ideology that perceived men as public actors and women as private performers.[4] Where domestic work had co-existed with commercial work in pre-colonial satellite households, a new form of domesticity, existing outside production, took over. Where land had been communally owned in pre-colonial societies, a tenure system that allowed for absolute and individual ownership in land took over. At the same time, politics and power were formalised and institutionalised with male public actors. The Western capitalist, political ideology (i.e. liberal democratic theory) that was imposed on the African people focused on the individual, submerging the African tradition that valued the collective. All these changes had a profound impact on African women's access to and control over resources.

Thus, womanhood became synonymous with domestic life – childbearing and rearing, cooking, subsistence farming, scrubbing, cleaning and other household chores became their inescapable destiny. These duties were and still are performed gratuitously, without formal recognition and remuneration. African women engage in the drudgery of domestic work for an average of seventeen hours a day. Domestic work is unacknowledged and invisible in traditional economics and GDP statistics, facts that attest to its denigration. The ideology of domesticity is so efficient that the majority of African women have internalised it and it informs their self-identity.

Domesticity as a Hindrance

Domesticity is deployed in the African context to systematically disenfranchise women from accessing and controlling resources. Indeed, the gendered public/private spaces carved out of and reaffirmed by the ideology of domesticity have overarching consequences for men and women in Africa. Domesticity confines African women, both conceptually and practically, in ways that limit their access to resources. Here, I analyse three important ways that domesticity restricts women's access to and control over resources.

Space as a resource

The gendered male 'public' space is the key to power, privilege, opportunities and wealth. The ideological boundary between the private and the public spaces was designed to limit and control women's access to the resources associated with the public space. It is important to note that while women are generally restricted to the marginal domestic 'private' space, men not only have free and easy access, but they are also the bosses in this space. Women's access to the public space, on the other hand, is extremely limited and controlled by men.

Patriarchy uses several tools, including culture, the law and religion, to safeguard the public sphere as a domain of male hegemony. It will resist any attempts by women to make the transition to the public sphere. Setting male values and interests as the norm in the public sphere easily achieves this purpose. Hence any woman who wishes to transcend into this sphere is forced to meet the male/masculine standards required in the public world (e.g., by employers, voters, etc.). Masculine standards operate as a delicate 'glass ceiling' that stops many women from entering the public world. In that world the female becomes the 'other' who is constantly confronted with obstacles that impede her access to and control of other resources.

Because of the marginalized nature of the physical and metaphorical space that women occupy, their legal and social status is subordinated to that of men.

Their mobility and erudition is significantly curtailed and their potential considerably limited. Where roles are divided into breadwinner and homemaker, the law decrees that the breadwinner is owner of resources. He can decide how these are to be allocated. For instance, it is the husband that has control over the proceeds derived from selling off the surplus produce grown from the sweating brow of the wife. He has automatic access to the outside world, not only through his employment but also through his ability to spend what he likes. She, by definition, has none of these things and is further confined by her prior responsibility for household tasks and childcare. In practice, African women's legal status, social standing, political participation, and national membership are largely appended to that of their male relatives.

In effect, African women are relegated to second-class citizenship. Domesticating women subordinates their citizenship, as women are less likely to participate in those activities that are associated with citizenship (e.g., participating in legislation, decision-making, voting, paying taxes, etc.). Society, which perceives them as wives and mothers, persistently refuses to register them in a non-domestic space. Moreover, the labour that they perform in the domestic arena (e.g., mothering) is not inscribed into the construction of citizenship. Thus, alienation, frustration, hostility and hopelessness characterize women's experience of citizenship – so much so that it becomes meaningless. The exclusion of the majority of women from effective control over and access to resources means that as yet Africa has not achieved full citizenship for all. In sum, the concept of separate spheres renders citizenship in Africa to be a gendered citizenship (Mcewan 2001; Gouws 1999; Werbner 1999; Gaizanuwa 1993; Lister 1997; Phillips 2000).

Political participation is an essential component of accessing, allocating and controlling resources. This points to two bottlenecks for African women. First, because women are generally excluded from what is conventionally regarded as politics, they miss out on this vital resource. Secondly, because what women do in the domestic domain is not regarded as politics, their 'participation' is outside the reach of vital resources. However, it is not enough to increase women's participation in politics without democratising the 'public' spaces where such politics is 'done.'

Patriarchal politics and the law dictate a policy of non-interference with the private sphere. Issues of the home and family are considered private to be dealt with confidentially. Most of the traditional wisdom in Africa teaches us that home affairs are not to be talked about in the public square. The law, for example, is dichotomised into public and private law. To date, in many countries across Africa, discrimination on the basis of sex in 'private laws' (e.g., marriage, divorce, inheritance and custody) is sanctioned by national constitutions.

Recently, the vice-president of Uganda publicly declared that the reason she separated from her husband was because he subjected her to physical violence.

The retort of many Ugandans – men and women – has been to say that such issues do not belong in the public arena (*'Eby'omunjju tebitotorwa'* meaning: 'Home issues are strictly classified'). However, a close analysis of domestic violence reveals that in fact by shielding the private sphere from state interference, patriarchy lends men considerable liberty to dominate women. Furthermore, studies have revealed the adverse effects that domestic violence has on national economies. In sum, the distinction between the public and the private serves the twin effects of keeping women in a relatively deficient space and ensuring that women lack both the capacity and the means to access and control material resources. I now turn to a more detailed discussion of how the latter aim is achieved.

The practical limits of domesticity

During the past four decades of post-colonial Africa, a small but significant percentage of women have managed to break through the glass ceiling that separates the private and public spheres. This has been possible partly because of women's own struggles against all odds and partly because of some deliberate policies (e.g., affirmative action) on the part of some 'benevolent dictators' to increase women's representation in the public sector. However, such women represent only a small drop in the calabash and are yet to make a significant impact on the 'gender trauma' barometer of African societies (Goetz & Hassim 2000).

A key element of domesticity is that it protects men's privileged access to resources. On the one hand, the ideology of domesticity in Africa marks the maternalization (and sexualization) of women's bodies. By so doing, it effectively stifles their potentialities, signifies their social isolation and increases their vulnerability to all forms of abuse. On the other hand, the dualism between private/ public life constructs social structures in a way that normalises gender inequality. Male domination as the status quo is constantly defended and protected.

So, how does African women's occupancy of domestic space inhibit their access to and control of material resources? It is important for us to understand the huge contradiction posed by African women's domesticity, especially as it relates to gender. Whereas women are always equated with the domestic or private sphere, they nevertheless constitute the most regulated (and thus non-private) social group on the continent. This point can be illustrated by discussing the primary resource and means of production in Africa – land.

In most of Africa, land ownership is the gateway to markets and other resources. The division of power between men and women is reflected in the unequal distribution of land. African states deliberately pursue policies that deny women ownership of land. An example from Uganda will adequately illustrate my point. While Ugandan women are responsible for 60 percent of cash crop production and 80 percent of the production of food crops, only 7 percent of registered landowners are women. This means that Ugandan women till and toil on land that they neither own nor control. Uganda underwent a land reform exercise in the late 1990s. Women saw this as a unique opportunity to address the problem of women's landlessness. Through aggressive campaigning and intensive lobbying, a coalition of women's rights groups succeeded in inserting an amendment to the 1998 Land bill that guaranteed spousal co-ownership of the matrimonial home. However, through political machination, the said amendment was missing from the final version of the Act! To date Ugandan women are fighting for the reinstatement of what has come to be known as the 'lost clause.'

The leadership in most African states is extremely paternalistic towards women and actively works to maintain the status quo of land ownership on the continent. Women from all corners of Africa have requested for joint ownership of land between spouses but the leadership has largely spat on such demands. President Mugabe is on record for advising Zimbabwean women in 1998 that they should not get married if they want to own land! But Zimbabwean women were thrown into total confusion when in February 1999 the Supreme Court emphatically reminded them that even unmarried women are more likely to be property than to own it. In the infamous case of *Magaya v. Magaya*[5] the court denied 58-year old Venia Magaya her inheritance right, holding that the 'nature of African society' dictates that women are not equal to men, especially in family relationships (ZLR 100 1999; WSLA 2001). It awarded the father's estate to her half-brother, making reference to African cultural norms, which say that the head of the family is a patriarch, or a senior man, who exercises control over the property and lives of women and juniors. The 5-0 ruling equated the status of a woman to that of a 'junior male' or a minor. On International Women's Day celebrations of 2000, President Museveni (2000) also warned Ugandan women to desist from 'commercialising marriage.' He designated himself the driver of the emancipation vehicle and implored women to slow down in their demands: 'Since I am the driver of the vehicle listen very carefully to my advice. Don't make the vehicle collide because of high speed.'

However, in this era of globalisation and neoliberal economic reforms, land is steadily losing its importance as a resource in some parts of Africa. Moreover, ownership of land for African women does not always translate into empowerment or real control of such land.[6] For instance, there are certain traditional practices among many African communities that limit women's working with heavy farm implements or where it is taboo for women to plant or harvest crops (because of the belief that it will adversely affect yields). In such cases female landowners have to rely on male labour, which compromises their control over this particular resource. Even here, Africa is replete with stories of wives who have been chased out of their matrimonial homes – homes they have helped build and/or improve; of mothers that have been thrown out of their homes by unscrupulous sons; of sisters that have been denied the right to inherit land by male relatives; of women who have been squeezed onto ever smaller and increasingly more unproductive plots of land.

Nevertheless, domesticity remains the norm for the majority of African women. Even where a handful of them manage to break the barriers and enter the public world of business and politics, their association with domesticity compromises their work. Because they are forced to work double-shifts (in and out of the home), such women have inevitably found that their domestic and reproductive functions have rendered them partial or imperfect actors in their public work. Thus, the ideological prescription that imposes domesticity on African women limits their control over resources, while engendering a political consciousness to their plight.

Gender and resources in Africa's adjusting economies

A common feature in all adjusting economies of Africa is the vigorous implementation of various poverty-reducing programmes. However, such programmes are often conceived in a top-down fashion without any input from the poor populations. Despite the fact that women experience poverty in higher numbers and in more debilitating ways than men, such programmes ignore important gender issues and fail to link them to national poverty. Often they only succeed in recreating domesticity by increasing rather than lessening women's work burden.

A good example of such a programme was the Heifer project introduced in Uganda in the 1980s by the US-based Heifer Project International (HPI). The main objective was to empower women economically. Women would be given a 'living loan' of an exotic cow. Each beneficiary was required to 'pass on the gift' – the first female offspring and animal care knowledge – to another needy family. In this way, each beneficiary becomes a donor and the benefits of the HPI project are replicated and sustained. Women that benefited from the project practised the 'zero-grazing' method.[7] It was not long before they discovered that the exercise was too labour intensive. Not only did the animals demand a lot in terms of their feeding habits, but they also required expensive veterinary care. Women found that by the time they were through with cutting grass, cleaning the cow's shed and tending to its other needs, half the morning had gone. In other words, the exercise simply added to her already backbreaking workload in the home and it was simply not sustainable. Many poor rural-based women were forced to abandon the project.

Another problem with poverty alleviation programmes is that they rarely reach women. This is because most of these programmes target 'the household' often ignoring the gender inequalities that exist within the household. Women, who neither have access to productive resources nor control over the outcomes, are indirectly written out of such programmes. Moreover, African women have borne the worst effects of structural adjustment economic programmes and emerged as the social 'shock absorbers' to deal with its worst consequences. Most significantly, more and more women have been forced to venture beyond the domestic space by engaging in 'informal' trade or small-scale urban entrepreneurship. This of course has increased their workload as they are forced to work double-shifts – inside and outside the home. This leaves women with virtually no time for lei-sure. Leisure and time too are resources. But even where women have managed to transcend into public spaces, patriarchal authority in the domestic arena has not lost its grip. In many cases, men still take control of women's finances and have the final say on how they are to be used.

Africa's integration into the globalised economy means that the continent has become party to many international trade agreements some of which are detri-mental to women's links to resources. Most prominent among these is the Trade-Related Intellectual Property Rights (TRIPS) Agreement of the Uruguay Round of the General Agreement on Tariffs and Trade (GATT). As the primary farm-ers and caretakers of the young and sick, African women are highly knowledge-able in seed preservation, herbal medicines and other ecology-related resources. By the stroke of the pen, TRIPS allowed for the patenting of such knowledge whereby African people would find themselves in the position of paying royalties to powerful multinational corporations say, for saving seeds of their crop yields or for administering herbal treatments based on indigenous knowledge that has been passed down for generations! The resource in African women's individual and collective intellectual property is not protected by TRIPS and is the subject of gross abuse and exploitation by foreign multi-national corporations.

Forging Ahead

In as far as 'domesticity' is inhibitive and perpetuates patriarchy, some feminists have rejected the terminology and replaced it with concepts that are more em-powering to women. Diane Elson (1992, 1997), for example, in attempting to capture the role that unpaid domestic labour plays in sustaining the economies of Africa, suggests use of the term 'care economy'. Such a concept not only recognizes the economic value in the work of care giving, but it also shifts such work from the deficient space of the domestic arena.

Public space is a crucial resource for African women – a social group that makes up 52 percent of the continental population and represent 70 percent of the agro-processing sector, and yet remain largely landless or own very small and fragmented holdings. They lack the power to decide on the use of the land or the means to improve its productivity. The gender-blindness in agricultural policies across Africa need to be seriously addressed with the view to promoting women's rights and lessening their domestic burden (Kasente, Lockwood, Vivian & White-head). The doors to the public space need to be flung open for African women to access freely and share in policy- and decision-making. Africa cannot afford to ignore women if it is to achieve democracy and sustainable development. The illogical artificial line that separates the public realm from the private sphere needs to be blurred with men and women sharing in the tasks performed. Paradoxically, hope for the African woman lies in the present unstable character of the African gender regime.

Enlarged women's spaces

Enlarging the domain that African women occupy would entail a total redefinition of womanhood and femininity in our societies. It would also require a redefinition of the concept of domesticity itself. As we speak now, the ideology of domesticity is undergoing some form of metamorphosis in the face of larger forces such as the HIV/AIDS scourge, the structural adjustment of African economies with its related entry of women into the economic sector (through micro-entrepreneurship) and, of course, the pressure from women's movements across the continent.

The reality of enlarged women's spaces is illustrated by the growing number of women across Africa that literally travel to the market place everyday with babies strapped to their backs. Charcoal stoves are permanently stationed at the market where women prepare their meals. For such women, the dichotomy between the 'public' and 'private' spheres is deconstructed. By shifting the ideological domestic space to the market public place, they are rejecting the artificial separation. These changes have thrown African social and gender systems into unprecedented flux. It has begun to upset the very meaning of domesticity and the *raison d'etre* of African women's identity. It is a paradox indeed that women's consciousness and spaces have enlarged through their added burdens and difficulties. Thus necessity, for African women, has truly been the mother of intervention.

To be sure, the current backlash against the women's rights movements on the continent has doubtlessly been unleashed by the fact that the position of women in the African family and society is no longer a given but an open-ended question at best, and at worst, a big threat to patriarchy. Yet, as noted earlier, women's performance in their enlarged spaces is still rendered invisible by their domestic and reproductive roles. Domesticity still ensnares women generally and continues to inhibit their control over and access to resources. Therefore, a lot more has to be done to completely change African women's station in life. For instance, women's domestic burden has to be eased somewhat. One important way of achieving this is through men taking a larger share of the burden.

Men sharing domestic work

Every programme that seeks to transform African economies must simultaneously seek to transform African masculinity, femininity and gender relations. Domestic work should be reconstructed into a valued occupation and calculated in official economics statistics. We need to enact laws and create initiatives that would make domesticity a desirable goal for African men too. Paternity leave, for example, would encourage fathers to actively participate in childcare; encouraging boys to engage in household chores and study domestic science would ease young men into domestic responsibilities. State incentives such as tax relief for fathers who share in housework may also work.

Most importantly, however, the ideological pressure that discourages African men from involving themselves in housework, childcare and care giving generally (through culture, the media, religion, education, etc.) must be checked. Transforming the masculine institutional culture and existing psychosocial attitudes towards a gendered domesticity would best be achieved by according domestic work a true valuation. Sharing domestic tasks between African women and men would ultimately tilt the scales to a more balanced workload, liberating women to contribute more meaningfully to sustainable development. It would represent an important watershed in beginning to address gender inequality in our societies. New emancipatory masculine identities would also go a long way in checking the heinous crime of domestic violence.

Reconceptualizing African citizenship

In all African countries citizenship is construed as a formal legal status, neglecting the practical notions of the concept. In fact, citizenship is currently confined to the male 'public' spaces of formal power structures and is largely absent from the female 'private' sphere. As I have demonstrated in this paper, structural, economic and social hurdles stand in the way of the majority of African women's enjoyment of full citizenship. All the hurdles reflect women's resource-less status. Thus, women's full citizenship depends on their accessing and controlling resources on equal terms with their male counterparts. Women's citizenship rights are further compromised by the absence or underdevelopment of democratic institutions in our countries.

Hence there is an urgent need to reformulate the notion of citizenship with the aim of making it less exclusive and much more inclusive for women as a social group. This would entail a re-conceptualization of social organization. Most importantly, we need to reject the artificial separation between the gendered public/private spheres. We should move away from the liberal democracy definition and borrow a leaf from legacies of African systems in re-formulating citizenship. For example, taking into account human survival and African philosophies (e.g., communitarianism).

Conclusion

Resources for African women constitute a complex and broad concept going beyond a laundry list of non-empowering assets. More important are the institutional and ideological factors that inhibit women's access to and control over resources. For any talk of a renaissance to hold substance in Africa, we must seriously address issues of gender inequalities. This means that African leaders and populations at large must be prepared for changes of revolutionary proportions. It is very sad indeed that we have to speak of 'a revolution' in reference to granting the continental majority their full dignity and rights. However, it is quite clear that without liberating the womenfolk, any attempts to rebuild Africa will be a truncated exercise in futility. In short, there is no short cut to Africa's liberation other than through women's empowerment.

Throughout the chapter I have deliberately used the term 'African women.' This is not because I am unaware of African women's heterogeneity and the significance such differences hold. I know that because of the rich and diverse socio-cultural and political differences across African societies, the statuses of women differ based on class, race, ethnicity, religion, age, sexual orientation and so forth. My reference to the collective of African women in relation to resource accessibility and control stem from two important factors. First, the glaring statistics that show that the overwhelming number of resource-less people on the continent are women—so much so that one loses track of the very few who actually have control over and access to resources. Secondly, and more important, is that regardless of the differences that may exist between and within African women, all are affected by and are vulnerable to the conceptual and functional space that they occupy in the domestic sphere. Moreover, no African woman can shield herself from the broad negative and gendered legacies left behind by forces such as colonialism, imperialism and globalisation. Thus, the term is used *politically* to call attention to the common oppression that African women endure by virtue of their simple membership to the social group called 'women'.

Ladies and Gentlemen, as you have all noted by now, there is nothing I have said in this chapter that has not been said before. Déjà vu is our collective affliction! It is TIME FOR ACTION NOW!

Notes

1   Another characteristic of NEPAD that reflects its snubbing of history is its strong neoliberal underpinnings which have in the last three decades spelled disaster and disempowerment for the majority of Africans.

2   In Luganda we have several proverbs that mirror domesticity. For example: '*Ekitibwa ky'omukyala ekisoka, bufumbo,*' meaning: 'Woman's principal dignity is derived from marriage'; '*Bulikugwa, obukyala si bumbejja,*' meaning: 'A woman loses her dignity when her husband dies or when she falls out of his favour.'

3   Gender as used here connotes the social and cultural meanings that are attached to the sex categories of male and female.

4   Such colonial structures were seen in the law and religion that were introduced backed by sound policies such as those in the educational sector.

5   See *Venia MAGAYA V. Nakayi Shonhiwa MAGAYA* 1999 (1) ZLR 100 (S).
    Venia Magaya had been married but was divorced and had returned to her
    parents' home with whom she had lived for over twenty years. For a detailed
    analysis of this case, see Women and Law in Southern Africa (WLSA) Re-
    search and Educational Trust, *Venia Magaya's Sacrifice: A Case of Custom Gone
    Awry*, Harare: WLSA (2001).

6   The concept of 'empowerment' as used in this paper is not in the restrictive
    notion reflected in the *power-over* conceptualisation. Rather, it is conceived as
    power-to (power which is creative and enabling), *power-with* (involving a sense
    of collective organizing and unity) and *power-within* (to do with self-respect
    and self-acceptance). Adopted from the *Oxfam Gender Training Manual*, Oxfam
    (UK) (1994).

7   The innovation of 'zero-grazing' requires that animals do not roam freely.
    They are kept in a shed or stall and the family brings fodder and water to
    them.

References

African Women's Forum (AWF), 2002, Preliminary Report of the Regional
    Conference on African Women and the New Partnership for Africa's
    Development (NEPAD), International Conference Hall, Africa Leadership
    Forum, Ota, Nigeria, February 3–5.

Elson, D., 1997, 'Gender-Neutral, Gender-Blind, or Gender-Sensitive Budgets?:
    Changing the conceptual framework to include women's empowerment and
    the economy of care,' *Preparatory Country Mission to Integrate Gender into National
    Budgetary Policies and Procedures*, London: Commonwealth Secretariat.

Elson, D., 1992 'From survival strategies to transformation strategies: Women's
    needs and structural adjustment,' In Benería, L. & Feldman, S., eds., *Unequal
    Burden: Economic Crisis, Persistent Poverty and Women's Work*, Boulder: Westview
    Press, pp. 26–48.

Gaidzanwa, R., 1993, 'Citizenship, Nationality, Gender, and Class in South Africa,'
    Alternatives vol. 18, No. 1, Winter

Goetz, A. & Hassim, S., 2000, *In and Against the Party: Women's Representation and
    Constituency-Building in Uganda and South Africa*, Geneva: United Nations Research
    Institute for Social Development (UNRISD).

Gouws, A., 1999, 'Beyond Equality and Difference: The Politics of Women's
    Citizenship,' *Agenda* No. 40.

Hansen, K. ed., 1992, *African Encounters with Domesticity*, New Brunswick, NJ: Rutgers
    University Press.

Kasente, D, Lockwood, M, Vivian, J. & Whitehead, A. (nd), 'Gender and the
    Expansion of Non-traditional Agricultural Exports in Uganda,' *UNRISD
    Occasional Paper*, http://www.unrisd.org/engindex/media/press/opb12.htm

King, E. & Mason, A., 2002, *EnGendering Development— Through Gender Equality in Rights, Resources and Voice*, World Bank <http://www.worldbank.org/developmentnews/stories/html/030801a.htm> (Accessed March 7, 2002).

Lister, R., 1997, *Citizenship: feminist perspectives*, London: Macmillan.

Mcewan, C., 2001, 'Gender and citizenship: learning from South Africa' *Agenda* No. 47.

Museveni, Y., 2000, 'Museveni Advises Women on Property,' *New Vision* March 9, p. 3.

OXFAM, 1994, *Oxfam Gender Training Manual*, Oxfam, UK.

Phillips, A., 2000, 'Second Class Citizenship', In Pearce, N & Hallgarten, J., eds., *Tomorrow's Citizens*, London: IPPR.

Werbner, P., 1999, 'Political Motherhood and the Feminisation of Citizenship: Women's Activisms and the Transformation of the Public Sphere,' In Yuval-Davis, N & Werbner, P., eds., *Women, Citizenship and Difference*, London & New York: Zed Books.

Women and Law in Southern Africa (WLSA) Research and Educational Trust, 2001, *Venia Magaya's Sacrifice: A Case of Custom Gone Awry*, Harare: WLSA.

Zimbabwe Law Reports (ZLR), 1999, *Venia MAGAYA V. Nakayi Shonhiwa MAGAYA* 100, ZLR.

3

Gender and Resources:
Some Macro and Micro Level Considerations

Godisang Mookodi

Introduction

In discussing gender manifestations of access and control of resources in Africa, we define resources as assets that may be harnessed productively to provide for human basic needs, including land, capital and labour. The distribution of resources depends to a large extent on power – the ability to own and control the processes that are key to providing, and/or denying access. Gender roles and status have been recognised as major determinants of access to resources and strategies for promoting gender equality have been extensively discussed by African social scientists and gender scholars. In particular, recommendations for advancing the economic, social and political status of women have accompanied these studies.

Three major movements have resulted from these recommendations: women in development (WID), gender and development (GAD) and gender mainstreaming. In the following sections, we discuss the historical development of these paradigms, their implications for gender equity and various challenges to their implementation. We also assess the paradigms based on a qualitative study of household organisation and economic relations in Botswana.

WID, GAD and Gender Mainstreaming

In the late 1970s and 1980s, under the auspices of the Women in Development (WID) paradigm, many advocated for the 'integration of women in development'. This approach arose out of concern by scholars and advocates that women, particularly in Third World countries, were being left out of the economic development processes. Ester Boserup's study (1970) which analysed women's labour force participation in Africa, Asia and Latin America is often noted as a major basis for the WID approach. Based on this and other empirical studies, mostly by international development agencies (United Nations and others), the WID concept was effectively globalised during the first United Nations Decade for Women (1975–1985). The major elements of the WID recommendations for women's integration in development include:

- Making women more 'visible' within national statistics, particularly as they relate to their labour force participation (in 'formal' employment as well as 'informal' sector activities);
- Effectively reducing the productivity gap between women and men through education and training;
- Providing policy measures for greater participation of women in decision-making positions in their respective governments.

Government-based women's focal points (Ministries, bureaux, departments and units) were established in the 1980s to facilitate the implementation of WID. Many of these focal points sought measures – largely through advocacy – for the recognition of women's participation in economic and social aspects of society. On the basis of western 'experts' advice, huge resources were provided for commissioned studies to provide gender disaggregated data and information on the status of women. These in turn formed the basis for the establishment of income-generating activities within various communities.

Critics of the WID approach see it as being inextricably linked to the modernisation[1] paradigm that visualised progress only as westernisation of economic, social and political institutions and processes (Mies 1986; Beneira and Sen 1981). WID was also criticised as having limited impact on the status quo due to its failure to examine the status of women within the context of issues of class, race and imperialism (SARDC 2000). An additional failure was seen in WID's 'superficiality' in the sense that its analyses did not include an acknowledgement of the underlying cause of gender inequality – patriarchy. Finally, the approach tended to leave men out of the analysis while having an isolated view of women as a socially, economically and politically homogenous group.

As an approach, Gender and Development (GAD) examines the impact of development on gender relations and how gender shapes women's and men's experiences of the development process. This concept, which became prominent partly out of disillusionment with the WID approach, centralises the power contests in the relationships between women and men. Within the GAD approach, some scholars engaged in developing global theories that named and analysed gender oppression systems (see Mies 1986; Rogers 1980). Others grappled with conceptualising 'gender' and 'inequality' within African societies. While the framework has been effectively used to *engender* the analysis of socio-economic processes at macro levels, it is increasingly being seen as the means by which qualitative insight can be gained into micro-domestic and individual dynamics hidden within the context of national data collection exercises.

Women in Development and Gender and Development paradigms have been applied at various times in different contexts in the African region. While they represent different methods of analysis and action, their primary aim is the advancement of the status of women. (SARDC 2000). Currently there is a shift towards 'gender mainstreaming', also associated with the Gender and Development (GAD) approach. Its major emphasis is the promotion of equality between men and women. Gender mainstreaming has resulted in the review of development policies and programmes. It has also led to the development of analytical tools for assessing and transforming policy, particularly as it relates to control over resources within the context of national budgets. One of these is the concept of reviewing national budgets through gendered lenses. The following section outlines the justification for gendered review of national budgets.

Gender Budgets

Gender responsive budgets are a variety of processes and tools aimed at assessing the impact of government budgets, mainly at national levels, on groups of women and men, by analysing gender relations in the society and the economy. They require an understanding of the economic, political and cultural situations of women and men in particular societal contexts. Gender budgets have also been referred to as 'gender sensitive budgets, 'women's budgets' and 'women's budget statements'.

Gender budgets date back to the Commonwealth's directive encouraging their member countries to integrate gender concerns into economic policy.[2] In 1989 the Commonwealth Expert Group called for interalia: 'the incorporation of gender concerns in the areas of public expenditure, taxation, credit policies, wage policies, trade liberalisation, and privatisation' (Hewitt 2001: 1). This entails a review of government policies that influence budgetary decision-making and an analysis of gender targeted allocations, including gender disaggregation of the impact of mainstream expenditures across all sectors and services and the review of equal opportunities policies and allocations within government services (Hewitt 2001).

Hewitt indicates that gender responsive budgets seek to create a direct linkage between social and economic policies through the application of a gender analysis to the formulation and implementation of gender budgets. These gender analyses would not only show the extent to which national budgets have either incorporated or overlooked gender (or be biased either towards women or men), but also demonstrate the ways in which institutions that seem 'gender neutral' may in fact transmit gender biases.

The justification for gender mainstreaming, and gender budgets has been provided by international and regional agencies, for example, the Commonwealth,

UNIFEM, UNDP, SADC, as well as gender activists and scholars (Kabeer and Subrahmanian 1996; Elson 1996 & 2000). The main argument presented is that although most macroeconomic policies aim to improve human development and reduce poverty, the achievement of these goals is jeopardised by inefficiencies resulting from the failure to take into account gender relations, as well as the specific needs of women and men. The efficient use of resources is important for improving the targeting of policies and the delivery of services.

Elson (2000) refers to benefits of gender budgets in avoiding 'false economies' which occur when attempts to reduce or contain financial costs in one sector may transfer or perpetuate actual costs in terms of time use for individuals and groups, lowering their productivity in the process. Studies (Kabeer 1994) have indicated that the introduction of agricultural technologies and better seed varieties which are aimed at improving productivity among farmers, and reducing government spending on the provision of agricultural inputs often have the opposite effect on women by increasing the time spent on various aspects of the agricultural cycle like weeding and bird-scaring. Structural Adjustment Programmes and other fiscal austerity measures caused a reduction of government spending on social services, particularly medical services in many African countries. The net effect is a transfer of burden of care to women as patients receive limited institutional care, and are often discharged into their communities early. Consequently, women's capacity for economic productivity or income-generation is lowered substantially.

Although information about poverty generated through household data may give a good indication of the income differentials between rich and poor households, the absence of an insight into intra-household dynamics of resource allocation and decision-making presents limitations by obscuring the larger picture.[3] The following section highlights some experiences and challenges to the gender budgeting process within the Southern African region, and specifically in Botswana.

Some Issues and Challenges to Gender Budgets in the SADC Region

In 1998 the United Nations Women's Fund (UNIFEM) organised a forum in Harare to discuss and debate the importance of engendering budgets. The workshop was attended by parliamentarians, senior government officials, women's organisations, researchers, activists and the SADC gender unit. The workshop identified some issues from the region that prompted the need for action. These are:

1. **Proportions of budgets spent on defence**: The workshop noted that nearly 1/2 of the fourteen SADC member states were at war. The expenditure of Zimbabwe (struggling under the weight of structural adjustment) on the war in the Democratic Republic of Congo, and South Africa on the conflict in

Lesotho were given as examples. It was duly noted that the effects of war on national economies, as well as their detraction from the advancement of the status of women should be documented.

2. **Proportions of budgets spent on social expenditure:** Many governments are under pressure from the International Monetary Fund (IMF) to cut social spending. However, this places additional burdens on the unpaid labour of women. It would be important to document the effects of cuts in social expenditure by gender, particularly the status of girls and women as evident in the provision of care of the disabled and infirm by women.

3. **Land:** Since women's limited access to land is a common problem in most countries, the detailed documentation of land ownership patterns by women and men, as well as the cultural dynamics that determine access should be prioritised. Secondly it would also be important to know the budgetary resources going into land reform, as well as the proportion of them spent on bridging the gender gap. It would be pertinent, therefore, within the context of the ongoing Zimbabwean and South African land reform processes to produce gender disaggregated data for the purposes of policy formulation and to support appropriate legislation.

4. **Credit:** Women's lack of access to credit is also a widespread phenomenon in African societies. This is further exacerbated by patriarchal legal traditions that relegate married women to the position of minors under the marital power of their husbands. Married women in Botswana, for example still face difficulties when opening bank accounts, or securing loans without their husbands' assistance. These issues need to be documented within the context of gender mainstreaming and national budgets.

5. **Regional Organisations:** Since this was a SADC forum, questions were asked about the proportion of the overall SADC budget spent on the advancement or women, or promoting gender equality. Regional organisations such as the Organisation of African Unity (OAU) should be challenged to undertake gender analyses of their budgets in order to assess their levels of commitment towards gender mainstreaming (Extracts from Budlender 1999).

One cannot refer to the national development planning process without addressing power relations and issues of governance. Gender mainstreaming and gender budgets often entail a radical departure from policy planning traditions perpetuated over many decades. Ideological shifts necessarily have to begin with the decision-makers within the state machineries. Here, the role of parliamentarians, particularly parliamentary finance committees, are central. In most countries where the representation of women in political decision-making roles is limited, this remains a key challenge. It is crucial, therefore, to examine the inroads that have been made in creating awareness among policy-makers, as well as the barriers that exist.

Another key challenge to the process of gender mainstreaming of national budgets is that of access to gender disaggregated data across all sectors. While the situation has improved over time, particularly with respect to demographic, employment, health and educational statistics, much remains to be done to ensure that all sectoral planning is on the basis of gender disaggregated information. In addition, the links between sectors, particularly as they affect each other should be established. A pertinent example is that of the effects of HIV/AIDS on national economies, communities, families and individuals.

The UNAIDS and WHO figures consistently show that four out of every five HIV-positive women live in the Sub-Saharan region (UNAIDS/WHO 1998), with the majority in Southern Africa. HIV/AIDS has been referred to as a national crisis by the Minister of Health in Botswana. AIDS Sentinnel Surveys[4] conducted by the Ministry of Health indicate that infection rates were highest among the age group 15–49 years, with women being in the majority. The economic implications of the pandemic are manifold – loss of productivity among breadwinners, possible declines in agricultural production, human capital, etcetera. While the implications are duly noted in the Botswana National Development Plan 8 (1997/98–2002/03), the inter-sectoral gender implications are not reflected. The absence of this discussion limits the ability of sectors such as agriculture, education, industry to emplace measures to adjust for the effects of the disease accordingly.

Gender mainstreaming requires researchers to identify gaps in gender disaggregated information while reviewing the different mechanisms that either promote or prevent the effective 'engendering' of our national budgets. This is particularly pertinent in the examination of poverty and life chances.

The Gender Dynamics of Poverty, and Decision-Making at Household Levels

The analysis of poverty and life chances focusing on the gender of the head of the household has recently been the subject of increasing academic research and debate in developing countries. Census and household surveys conducted in Botswana reveal that almost half of all households in the country are headed by women, with a significant proportion of them falling into the lowest income categories. This section examines some of the dynamics of access to and control over resources among low-income households in Botswana. The evidence is from a quantitative study that I conducted in 1996 in Botswana. The study examined the implications of household organisation and gender relations of economic production and social reproduction on the life chances of women and their dependants.

Research was conducted within a pool of low-income female and male headed/supported households in Manyana, a rural village and Gaborone. It compared similarities and differences in composition, sources of income and survival strategies employed by women and men within study households. Interviews with women and men reveal the complexity of domestic organisation and the significance of gender hierarchies that are often obscured by focusing on discrete notions of 'headship'. Based on the evidence from this empirical study, as well as that presented by other studies, I will argue that the utility of the concept (of household headship) within the context of Botswana is diminished by a lack of in-depth account of the culturally-based *gendered social relations* that shape identity and life chances.

Gender Disaggregated Household Income Data and Household Headship

During the United Nations Decade for Women, researchers commissioned by UN agencies,[5] working in collaboration with national machineries and local researchers in developing countries, identified the gaps in data on the status of women, and sex biases in national statistics. The research pointed to the under-enumeration of women's work in the subsistence agriculture, the informal sector and unpaid work performed within the home by women in developing countries of Africa, Asia and South America (United Nations 1984).

On the basis of results of empirical studies conducted in different countries, various United Nations agencies (eg., International Research and Training Institute for the Advancement of Women and the United Nations Statistical Office) collaborated to develop social indicators on the situation of women, and guidelines for the generation of gender disaggregated data at national levels. The social indicators and guidelines facilitated the generation of data on the economic status of women; focusing primarily on their participation in the labour force and their access to productive resources.

In addition to identifying gaps in data on the status of women in the economy, WID advocates pointed to gender biases in data collection at the household level. Attention was focused on male biases in the identification of the household head in data collection exercises:

> The concept of family head is based on the assumption that men head all nuclear families and provide for their economic needs while women take care of reproduction and home-care functions...The assumption of economic support by a male family head has become increasingly unrealistic as larger numbers of households are made up of single persons, particularly women living alone, and of women and children only. Also women are frequently the main or only providers for themselves and their chil-

dren and larger proportions of women in all households are entering the paid labour force and contributing significantly to household income (United Nations 1984: 26).

WID advocates lobbied for gender disaggregation of household headship primarily to bring the attention of policy-makers to the existence of these household types and establish the link between the subordinate status of women and the economic welfare of the households that they head. This led to the emergence of the concept of 'female headed household' emerged in policy-oriented household surveys in developing countries. Consequently, evidence compiled during the last two decades estimates that at least one third of the world's households are headed by women (Moser 1989). The research also show an increasing prevalence of these household types in Third World countries of Latin America, the Caribbean and parts of Africa (Rosenhouse 1989; Folbre 1991; Mencher and Okongwu 1993; Kabeer 1994).

Debates on Female Headship

The generation of gender disaggregated household income data arguably had the benefit of making women more visible within the context of poverty analysis. However, literature on female-headed households in developing countries illustrates the ongoing struggle to define female headship. Scholars have encountered difficulties in reconciling:

a) the definitions of headship adopted by policy-oriented national surveys;
b) the criteria used by individuals in their identification of household heads ; and
c) the lived experiences of women and men with regard to resource provision, household management and decision-making in different cultural contexts.

Sandra Rosenhouse (1989) and Nancy Folbre (1991) posit that while the use of the headship concept in censuses and household surveys partly serves to identify a reference person to whom to relate the various household members, the application of the concept is loaded with implicit assumptions about decision-making processes and resource provision within households. The identification of one household head, whether female or male, is based on unitary models of household organisation which assume that one person is the primary income-earner and decision-maker. This approach under-emphasises the complexity of economic provision under conditions where there are multiple earners and decision-making within households, and socio-economic cooperation between individuals, especially those with limited economic resources.

Another key criticism raised by feminist scholars refers to the asymmetry of headship. This means defining households as female headed only if no adult male is present, while defining a household as male headed whether or not an adult female is resident (Rosenhouse 1989; Folbre 1991; Kennedy and Peters 1992; Moser 1993; Kabeer 1994). While various household members (female spouses/partners, children and relatives) may not readily identify themselves as household heads, or be identified as such by national censuses and household surveys, their contribution of economic resources in households often has direct implications for the allocation of resources within those households.

Rosenhouse's discussion illustrated the limitations of reported headship as a reliable identification of the economic support base of the household. Women who identify themselves as household heads due to the temporary or permanent absence of husbands or cohabiting partners may have limited authority due to their reliance on non-resident male kins for representation in matters relating to their or their children's well-being. Case studies conducted in rural Egypt (Saunders and Mehanna 1993) and rural Bangladesh (Islam 1993) illustrate that while widows identified themselves as heads of their households, they were reliant on senior male kin representation in public matters, especially those relating to acquiring land for agricultural purposes.

Typologies of Female Headship in Botswana

During the 1980s, a number of scholars (Izzard 1982; Brown 1983; Kossoudji and Mueller 1983; Kerven 1982) pointed to the prevalence of female headed households in rural Botswana. These scholars developed typologies of headship based on the marital status of women, their ages, as well as temporary and permanent male absence utilising data from various government surveys. Additionally, the National Migration Study (NMS) was conducted in the late 1970s to document patterns of internal migration between rural areas, and between rural and urban areas in Botswana. Since migration resulted in the fluidity of household membership over time, the NMS adopted the following definitions for their classification of household membership:

a) **De Jure**: household membership referred to those individuals who were regarded as 'usual' household members; *De Jure* female household heads were defined as those individuals who were identified as the 'usual' or 'permanent' heads of their households

b) **De Facto**: household membership referred to those individuals who were present at the time of the study. De *facto* female household heads were identified as women who assumed temporary headship in the absence of *de jure* male household heads.

Using anthropological accounts (Schapera 1933; Comaroff and Roberts 1981) of the lengthy process of marriage and the fluidity of consensual unions in Botswana, Peters (1983) identified the limitations of utilising marital status as a central criterion for defining female headship in the country. She argued that female headship may be ephemeral, rather than a permanent phenomenon within women's life cycles since many women who may be identified as *de jure* or permanent household heads could later be incorporated into male-headed households through marriage. She also alluded to the fact that the discrete headship typologies largely ignore the social and economic relations that occur between women with men who may not necessarily reside within them.

Athaliah Molokomme (1991) also pointed to the limitations of the female headed household concept within Tswana culture: A household may, *de facto*, appear to be headed by an unmarried adult woman in the sense that there is no adult male who resides in it and exercises decision-making functions on a daily basis. At the same time, some man somewhere such as a father, brother or uncle who makes important decisions may head it, *de jure*. This happens in patriarchal societies where only males can legally make certain important decisions (Molokomme 1991: 59).

Molokomme's objection to the labelling of such households as female-headed is based on the implication that headship suggests an embodiment of power, which many women do not wield under cultural circumstances. She therefore recommended a cautious application of the term by analysing headship and single motherhood separately.

The Ambiguity of HIES Classification

The Household Income and Expenditure Surveys (HIES) of 1984/85 and 1993/94 disaggregated household data by the gender of the household head. While the data from the latter survey were used in the analysis of poverty by the Botswana Institute of Development Policy Analysis (1996),[6] the HIES 2 did not provide a precise definition of headship. It utilised the *de facto* approach to household membership because population mobility would create problems in the operationalisation of the concept of 'usual member' since it would entail detailing exact or appropriate proportions of time spent at each of the places where members reside (Government of Botswana 1995a).

There is no clear indication of the basis of conceptualisation of the 'household head'. The following background information was obtained from several sources including a paper on methodology that was presented by a CSO official at a seminar held to disseminate Census findings (Government of Botswana 1995a), a report on living conditions in Botswana from 1986 to 1994 (Government of Botswana 1996) and the enumerators' manual for HIES 2 (Central Statistics Office 1993). The HIES 2 utilised a very broad framework for household headship:

Logically, every household must have a head. The head of a household has to be a member of the household...It was the responsibility of the household members to name from amongst members who their head was. In the case of couples, where either the wife or husband is present, one of them is the head. There were exceptional instances where from amongst the members, none, due to age, qualified to assume headship of the household. In such cases, the oldest was appointed head of household...(Government of Botswana 1995a: 32).

While the Central Statistics Office does not provide a detailed definition of household head, it is evident that the concept is based on the notion that the household head is the 'focal point' of decision making within the household (Government of Botswana 1996: 11). Although no reference is made to the head's central role in procuring resources for the household, it is implied in the focus on certain demographic aspects of the household head, for example, gender, age, educational status, and so on. This ambiguous conceptualisation of headship raises questions about its utility as an indicator of economic welfare and household organisation over time.

The vague definition of headship within the HIES, reflected in the absence of an indicator of relevance of decision making to economic welfare at the household level, supports the critiques levelled by Rosenhouse (1989) and others. Even when disaggregation of household data by the head's gender is used to identify gender-based income inequality at the household level, the evolving question is the reliability of broad conceptualisation of headship, based on the HIES data, for the analysis of gender and socio-economic inequality at the household level in Botswana.

What Is a Household Head?

My study of household organisation within forty households in Gaborone and Manyana provided the opportunity for a closer examination of the concept of household head or *tlhogo ya lolwapa*.[7] It would expose perceptions and experiences that link income generation and decision making as well as the social contexts within which these processes take place. The guide for the in-depth interviews included questions that were aimed at understanding decision-making processes, particularly the definition of household head. I asked women and men to define the term *tlhogo ya lolwapa* and to describe the responsibilities that were associated with this role.

The discussions showed that the designation of household headship is determined by a complex interplay between cultural norms, economic conditions and gendered individual agency. They also showed that the designation of headship is often determined by significant social relationships that extend beyond the boundaries of the physical residence. The views and experiences of the respondents have been divided into three main spheres of decision-making. The first was culturally-sanctioned male authority; the second was social reproduction, while the third was economic provision and income generation. The terms *tlhogo ya lolwapa* and *tlhogo*[8] are retained throughout the discussion in order to keep their socio-cultural and linguistic significance.

Culturally-Sanctioned Male Authority

When asked the question 'What does *tlhogo ya lolwapa* mean?', nineteen women and three men immediately gave the following response: '*Go raya Monna*' ('It means a man'). Among the women, the response was given by ten self-identified household heads, as well as by five individuals who had identified women as the heads of their households. From these immediate responses, it was evident that the term *tlhogo ya lolwapa* had specific gender connotations—and was synonymous with 'man or maleness' within the context of cultural beliefs and practices.

Men continue to assume dominance in public political affairs, such as active participation in *kgotla*[9] meetings. Although women are now permitted to attend meetings in the traditional meeting forum, their participation is largely passive. Men control discussions and make overall decisions. At the family level, men also play a key role in marriage negotiations, funeral rites and other significant cultural practices. The synonymy of *tlhogo ya lolwapa* and *monna* (man) is constantly reinforced in these cultural rituals.

Kgalalelo,[10] a widowed single mother in Manyana who lived in her younger brother's compound identified him as the head of the household during the screening survey. During the in-depth interview she alluded to the role that her non-resident elder brother played as head of the family, showing the importance of gender and age-based hierarchies in the determination of household headship. She mentioned that when important traditional events such as wedding negotiations and funerals take place in her family and community, her non-resident elder brother would represent her household as the most senior male member of the family:

> The head of this household is my older brother who lives on the other side of the village. He is the one who is consulted as the elder in the household. He often arbitrates in issues that are relegated to the uncles (*bo malome*). He is older than both of us [herself and her younger brother]. When someone from the *kgotla* brings an important message, they will want to consult a man, even if he is younger than me, to give him the message from the elders. He is my *kgosi* (chief). I cannot supersede him in authority. If he is absent, I can receive the information as a woman only if

he doesn't have a wife. If he is married, the message will be delivered to his wife, who in turn will deliver it to my brother.

Kgalalelo pointed to the subordinate status of women in culturally-based gender and age hierarchies. During marriage, she had been under the authority and guidance of her husband. After the death of her husband, she had been forced to return to her natal compound that had been bequeathed to her younger brother following the death of their parents. She effectively fell under the immediate guidance and authority of her younger brother. Her younger brother was in turn superseded in authority by her elder brother in terms of age and by virtue of his having completed the passage into adulthood through marriage. Another woman in Manyana who resided in her natal home initially identified her mother as the head of the household. She later indicated that her elder brother who lives and works in Gaborone was *tlhogo ya lolwapa* because he was *kgosi* (chief), even though he had virtually no input in maintaining the household financially.

Some respondents alluded to their dependence on *tlhogo* for guidance, and saw that position as being associated with dealing with and resolving disputes within the homestead, as well as dealing with problems that faced household members from outside. These roles were largely associated with men. Moatlhodi, a self-identified male household head in Gaborone voiced this view:

> The main thing that I am responsible for in the household as *tlhogo ya lolwapa* is to ensure that the male responsibilities are taken care of. Care of the children and their mother. I am the one responsible for maintaining discipline in this home.

Moatlhodi's views indicate that there are defined power relations within consensual relationships and that women occupy subordinate positions in relation to their consensual partners. The culturally-defined gender-specificity of the concept was also reflected in the men's immediate reference to themselves as heads, while many women were ambivalent about the implications of bestowing the title upon themselves within the context of culture. When asked whether a woman was ever regarded as *tlhogo ya lolwapa* within the context of Tswana culture, many indicated that women could only assume that role in the absence of men; especially if their partners were deceased. Many said that these women would still be required to consult with male relatives when making important decisions considered to fall within the male domain, as was clearly illustrated in Kgalalelo's case. A woman in Gaborone indicated that while culture was changing, she was still expected to contact her uncle in the event of a death in her nuclear family, as the arrangement of funeral rites is the responsibility of men.

These respondents' views illustrate the patriarchal assumptions reflected in cultural definitions of household headship alluded to by various scholars (Folbre 1991; Chant 1991. They also support the concerns raised by Molokomme (1991) regarding the applicability of the term 'female headed household' within the context of Tswana culture. Molokomme's views relate to the cultural framework that continues to promote patriarchal relations of power and authority, whereby men are the key players in matters of cultural importance such as marriage negotiations and inheritance practices. While single women are considered to be legal majors in the acquisition of property under the law, they continue to be subjected to the authority of male relatives within the cultural context. Married women are doubly disadvantaged by being subjected to traditional male authority within marriage, as well as under statutory legal practices that relegate them to the position of minors in relation to their husbands.

It can be argued that a growing proportion of single women who spend the majority of their adult lives and establish homesteads in the urban areas are affected less by kinship influences than those single mothers whose lives remain embedded in their natal families out of economic need. The degree of autonomy that women exercise over their lives and the lives of their dependants is highly contingent on the degree of economic power that they possess. While the autonomy of some of the single women may be adversely affected by economically-motivated cohabitation as in 'marriage for maize meal', there is a large proportion of women who remain alone by choice or due to the failure of co-resident consensual unions.

Domestic Social Reproduction

For the purposes of my study, domestic social reproduction was defined as including childbearing, child-rearing and the performance of activities that are related to the daily maintenance of household members as described by Laslett and Brenner (1989) and Fox (1993). These activities are often subsumed under 'housework' within national household surveys and labour statistics, and are not considered to be economic activities. The Botswana Labour Force Survey of 1995/96 mentioned the following about female labour force participation rates and housework:

> Females generally show lower rates of economic activity than males and many are engaged in housework which is still very much work but is not included as an economic activity internationally largely because of the problems of putting monetary values on such activities (Government of Botswana 1996: 3).

Respondents pointed to the central significance of social reproduction especially with regard to the maintenance of life. In addition, it was clear that the realm of housework extends far beyond domestic chores to include the procurement of resources, especially food that is consumed by household members. Several respondents remarked that *tlhogo ya lolwapa* is the person who takes responsibility for the daily survival and welfare of members of the household. The qualification of the terms 'survival' and 'welfare' varied according to the gender of the respondents, with men alluding more to general welfare, while women provided details regarding home-management tasks ranging from catering for their children's' nutritional and educational needs to food acquisition and preparation. Men subsumed 'welfare' under their culturally-sanctioned authority. Three men in Gaborone alluded to their responsibility for the overall material welfare of their families, indicating that they were responsible for 'bringing home the food'.

The views expressed by women reflected their pre-occupation with making ends meet on a daily basis. Most of the female heads of households indicated that they undertook these responsibilities single-handedly, while the women who were married and cohabiting indicated that they consulted their husbands and partners since they were partly responsible for meeting the financial requirements for household expenses.

Provision of Resources

The provision of resources includes the production and/or acquisition of cash, goods and food for consumption within the household, as well as the procurement of basic necessities like shelter. Some of the respondents alluded to the links between culturally-sanctioned authority and resource provision. It appeared, however, that the link between social reproduction and resource provision was stronger. Couples, and women who were single due to the disintegration of resident consensual unions, or the deaths of consensual partners identified the link between culturally-sanctioned authority and resource provision. On the other hand, the link between social reproduction and resource provision was identified in the views of women who had never cohabited; some of whom had established their own households, and those who resided in the households of their single mothers. The discussions also highlighted the complexity of provision of resources and ownership of assets between and within households, and the likelihood that households headed by women would rely on informal networks that sometimes had direct implications for their personal power and autonomy.

Several widows referred to the fact that their late partners had been the primary income earners in their households. A widow in Manyana mentioned that if her husband were still alive, he would assume responsibility for supporting the household financially. She indicated that she was the head of her household because she was a widow, and had assumed primary responsibility for catering for the needs of her children. While seeming to be certain about her role, she felt that her migrant son could be regarded as *tlhogo* due to his regular contribution to her welfare as well as that of his siblings.

Several widows in Manyana indicated that they relied on their non-resident adult children for the upkeep of their homes. An elderly widow who had originally identified herself as the head of her household in Manyana indicated that she depended on her son to provide food for her, and saw him as the main decision-maker. Another elderly widow mentioned that it was difficult to determine who the head of her household was, as her sons assisted her financially. She finally said that she thought it was her eldest son, as he was the one that she appealed to for financial assistance. Another widow who lived with her daughter and several grandchildren said it was difficult to determine who the head of her household was, as her resident daughter and non-resident sons contributed to her welfare.

The complex interface between economic provision and headship was also reflected in the households of cohabiting and married couples. While men assumed the role of breadwinner and principal decision-maker, it was evident that women played a prominent role in food provision. This was reflected in the case of Mmantho and Mmoshe, a couple in Manyana. While Mmantho had originally indicated that her household relied on her partner's income from casual work, she later indicated that she had been feeding her family of ten with maize and sorghum that she jointly produced with her mother. She indicated that the little income that Mmoshe made was used to supplement the food supply, pay for the children's educational expenses, clothing needs, and to purchase fuel for lighting.

Ownership and control over major assets are important aspects of headship. Several respondents referred to *tlhogo* as *monnga lolwapa* (the owner of the home). The patterns of home ownership were largely determined by partnership and marital status in both locations. The proprietary consequences of marriage in Botswana subject married women to the marital power of their husbands, who are appointed the legal administrators of their marital estates. Husbands effectively have the right to acquire and sell property without reference to their wives (WLSA 1994). These proprietary consequences of marriage have dire implications for women.

Another area of complexity in the ownership of housing is reflected in the lives of single mothers who reside within the households of their natal families. Kgalalelo, a widowed mother of five in Manyana was compelled to return to her deceased parent's home when her marital homestead had physically collapsed. She indicated that the home was left to her single younger brother who is a migrant worker in South Africa. Kgalalelo is unemployed, and does not have the financial means to build a home for her family. She said that while she was occupying and looking after the home for her younger brother, she was concerned about the welfare of her family once her brother returned and established a family in the compound.

Observations

The foregoing discussion has illustrated the complexity of household headship and decision-making within and between households. The predominance of patriarchal patterns of authority continues to be reproduced through cultural norms and legal traditions. The dependence of women on men has largely been reinforced by gender patterns of wage employment and the creation of the male breadwinner ideology over time.

The prominence of single women as decision-makers in their households is largely due to the absence of senior male adults in the household, and the economic 'independence' that they gain from earning their own income. While many of these women are subjected to male authority within the context of traditional rites, and many identified men as the heads of their households, they assumed primary responsibility for the daily provision of resources and the welfare of their dependants.

The contribution of wives, female cohabitees and other household members to economic provision and social reproduction largely goes unnoticed within conceptualisations of headship. The delineation of the different spheres of headship pointed to the close interface between social reproduction and economic provision through processes of mothering.

Conclusions

Mainstreaming gender into national policies, budgets and programmes remains a challenge for African countries in the new millennium. Many barriers to achieving this objective lie in the paucity of resources for development in general as a result of SAPs, conflicts and ongoing crises like HIV/AIDS. It is important for scholars, researchers and gender activists to ensure that active inputs in the gender mainstreaming process is made by undertaking studies that will:

- Generate gender disaggregated data across all sectors of our economies
- Investigate the dynamics of resource allocation within policy and national budgetary exercises;
- Participate in the gender sensitisation of other researchers to add to the body of literature on resource allocation at macro and micro levels within our different contexts.

Lessons learned from a study focusing on the economic production and social reproduction roles of individuals within domestic units stem from their ability to provide a more holistic picture of the interface between structural factors (for example, culture and the economy), patterns of social and economic co-operation at the domestic level, and the shaping of individual ideology over time. The strength of this type of analysis rests in the ability to look beneath convenient conceptualisations such as household headship in order to examine the different configurations of gender relations and socio-economic welfare; particularly the dynamics of access and control over resources among women and men.

Notes

1 Associated with western economic development theories of scholars such as Myint, Myrdal and Rostow.

2 The impetus dates back to the report of the 1989 Commonwealth Expert Group *Engendering Adjustment for the 1990s* and the *Ottawa Declaration on Women and Structural Adjustment* which was endorsed by the Heads of Government in 1991.

3 A more detailed discussion of the gendered dynamics of access to and control over resources in domestic units will be presented later in the paper.

4 Sentinel Surveys are conducted every year among a selected sample of pregnant women and men presenting Sexually Transmitted Diseases and Tuberculosis.

5 The Department of International Economic and Social Affairs Statistical Office, the International Research and Training Institute for the Advancement of Women.

6 The study indicated that 47 per cent of households in Botswana are below the poverty datum line, and interalia that female-headed households constitute the majority of income-poor households.

7 *Tlhogo ya Lolwapa* refers to 'head of the household' in Setswana

8 *Tlhogo* refers to 'head' in Setswana

9 *Kgotla* is the village political forum.

10 Pseudonyms were used to protect the identities of the respondents.

References

Beneria, L., 1982, Accounting for Women's Work, in Beneria, L. ed *Women and Development, the Sexual Division of Labour in Rural Societies*, New York: Praeger.

Beneria, L., 1983, *Women and Development: The Sexual Division of Labour in Rural Societies*, New York: Praeger.

Beneria, L., 1992, 'Accounting for Women's Work: The Progress of Two Decades', *World Development*, vol. 20, no. 11, pp. 1547–1560.

Beneria, L.& Roldan, M., 1987, *The Crossroads of Class and Gender: Industrial Homework, Subcontracting, and Household Dynamics in Mexico City*, Chicago: The University of Chicago Press.

Beneria, L. & Sen, G., 1981, 'Accumulation, Reproduction and Women's Role in Economic Development: Boserup Revisited', *Signs*, vol. 7, no. 21, pp. 279–99.

Boserup, E., 1970, *Women's Role in Economic Development*, London: George Allen and Unwin.

Botswana Institute for Policy Development Analysis (BIDPA), 1997a, *Study of Poverty and Poverty Alleviation in Botswana Volume 1: Overall Assessment of Poverty*, Gaborone: BIDPA.

BIDPA, 1997b, *Study of Poverty and Poverty Alleviation in Botswana Volume 2: Analysis of Income Poverty Using the Poverty Datum Line*, Gaborone: BIDPA.

BIDPA, 1997c, *Study of Poverty and Poverty Alleviation in Botswana Volume 3: Rapid Poverty Profile*, Gaborone: BIDPA.

Brown, B., 1983, 'The Impact of Male Labour Migration on Women in Botswana', *African Affairs*, vol. 28, no. 328, pp. 367–388.

Budlender, B., ed 1999, *Engendered Budgets: The Southern African Experience*, Harare: UNIFEM.

Chant, S., 1991, *Women and Survival in Mexican Cities: Perspectives on Gender, Labour Markets and Low-Income Households*, New York: Manchester University Press.

Comaroff, J.& Roberts, S., 1977, 'Marriage and Extra-Marital Sexuality: The Dialectics of Legal Change Among the Kgatla', *Journal of African Law*, vol. 21, no. 1

Elson, D., 1996, 'Gender Neutral, Gender Sensitive Budgets: Changing the Conceptual Framework to Include Women's Empowerment and the Economy of Care'. *Paper prepared for Fifth Annual Conference of Ministers Responsible for Women's Affairs*, Trinidad.

Folbre, N., 1991, *Women On Their Own: Global Patterns of Female Headship*, Washington DC: International Centre For Research on Women

Government of Botswana, 1995a, *1991 Population and Housing Census Dissemination Seminar 1–4 May*, Gaborone: Central Statistics Office.

Government of Botswana, 1995b, Household Income And Expenditure Survey 1993/94, Gaborone: Central Statistics Office.

Government of Botswana, 1996, *Stats Brief No 96/5*, Gaborone: Central Statistics Office.

Government of Botswana, 1997, *National Development Plan 8: 1997/98–2002/3*, Gaborone: Ministry of Finance and Development Planning.

Hewitt, G., 2001, 'Commonwealth Gender Responsive Budget Initiative', *Report of Capacity Building Exercise for the Parliament of Botswana*, London: Commonwealth Secretariat.

Islam, M., 1993, 'Female-Headed Households in Rural Bangladesh: A Survey', In Mencher, J. & Okongwu, A., (eds) *Where Did All The Men Go?: Female-*

Headed/Supported Households in Cross-Cultural Perspective, Boulder: Westview Press, pp. 233–42

Izzard, W., 1982, The Impact of Migration on the Roles of Women, Gaborone: Central Statistics Office.

Kabeer, N., 1993, Reversed Realities: Gender Hierarchies in Development Thought, London: Verso.

Kabeer, N., 1994, 'Revisiting the Links Between Gender and Poverty' *IDS Bulletin*, vol. 28, no. 3, pp. 1–13

Kabeer, N and Subrahmanian, R., 1996, 'Institutions, Relations and Outcomes: Framework and Tools for Gender-Aware Planning' *IDS Discussion Paper 357 September*, Sussex: University of Sussex.

Kennedy, E. & Peters, P., 1992, 'Household Food Security and Nutrition: The Interaction of Income and Gender of Household Head', *World Development*, vol. 20, no. 8, pp. 1077–86.

Kerven, C., 1982, *The Effects of Migration on Agricultural Production in National Migration Study Vol. 3*, Central Statistics Office, Gaborone, pp. 527–653.

Kossoudji, S. & Mueller, E., 1982, 'The Economic and Demographic Status of Rural Households in Rural Botswana', *Economic Development and Change*, vol. 3, no. 4, pp. 831–59.

Mencher, J & Okongwu, A., eds., 1993, *Where Did All The Men Go? Female Headed/ Supported Households in Cross-Cultural Perspective*, Boulder: Westview Press.

Mies, M., 2000, *Patriarchy and Accumulation on a World Scale: Women in the International Division of Labour*, London: Zed Books.

Molokomme, A., 1991, Children of the Fence: Maintenance of Extra-Marital Children Under Law and Practice in Botswana, *PhD Thesis*, Leiden: University of Leiden.

Mookodi, G., 1999, 'We Are Struggling': Gender, Poverty and The Dynamics of Survival Within Low Income Households in Botswana, *PhD Thesis*. Toronto: University of Toronto.

Moser, C., 1989, 'Gender Planning in the Third World: Meeting Practical and Strategic Gender Needs', *World Development*, vol. 23, no. 11, pp. 1799–1825.

Moser, C., 1993, Gender Planning and Development: Theory, Practice and Training, London: Routledge.

Peters, P., 1982, 'Gender, Development Cycles and Historical Process: A Critique of Recent Research on Women in Botswana', *Journal of Southern African Studies*, vol. 10, no. 1. pp. 10–22.

Rogers, B., 1980, *The Domestication of Women: Discrimination in Developing Societies*, London: Tavistock Publications.

Rosenhouse, S., 1989, 'Identifying the Poor: Is 'Headship' A Useful Concept?', *World Bank Living Standards Measurement Study Working Paper No. 58*, The

International Bank for Reconstruction and Development/The World Bank, Washington DC.

Schapera, I., 1933, 'Pre-Marital Pregnancy and Native Opinion: A Note on Social Change', *Africa*, vol. 6, no. 1, pp. 59–89.

United Nations, 1982, *Compiling Social Indicators on the Situation of Women*, New York: United Nations.

United Nations, 1983, *Handbook on Social Indicators*, New York: United Nations.

Saunders, W., Mehanna, L. & Mehanna, S., 1993, 'Women-Headed Households from the Perspective of an Egyptian Village', In Mencher, J. & Okongwu, A., eds *Where Did All The Men Go?: Female-Headed/Supported Households in Cross-Cultural Perspective*, Boulder: Westview Press, pp. 193–202.

Southern African Research and Documentation Centre (SARDC), 2000, *Beyond Inequalities: Women in Southern Africa*, Harare: Cannon Press.

UNAIDS and WHO, 1998, *Report on the Global HIV/AIDS Epidemic*, Geneva: United Nations.

Women and Law in Southern Africa Research Project (WLSA) Botswana, 1992, *Women Marriage and Inheritance*, Gaborone: Botswana Printing and Publishing.

4

Accessibility of Resources by Gender: The Case of Morogoro Region in Tanzania

Christine G. Ishengoma

Introduction: The Concept of Gender

Gender has been defined in a variety of ways, both in research and generally. While it usually refers to men and women, it encapsulates more than the differences between them. Early definitions use gender to describe social and biological differences between women and men. It is particularly applied to social meanings of biological sex differences or behavioural aspects of men and women shaped by social forces (Riley 1997).

In this study, we use a definition by Riley (1997) focusing on the socio-economic aspects of gender. Three major points emanate from Riley's definition. First, gender is a social institution. It is central to the way a society is organised and, like the family, religion, race and other social institutions, affects the role men and women play in a society. Gender also establishes patterns of behaviour through interaction with other institutions.

Secondly, gender involves differences in power. Gender orders social relationships, giving some individuals greater power than others. It affects both 'power to' and 'power over'. 'Power to' refers to the ability to act in society and often requires access to social resources such as education, money, land and time. Individuals with 'power over' are able to assert their wishes and goals even in the face of opposition from others. In every society, the roles assumed by women and men determine their opportunities and privileges. Women usually have less 'power to inherit land, for example. They are also less likely to develop individual characteristics (such as higher education) that would give them access to better paying jobs or political office, thereby enhancing their power. In the same vein, women generally have less 'power over' than men. They usually have less power than their husbands in family decision-making and less authority than men in the work place. Because women hold far fewer positions in governing bodies, they tend to have little impact on decision-making or public policies. Gender inequality may also be structured and perpetuated by the economy, the political system, and other social institutions. Civil law and religious customs in various countries, for example, may restrict a woman's ability to own property, work in certain occupations, or serve as a religious leader.

Thirdly, gender is a cultural construct. It refers to the cultural construction of male and female identities, often cast as binary opposites: for example, male dominance versus female submissiveness or the male's sphere of public activities versus the female's private sphere within the home (Creighton and Omari 1995). Gender is also organised differently in various societies. Accordingly, the expectations for women and men vary throughout the world. These differences are perhaps most clearly illustrated in intercultural comparisons of what is considered male and female work. For example in sub-Saharan Africa, female farming systems predominate, and women are involved in most aspects of agricultural production.

Background Information

In most developing countries, stereotypes of male difference and privilege over women are dominant (Mosha 1992). The difference is mostly reflected in the areas of work intensity, decision-making and access and control of, resources. Men control most resources and decision making in the family. Although FAO/WHO (1992) argues that women's access and control of resources may be increased if they earned income, this is not always the case. Despite women's important roles as producers and household managers, they are often marginalised in the allocation of resources and decision making. Their lack of direct access to resources, such as land, capital and credit, and information reduces their net productivity (FAO, 1990; Dankelman and Davidson 1988; 1991; FAO 1996; Mngodo *et al.* 1996).

In Tanzania, as in most communities of Africa, women's lack of access and control of resources reflects their subordinate status in society (Jonsson 1986; URT and UNICEF 1990; FAO/WHO 1992). The prevailing patriarchal system determined access to resources and enhanced traditional systems of male dominance in most communities. Therefore, inheritance of resources such as land, or assets such as houses and trees passed through male hands. In a few matrilineal societies however, women have rights to land and relatively more economic autonomy over its proceeds, particularly food crops (Mwaipopo 1994). Yet, even here, the overall overseer of those resources was male: the maternal uncle.

Historical analyses of the development of social relationships in Tanzania suggest that colonial economic policies and the commoditization of indigenous economies, capitalized on existing patriarchal systems in facilitating indirect rule at the local level. At the household level, it strengthened male dominance by confirming men as heads of households and owners of its property (Mascarenhas and Mbilinyi 1983). In this way, they enhanced inequities in access to resources between men and women (Becker 1995). Yet, women are the main farmers/food producers in Africa. Depriving women access to land seriously constrains their productivity and the household's access to important foods produced by women (Dey 1988). Consequently, male dominance and control of resources limits women's decision making, efficiency and productivity at household and societal levels (Makundi 1996).

Access to Land, Labour Time and Agricultural Inputs

Legally, women and men of Tanzania have equal access to land, livestock and productive assets. In practice however, such access is often reserved for males. Patriarchal relations of production exploit women and perpetuate the control of land and women's labour time by men. Men mostly inherit the land and control the critical inputs for agricultural production as well as proceeds from the sale of crops, produced by all adults and children (Wagao 1991). Although married women can access land through husbands, their ability to optimally utilize the land is limited since they are still answerable to their husbands. For example, they have no power to sell the land (Muro 1988; Ministry of Agriculture 1996). Issues of access to land also go beyond calculations of acreage. They include the distance to the fields and the quality of the soil (Aarnik and Kingma 1991).

Access to New Technology

Women's disadvantaged access to resources limits their ability to respond to new economic opportunities. Modern or improved technologies were introduced in developing countries to reduce drudgery in farm operations while improving production. However, it has been observed that modern technology has done little to improve the welfare of women (Lamming 1983; Lewis 1984; Trenchard 1987; Rwambali 1991). Women are still working with traditional and rudimentary tools like hand hoes, mortars and pestles. They often do not have enough cash to hire or buy new technology such as ploughs, oxen, manure or chemical fertilizer. On the other hand, the new devices and equipment have been benefiting men (Lamming 1983). Consequently, women's productivity is often low and sometimes left out in development planning (Mwaipopo 1994).

Access to Capital and Credit

In Tanzania, public credit programmes depend on physical collateral. They are therefore heavily biased towards men, the *de jure* owners of family assets. Women are usually unable to accumulate assets that would serve as collaterals and therefore receive very little credit from the banks (Virji and Meghji 1989). Women's weak land rights result in an inability to use land as collateral to obtain credit. Commercial and development banks provide loans to sectors mostly dominated by men. For example, credit technological services have been provided mostly for export crops controlled by men while denying such services to women (Virji and Meghji 1989; FAO 1996). Social and cultural barriers, women's lower education levels relative to men and their lack of familiarity with loan procedures may also limit their mobility and interaction with predominantly male credit officers or moneylenders. All these have increasing negative impacts on women's productivity.

The cooperative and rural development bank (CRDB), in conjunction with international organization, has tried to provide credit facilities to women in Tanzania on concessionary lending terms to enable them establish small-scale income generating projects. However, problems like lack of property ownership by women, lack of guarantors to women economic units by village leaders and limited entrepreneurial knowledge by women, have hindered implementation of these programmes. Consequently, only few rural women have benefited from the bank's credit programmes (Virji and Meghji 1989; FAO 1996).

Access to Markets

Women also have limited access to markets in comparison to men (FAO 1988; 1990). Inferior education and training superimposed on deep-rooted traditions and institutional arrangements create barriers for women to access markets (Clones 1992). According to Nkonoki's (1994) study in Tanzania, while nomadic women have fewer domestic tasks and greater prospects for owning cattle and producing ghee for sale, they are prevented from taking advantage of these conditions due to their lack of access to markets and political clout.

Access to Education, Innovation and Extension Services

According to Wiley (1984), although Tanzanian women provide over 60 percent of all required farm labour, agricultural and development-related information largely bypass them. Women lack information and opportunities for further training. Agricultural information and extension work are seldom directed to women's domains. In fact, most agricultural extension programmes concentrate on educating males thereby increasing women's dependency on their husbands, rather than extension agents, for access to such information (Rafferty 1988). In addition, because women are usually busy on the field, or preparing food, or collecting firewood or water, they are not always available to participate in extension education in the villages (CARE International/Tanzania 1995). In relying solely on husbands or neighbours for agricultural development information, women suffer significant disadvantages due to proven low trickle down of such information (Shayo 1991; Wambura 1992; Weidemann 1987; Van Den Ban and Hawkins 1988; Gabriel 1989). Furthermore because extension workers generally target household farms under male heads, it is mostly men that benefit from extension work (FAO 1987; Nikoi 1990; Malima 1993; Mwaipopo 1994; FAO 1996).

Access to Decision-making Power

Decision-making in Tanzania depends on the dominant organizing structure in the community. In patrilineal societies women are subordinate to men and play very limited role in household or communal decision. We had mentioned earlier that while matrilineal communities privilege women, such privileges are still subject to censure or approval by a 'custodian uncle'. Consequently, many crucial decisions affecting women are made by men with little or no input from women (URT and UNICEF 1990).

In order to increase awareness and draw policy attention to these issues, this study sought to investigate access to resources by gender based on the role of women in household food security.

Methodology

The study was conducted in six villages in Morogoro Rural and Kilosa districts. A longitudinal survey design, covering two cropping seasons was used. The study population were men and women household members. A purposive sampling technique was adopted to select three villages in each district. They are Fulwe, Melela and Msufini in Morogoro Rural district, and Kidoma, Kimamba and Dumila in Kilosa district. A representative sample for the study from each village was based on Boyd's (1981) formula $n/N \times 100 = C$ where C represents a figure greater or equal to five percent of the village household population; N is the total households in the village and n is the number of selected households. Selected households were used to get the information needed in the basic survey (data collection). A village register provided the sampling frame while respondents were selected by random sampling procedure (Table 1).

Primary data were collected through structured questionnaires. This was conducted in stages. First, a preliminary survey was conducted to obtain general information about the villages and familiarize and introduce the study to the village government. During the preliminary survey, a list of relevant guidelines and questions guided discussions with respondents. To ensure validity, ten members from five households in Mikese village were interviewed to pre-test the survey instrument, identify any shortcomings and make modifications in some questions before the actual data collection.

The second stage was the basic data collection which included written information on personal characteristics, accessibility of resources and decision making by gender as well as interviewers' observations of events in the homes and fields, and the general appearance of the area were recorded. Open-ended questions were added to probe deeper for additional insights into the information collected.

Table 1: The village households (N), household sampled (n) and percentage of sampled households

Districts	Villages	Number of village households N	Number of sampled households n	Percent of sampled households
Morogoro	Fulwe	1137	57	5.0
Rural	Melela	800	40	5.0
	Msufini	388	20	5.2
Kilosa	Kidoma	615	31	5.0
	Kimamba	850	43	5.1
	Dumila	1031	51	5.0

Source: Survey data 1994/95

Secondary data were obtained from reports and other official documents. Data collected was analyzed by using the Statistical Package for the Social Science (SPSS). Descriptive statistics, Chi-square and Multiple regressions were used in the analysis.

Results and Discussion

Women's Access to Resources
This study identified lack of access to capital (49.6 per cent) as the major factor limiting women's contribution to household food security in Tanzania.

Limitation to time (12.0 per cent) was the second limiting factor. Lack of decision making power (8.2 per cent) featured as another limiting factor but to a lesser extent. Limited agricultural knowledge and food (1.2 per cent) also was identified as a constraining factor.

Access to Land by Gender
Lack of access to land (5.4 per cent) was specifically important in Kimamba village in Kilosa district (42.9 per cent), and applied to men and women farmers. Generally, villagers rented land for cultivating food crops cultivation the Sisal estate under agreement of paying back, post-harvest, a bag of maize per culti-vated hectare of land. As a patriarchal community, land ownership was com-pletely reserved for men. Even in a matrilineal community like Morogoro Rural, cultural norms of women inheritance have become reversed, undermining wom-en's ability to own land by insisting that only household heads can own land (Table 3).

Table 2: Women lack accessibility to resources

Factors	Number	Percent
Lack of access to land	13	5.4
Lack of access to capital	120	49.6
Lack of decision making power	20	8.2
Limitation to time	29	12.0
Limited agricultural knowledge	3	1.2
All the above	4	1.7
Lack of access to capital, decision making power and time	37	15.3
Lack of access to land, capital, decision making power and time		
Lack of access to land and capital	6	2.5
Lack of access to land, capital and decision making power	3	1.2
	7	2.9
Total	242	100.0

Table 3: The head of household by gender

| Response | Female | | Male | |
	Number	Percent	Number	Percent
Yes	21	8.7	227	93.8
No	221	91.3	15	6.2
Total	242	100.0	242	100.0

As noted in Table 3, males dominated (93.8 per cent) as heads of the households among the respondents. Only 8.7 per cent females were heads of the households. These were either single, widows, divorce or separated couples. There were few married women who claimed to be heads of households. Consequently, women were marginalized in terms of access to land or household decision-making, since they were not heads of the households. These findings corroborate those encountered by Aarnink and Kingma (1991) who reported that women's span of manoeuvre in household decision making is drastically curtailed by customs and patriarchal traditions but enhanced in matrilineal societies. Surprisingly, however, the amplifying effect expected in a matrilineal community like Morogoro Rural was actually lacking. Women had no more access to land here than their counterparts in other patrilineal communities. This could have resulted from two possible reasons:

1. In-migration and intermarriages of different ethnic groups and
2. Economic changes

Similar observations have been reported by Swantz (1998) in Mtwara and Lindi communities where little or no in-migration has taken place.

These findings resemble those by FAO (1990 & 1996) and Mngodo *et al.* (1996). Despite limited involvement in the ownership, more than 50 percent of the women revealed that no restrictions were placed by their husbands on their use of the land. About 42.9 percent claimed that their husbands placed restrictions on them. Both situations affect women's productivity in different ways. As argued by Dankelman and Davidson (1988), Aarnik and Kingma (1991) and FAO (1996), since women play a major role in food production, without adequate access to land, it will not be possible for these women to cultivate enough land for food production.

Access to Capital and Credit by Gender

Lack of access to capital (49.6 per cent) was found to be the major constraining factor to women farmers. In contrast with men, women's agricultural activities focus on subsistence crops. This leaves women with limited cash income. When women do earn cash from trading activities, the husband usually controls all family income, including his wife's earnings. Consequently, women in the study area had limited access to cash. Without cash, they have difficulties purchasing agricultural inputs and other foods they cannot produce on their farms. This has serious consequences on their net productivity and ability to strengthen the family's food security. The findings of this study are similar to Clone, (1992) findings. In order to increase women's access to liquid capital, income generating activities of women should be strengthened. Due to limitations of time (12.0 per cent) women concentrate to those activities which are to be conducted at their homestead. Men dominated in petty business (58.3 per cent), crafts (57.5 per cent) and vegetable growing (54.2 per cent).

Table 4: Involvement in income generating activities by gender

Task	Female	Male	Total Percent
Petty business	41.7	58.3	100.0
Vegetable growing	45.8	54.2	100.0
Fruit growing	58.0	42.0	100.0
Brewing	60.4	39.6	100.0
Baking	56.5	43.5	100.0
Crafts	42.5	57.5	100.0

Additionally, women's lack of control over land is a key factor in the chain of gender disparities embedded in the economic system. It impairs women's eligibility for credit, since traditional lending institutions require collateral, often in the form of land. Even in cases where women do have titles to land, there is evidence that women cannot take full advantage of the established credit system because credit institutions tend to be male-oriented and discriminate on a cultural and social basis against women.

Women's Source of Income

The most common sources of women income in the study villages were mat making, beer brewing, petty business and hired labour. Cash crop and livestock production are dominated by men and provide an insignificant source of income for women. So, while women in Kilosa and Morogoro Rural have engaged in various activities to generate income, the scope of those activities remains low. The income generated was also generally low: about 60 percent of the respondents were getting between 501–3,000 Tanzanian Shillings per week, equivalent to US $ 0.5 – 3 per week (Table 5).

In order to adequately strengthen women's income generating activities, support has to be provided to appropriate women's group. This is because, in Tanzania, credit or loans suppliers are interested in groups rather than individuals. Additionally, since thorough economic analyses are required by lenders to assure profitability of their loan activities, women also have to be supported with feasibility studies of potential businesses. Ousmane (1996) study has similar conclusions.

Table 5: Average weekly income from income generating activities

Average weekly income (Tsh)	Number	Percent
Below 500	37	8.6
501–1000	115	26.7
1,001–2000	121	28.1
2001–3000	68	15.8
3001–4000	23	5.3
4,001–5000	34	7.9
Above 5,000	33	7.7
Total	431	100.0

1 US $ is equivalent to about 1000Tsh.

Decision Making on Household Income Expenditure by Gender

Decision-making regarding household necessities like salt, sugar and kitchen items were dominated by women. Purchase of items like furniture and luxury things like radio were determined by men. These results indicate that while some decisions were jointly made by spouses, there was a gender-based division for decision-making on certain household areas. This is different from conclusions reached for Tanzania and Zambia respectively by Due and Anandajayasekeram (1982) and Phiri (1990) stating that decisions on income expenditure was made jointly between spouses.

Decision Making on Family Income by Gender: Who Keeps the Funds from the Different Sales?

In general, husbands kept family income from different sales except off-farm income kept by the wife. A greater part of family income was therefore controlled by men even when the main producers were women (FAO, 1989). These confirm findings by Mung'ongo et al (1990) that women were accustomed to subordination and play very little role in decision making.

In all cases, decisions were made by the family (husband and wife) although the husband always had the leading role. Decisions made by solely women were negligible. This could be a constraint to women farmers if they play a big role in food production but cannot make decisions on different production activities. The findings of this study compare with Aarnink and Kingma (1991) that women's range of household decision making is drastically affected by customs and patriarchal power.

Decision Making Related to Resources Allocation by Gender

Women's contributions were generally marginalized in all activities. Most of the contributions to decisions were made by men. They confirm statements by URT and UNICEF (1990) that, at all levels, in developing countries, women are not provided equitable voices in decision making.

Access to Education, Agricultural Knowledge and Extension Advice by Gender

Women generally reported limited possibility of getting agricultural development advice from extension workers. This is supported by Makundi (1996). The fact that there was an inadequate number of extension workers, also reported by Wambura (1992), was cited as a reason. In addition, available extension workers were said to concentrate on predominantly male target groups or contact farmers who were only a small proportion of the rural population. Other reasons for limited extension support for women include unreliable transportation for village extension workers and poor pay that diverted extension workers to other avenues to increase their earnings. Consequently, information on improved technology did not reach women farmers in time, thereby reinforcing their decreased productivity.

Conclusions and Recommendations

This study confirms the results of many similar studies highlighting women's comparatively limited access to resources and decision making power. Lack of access to capital was a major factor limiting the contribution of women to household food security. Other factors, such as time constraints, lack of access to agricultural knowledge and land were also reported.

While decisions were reportedly made jointly by the family, there was a gender-based dichotomy in designating spheres of influence for decision-making. Women controlled decisions regarding domestic activities but overarching control was exercised by men in all other areas. In addition, income from the sale of cash crops, food crops, livestock and land was controlled by men. Women only handled cash obtained from sale of local beer and crafts.

It is therefore recommended that there is need to involve women in decision making and improve their accessibility to resources. Women should be assisted to engage in income generating activities. Extension services need to be improved, made reliable and be conducted in time. To increase their access to credit facilities, women can be supported to form groups.

References

Aarnik, M. and Kingma, K., 1991, 'The Shamba Is Like a Child' in *Women and Agriculture in Tanzania*, Vol. 1. Women and Autonomous Centre: Leiden University.

Becker, A., 1995, 'A Task for the 1990s: Promotion of Women', in *DC (Development and Cooperation)*, No. 4, July/August.

Body, H. *et al*, 1981, *Marketing Research: Text and Cases*, Illinois: Richard D. Irwin.

CARE International/Tanzania, 1995, *Rapid Food and Livelihood Security Assessment in Shinyanga, Mara and Mwanza Regions*, Dar-es-Salaam: CARE.

Clones, P., 1992, *The Link between Gender Issues and the Fragile Environments of Sub-Saharan Africa*, Women in Development Unit, Poverty and Social Policy Division, Technical Department, Africa region, the World Bank

Creighton, C. and Omari C., 1995, *Gender, Family and Household in Tanzania*, Hants, England: Avebury Ashgate Publishing Limited.

Dankelman, L. and Davidson, J., 1988, *Women and Environment in the Third World: Alliance for the Future*, London: Earthscan Publications Ltd.

Dankelman, L. and Davidson, J., 1991, 'Land: Women at the Centre of the Food Crisis' in S. Sontheirmer, ed., *Women and Environment in the Third World: A Reader*, London: Earthscan Publications.

Dey, J., 1988, *Women in Food Production and Food Security in Africa*, Human Resources, Institutions and Agrarian Reform Division, Rome: FAO.

Due, J. and Anandajayasekeram, P., 1982, 'Women and Productivity in Two Contrasting Farming Areas of Tanzania', *Canadian Journal of African Studies*, 18, 3

FAO, 1987, 'Effectiveness of Agricultural Extension Services In Reaching Rural Women. A Synthesis of Studies from Five African Countries', *Report of Workshop*, 5-9 October 1987, FAO, Harare.

FAO, 1988, 'Effectiveness of Agricultural Extension Services in Reaching Rural Women in Africa', Report of Workshop, Human Resources, Institutions and Agrarian Reform Division, Harare: FAO

FAO, 1989, *Household Food Security and Forestry: An Analysis of Socio-economic Issues*, Rome: FAO.

FAO, 1990, *Women the Key to Food Security: Women and Sustainable Food Security*, Women and Population Division, FAO

FAO, 1996, 'Food Grains Marketing Improvement in Tanzania', *Report of Technical Cooperation Among Developing Countries (TCDC) Experts on Grain Marketing Visit in Tanzania*, September 20 – October 6.

FAO/WHO, 1992, 'Improving Household Food Security: Major Issues for Nutrition Strategies' *International Conference on Nutrition*, FAO.

Gabriel, T., 1989, 'A Forgotten Asset for Development Women and Extension Services', Development *and Cooperation Newsletter* 4:

Jonsson, U., 1986, 'Major Problems of Women and Children in Tanzania', *Paper Presented at the TFNC Regional Course on Food and Nutrition Planning*, February 3 – 15 1986, Morogoro, Tanzania.

Lamming, G., 1983, *Women in Agricultural Cooperatives: Constraints and Limitations to Full Participation*, Human Resources, Institutions and Agrarian Reform Division, Rome: Food and Agriculture Organization of the United Nations.

Lewis, B., 1984, 'The Impact of Development Policies on Women', in Hay and Sticher eds., *African Women South of the Sahara*, Hong Kong: Longman.

Makundi, F., 1996, *House Food Security in Rural Tanzania: A Case Study of Moshi Rural District, Kilimanjaro Region*, Oslo: Agricultural University of Norway.

Malima, V., 1993, 'Agricultural Extension Services for Women Farmers: The Crucial Role of Women Farmers in Food Security', *Paper Presented at the African Women Farmers Workshop, the Mbagala Spiritual Centre*, October 11 – 16.

Mascarenhas, O. and Mbilinyi, M., 1983, *Women in Tanzania: An Analytical Bibliography*, Stockholm , Scandinavian Institute of African Studies.

Ministry of Agriculture, 1996, *Country Position Paper*, World Food Summit, November 13–17, Rome.

Mngodo, J. *et al.*, 1996, *Food Security in Tanzania: Transport, Markets and Poverty Alleviation*, Ministry of Agriculture and Cooperatives, United Republic of Tanzania.

Mosha, A., 1992, 'Decision Making on Resource Allocation in Rural Households for Food Security', in Shinyanga Rural District', *Tanzania Food and Nutrition Centre (TFNC) Report*, Dar-es-Salaam.

Mung'ongo, C. *et al.*, 1990, *A Socio–economic Assessment of North Eastern Parts of Tanzania*, IRA, University of Dar-es-Salaam

Muro, A., 1988, 'Rural Women and Agriculture: A Situation Analysis', Paper Presented at World Food Day Workshop, in A. Njau and T. Mruma eds., *Proceedings of the Women Research and Documentation Project*, Gender Seminar Series, Dar-es-Salaam

Mwaipopo, R., 1994, *The Impact of Commodity Relations on the Status and Position of Women in Peasant Households: A Case Study of Syukula Village, Rungwe District, Mbeya Region.*

Nikoi, G., 1990, 'Women's Initiatives in African Food Security: The Link between Micro Activities and Macro Policies: Advocates for African Food Security', *Lessening the Burden for Women Symposium* Held at the United Nations, November 15.

Nkonoki, S., 1994, 'Gender, Technology and Agricultural Development', in Njau and T. Mruma eds., *Proceedings of the Women Research and Documentation Project*, Gender Seminar Series, Dar-es-Salaam.

Ousmane, D., 1996, 'Food Security and Nutrition: The Role of Women', in *NGO Working Group on Nutrition on the Status of Women: A Paper for the World Food Summit*, Geneva

Phiri, E., 1990, 'Women in Agricultural Extension: Problems and Prospects: Zambia case Study', *Paper Presented at the Regional Course on Administration and Management of Agricultural Extension Services*, Morogoro, Tanzania.

Rafferty, M., 1988, 'Women Development and Adult Education in Tanzania', in M. Hodd ed., *Tanzania after Nyerere*, London: Printer Publishers Ltd.

Riley, N., 1997, 'Gender, Power and Population Change' in M. Kent ed., *Population Bulletin*, Vol. 52: 1.

Rwambali, E., 1991, 'Women and Agricultural Extension, Has It By Passed Them? Experiences from Morogoro Region', Paper Presented at the *Workshop on Women in Agricultural Extension* held at Dodoma, Tanzania, November 26–27.

Shayo, E., 1991, 'Women in Agricultural Extension', Paper Presented at the *Workshop on Women in Agricultural Extension* held at Dodoma, Tanzania, November 26–27.

Trenchard, E., 1987, 'Rural Women Work in sub Saharan Africa and the Implications for Nutrition' in J. Monsen & J. Townsend eds., *Geography of Gender in the Third World*, London: Butler and Tanner Ltd.

URT and UNICEF, 1990, *Women and Children in Tanzania: A Situation Analysis*, Dar-es-Salaam.

Van Den Ban, A. and Hawkins, H., 1988, *Agricultural Extension*, Essex: Longman Scientific and Technical.

Virji, M. and Meghji, Z., 1989, A *Study of Credit Facilities to Women in Tanzania*, Mimeo.

Wagao, J., 1991, *Household Food security and Nutrition in Tanzania: A Consultancy Report* submitted to UNICEF Regional Office, Nairobi.

Wambura, C., 1992, *Accessibility of Agricultural Technical Information to Rural Women in Morogoro Rural district.*

Weidemann, C., 1987, 'Designing Agricultural Extension for Women Farmers in Developing Countries', in M. Rivera & S. Scram eds., *Agricultural Extension World Wide*, London & New York: Croom Helm.

Wiley, L., 1984, 'Tanzania: The Arusha Planning and Village Development Project', in C. Overholt & M. Anderson eds., *Gender Roles in Development Projects*, Connecticut: Kumarian Press.

5

Trajectories of Women, Environmental Degradation and Scarcity: Examining Access to and Control Over Resources in Ethiopia

Zenebe N. Bashaw

Introduction

The degree of access to and control over resources within a society play significant roles in differentiating members of a society in policy and decision-making processes. Not all societies have legal, organizational and political frameworks that promote fair access to and control over resources. Concepts ranging from deprivation to marginalization, exclusions and alienations are employed to indicate the extent of denying latitudes in controlling resources within a society. The extent of the problems of 'who gets what, when and how' (Laswell 1969) is highly critical in agrarian societies with scarce resources where the majority of the population live in highly degraded rural areas. The bargaining power of men and women crucially shapes the resource allocation decisions of rural households (International Food Policy Research Institute 2000: 1). It has been recognized that access to and control over resources molds the bargaining power and status of women (Thomas 1990; Hopkins, Levin and Haddad 1994). The status of women within such a context is more precarious and sordid than that of other members of the society.

Gender analysis refers to a multitude of methods and approaches that look into the roles and relationships between women and men, and their access to and control over resources. It is not only a cognitive tool for structuring and framing the interactions and relations between the sexes, but also a practical tool that cuts across needs assessment, activities and responsibilities, resources, access and control, benefits and incentives analysis, and institutional constraints and opportunities. As such gender analysis has passed through a multitude of paradigms and approaches. The past decade witnessed the Gender Roles Framework (GRF); the University College-London Department of Planning Unit (DPU) Framework – 'triple roles model'; the Social Relations Framework developed by the Institute for Development Studies (IDS), Sussex; and the approaches of feminist economics.

In gender analysis access to and control over resources is 'one of the principal factors determining the economic and social well-being of women, especially in situations of conflict and reconstruction, when their rights are violated on a mass scale' (United Nations Center For Human Settlements 1999: 4). This is especially true in countries with an arduous and protracted history of war, famine, environmental degradation, resource scarcity and highly conservative and male dominated societies like Ethiopia. However, such calls for resource access and control should focus on feasibilities of deriving benefits from ownership of resources. Rhetorical calls just for the sake of granting titular ownership of resources boil down to zero sum results. From the political dimensions, reforms and policy advocacy need to appreciate the conditions at the micro level and the structures of agrarian societies.

The population of the country was estimated to be 63,494,702 in 2000. Ethiopian society is highly agrarian, with 85 per cent of its people living in rural areas. What is more significant is almost 50 percent of the rural population, 26,876,699, constitutes women (Central Statistics Authority 1994). As a patriarchal society, women's status and condition is one level worse than that of other members of the society in spite of their significant number and role in the country's agrarian economy. Women constitute the majority of the population living in absolute poverty. The United Nations reiterated that there is growing evidence that in the past decade, the number of women living in poverty has increased disproportionately to that of men (United Nations 1996). The extent of poverty, the state of the environment and the conditions of women therefore proved to be far more acute, far more deteriorated, and far more precarious than a couple of decades ago despite limited and unsteady positive changes. The trajectories of acute poverty, degraded environment, alienated and deprived women have today become one of the most deplorable trends within the structures of agrarian societies. Such a phenomenon has particularly marked an unprecedented proliferation of cases where acute poverty, access to and control over resources, and degraded environment have significantly been influencing and shaping the role, condition and status of women within agrarian societies like Ethiopia.

Study Objectives

This study aims to look into the paths of access to and control over resources – mainly agricultural land – by women in two rural communities of Tigray and Wello in northern Ethiopia. The study is based on research projects of the Netherlands-Israeli Research Programme (NIRP) and the Peasant Production and Development project in Ethiopia (PPDE). Is it worth calling for access to and control over resources, mainly land, by women in the mainly agrarian society of Ethiopia? Do women with access to and control over land resources have actual control and benefits of land ownership? This study attempts to answer these research questions.

From a multicausal approach, it is believed here that any analysis of the trajectories of access to and control over resources by rural women in Ethiopia should focus on the feasibility and actual benefit of control over and use of land resource. Policy and socio-cultural factors significantly account for the downturn trend, also influenced by the structure of the agrarian Ethiopian society. The multicausal nature of the problem is reflected in women's position and status, which, according to Lawrence Haddad, is formed around a series of cultural and economic factors such as resource use, ownership, control, legal and ideological structures, and education and information (Haddad 1999: 96-97). Acute environmental degradation and resource scarcity also contribute to the increase in the value of land and struggles for its control as a resource. These causalities have been aggravated by the inadequacies of successive governments' practical concern for appropriate gender approaches that could facilitate, as Charlotte Johnson-Welch puts it, 'the process of identification and change of inequities – in power relations, decision-making and resource access and use' (Johnson-Welch 2000: 6).

Study Methodology

This study uses a case study approach. Among others, three major types of case studies may be identified: correlational analysis, controlled-case comparison and process tracing (Van Evera 1997). Specific to the study of trajectories of access to and control over resources, correlational analysis involves collecting large amounts of quantitative data on the extent of practically using and controlling land by women across many societies and over time. In controlled-case comparison, cases are selected that vary on the independent variable, for example political, socio-cultural or environmental degradation and scarcity, but that are essentially the same for all other variables that might affect the incidence of actual benefits and control over resources. Finally in process tracing, cases with a prima facie assumption of women with access to land but with limited actual benefits as result of political, socio-cultural and environmental degradation and scarcity are selected for further analysis and examination (Van Evera 1997). In this study, the case selected is more related to the process tracing methodology of case study.

Primary and secondary sources of data were employed. Intensive interviews, structured questionnaire, informal discussions were held with 250 farmers and women. The study also held interviews and discussion with regional and local government officials, non-governmental representatives and elders. Books, journals, official documents, Internet documents were used as secondary sources of data.

Environmental Degradation and Scarcity: an Overview

Ethiopia is an ancient country, historically dated as 3000 years. However, the writing of history in the country, to use Gebru Tareke's words, 'has been a contested terrain' as recently as the past few decades. Disagreements have been budding between nationalist-hegemonists and cultural pluralists. 'Whereas the first group traced the lineage of the modern state to the ancient Axumite civilization, thereby laying claim to some three thousand years of history,' writes Tareke, 'the latter group dismissed that claim as historical mythology' (Tareke 1996: 217–18). Nonetheless, what is not contested is that the country's history has been full of arduous conflicts, wars, rebellions and famines despite its being portrayed as the cradle of human kind and land of plenty!

Donald Levin captures five general categories of images of Ethiopia over the centuries. The country has been illustrated as a far-off land; a home of pristine piety; a magnificent kingdom; an outpost of savagery; and a bastion of African independence (Levin 1974). Miles Bredin adds to the list as follows: '[t]oday, as then, Ethiopia is a surprising place. Where you expect Live Aid-style deserts and starving children, there are monumental mountain ranges and one of the most ancient cultures in Africa' (Bredin 2000, 48–55). In the eyes of John Markakis, the Ethiopian 'homeland suffers from an age-old process of physical degradation, the work of natural forces abetted by human and animal action…. Continuous cultivation and grazing stripped the earth of its natural cover, leaving it unprotected against the torrential rains that beat on the inclined surfaces of the highlands' (Markakis 1987: 8).

The country suffers from acute environmental degradation and scarcity, understood in the Ethiopian sense broadly as land degradation (Djene 1990: 49). Agricultural produce in the country fails to meet subsistence needs of the population with an annual growth rate of 3 percent (Food and Agricultural Organization 2000). A mix of factors ranging from population pressure to unfavorable land tenure system, over-ploughing, over-grazing of farm lands, mismanagement of land resource, deforestation, soil erosion and inappropriate land use systems are responsible for the deteriorating productivity of land in Ethiopia. For over one year, the production of major crops such as *teff* (indigenous grass), wheat, maize, barley and sorghum is barely enough to feed the population.

Historically, famine occurs been every 6–8 years in northern Ethiopia and every 8–10 years for the whole country (Haile 1988: 90). Richard Pankhrust outlined an average of one famine incidence every decade between the fifteenth and nineteenth centuries (Pankhrust 1985: 26). There have been forty major famines and food shortages in total, with fourteen occurring in northern Ethiopia, particularly in Tigray and Wello, areas where this study is focused (Webb & Braun 1994: 20–21). For years, the country has not produced sufficient food to feed its people. Almost 90 percent of the population live in rural areas where the predominant economic activity is rain-fed agriculture.

The ever-increasing population number and the overwhelming dependence on rain-fed agriculture put tremendous pressure on the carrying capacity and productivity of the land. Berry Hughes argues that 'population prediction at least for a period of 20–30 years tends to be more accurate than predictions in other issue areas' (Hughes 1993: 15). The present international consensus is that in the next thirty years the world population will swell to at least 8.2 billion (Novartis Foundation for Sustainable Development 2000). In the words of Thomas Homer-Dixon, it is not only a mere scarcity of resources that create challenging conditions to sustenance and development without conflicts and instabilities, but also demand sides as a result of population increase (Homer-Dixon 1999).

It is hardly difficult to discern the status of women within a degraded, highly sensitive, conflictual and male dominated agricultural resource of land. It has been an underlying triggering factor for series of peasant revolts against successive governments in the country. Leslie Gray and Michael Kevane show that 'when land becomes scarce or rises in value, or when rights are formalized through titles or registration, these rights to use land are revealed to be secondary and tenuous' (Gray & Kevane 1999: 2). The impact of resource degradation and resources on politico-economic factors in Ethiopia is highly debated (Meadows *et al.* 1979; Djene 1990; Lanz 1996; Semait 1989; Rahmato 1999; Homer-Dixon 1999; Wolde Mariam 1984; Cohn 1987; Duetch 1996; Tareke 1996; Young 1997; Kebbede 1992; Molver 1991; Tvedt 1993; Myers 1993; Cohn & Anderson 1999; McCann 1991; Picket 1991).

Specifically, impacts through feedback loops on political and policy decisions are very interesting to examine, for they have close relationships with limiting or restricting policy choices in land (re)distributions. The causality is mutual when politico-economic policies bring diverse impacts on the environment. Increased resource degradation and scarcity entails dismal prospects for women. Access to and ownership of agricultural land holds the key to access to other sources of income and assets. The dependence of women on men becomes complete, and rural households will be seen as unitary thereby discounting and blurring the contributions and conditions of women.

Paradoxically women are more active in environmental and resource conservation activities, which are widely recognized and documented (Merchant 1995; Steel 1996). The United Nations gave credence to women as closely associated with local ecological resources and management of biodiversity on a daily basis (UN 2001: 6). Women play significant roles in intervening against the problem of food insecurity mainly caused by environmental degradation and resource scarcity. Chris Udry's assessments indicate that women's contributions towards increasing food security amount to as much as 15 percent of household income (Udry 1996). Identifying individuals' differential access to and control over resources and benefits is the fundamental feature of gender analysis, and ensuring equitable access and distribution will enhance food security (Johnson *et al.* 2000: 10).

Women And Access to and Control Over Land Resource: Overview of Findings

There appears to be increasing evidence that 'greater gender equality correlates with higher economic growth and ... poverty reduction strategies must pay serious attention to reducing gender disparities' (Zuckerman 2001: 2). Even if the causality needs thorough investigation, the incidence of poverty is highly correlated with lack of access to land (Mearns 1999: 1). Nothing is more important in a society where rural population make up the overwhelming majority than the availability of productive land (Young 1989: 199). Access to and control over land as a resource have received the greatest amount of attention because, as a fixed asset, it is easier to define the boundaries of the resource unit (Meinzen-Dick *et al* 1997: 13). The World Bank succinctly summarizes the broader importance of owning land. It states that access to and control over land shapes equity because land is still one of the major assets held by households; influences efficiency because land is one of the economy's main productive assets; underlines sustainability of resource use, for it is important for agricultural production and the provision of nationally-important ecosystem services; and affects governance because there is a strong link between land tenure and the prevention of conflict (World Bank 2001).

In many parts of Ethiopia poor access to resources is widely acknowledged as a major cause of food insecurity (Amare *et al* 2000: 2). The 1975 'land to the tiller' Proclamation No 31 of Ethiopia brought fundamental changes in terms of allowing land 'ownership' to the majority of the rural population. Under the 'Public Ownership of Rural Lands Proclamation' the tenancy system, hired farm labor and private ownership of land were abolished while placing a limit of 10 hectares of cultivatable land for any given farm and making provisions for the establishment of a peasant association (Yefru 2000: 362). The recognition of the intricate relationships among these factors has led to the growing interest in examining the nature and status of rural women access to and control over resources like land. Consequently, women's access to and control over land, and their property rights have received considerable attention internationally, regionally and locally (United Nations Development Fund for Women 2001: 8). So is a growing interest to address the impediments of women access to and control over resources, as indicated in the Beijing Declaration and Platform for Action (1995), the Nairobi Forward-Looking Strategies for the Advancement of Women (1985) and the twenty-third special session of the General Assembly titled 'Women 2000: gender equality, development and peace for the twenty-first century'.

However, these calls have unfortunately been mostly rhetorical and political, and really far from the critical questions of locating the real locus of power. In other words, when access to and control over land is problematized, it creates disparities regarding who has real control over the produce of the land. A call for greater access to land ownership is one thing. But addressing and locating concrete problems of power in land ownership, although transcended in many aspects by gender analysis, has been elusive over the past decades. The great majority of women in rural Ethiopia do not have access to and control over resources, mainly land. Even women with access to land ownership do not have actual control over their resources. They receive a significantly lower amount of the produce of their land, for they are dependent on male labor, which is locally termed as 'ye equil'. Feleke Tadele succinctly writes that despite their equal share with men in socio-economic life, Ethiopia women have little decision-making power and a smaller share of resources and benefits. Eighty-seven per cent of women in Ethiopia are engaged in agriculture, contributing about 50 per cent of income based on subsistence agriculture. However, little attention has been given to involving women in rural development efforts and enabling them to benefit directly from agricultural extension services (2001: 16).

In this study, access to and control over resources, mainly agricultural land, is viewed as the right or opportunity to use, manage, or control land and its resources. It includes the ability to reach and make use of the resource and constitutes two parameters: quantitative parameters (such as the nature of tenure, the size of the parcel and its economic value) and qualitative parameters (for example, legal security, and documented, or registered evidence of rights to land). These parameters play an important role in 'measuring' access to land before, during, and after development projects or land administration programs (Komjathy & Nichols 2001: 2). During the study, intensive interviews were conducted with more than 250 farmers and women in the two research regions over a four-year period. In Tigray region Atsbi Wonberta and Humera areas were covered while in Wello region Kalu 'wereda' (district) was selected as a research site. Almost two third of the respondents (127) were women with access to land resource. The study mainly aimed to assess the extent to which women with access to land actually have control over their ownership of land. It also attempted to examine the feasibility and viability of increased calls for greater access to and ownership of land by women.

Findings from the studies indicate that recommendations for increased access to and control of resources by women should focus on assessing who actually controls and draws benefits from land. The status and rights of women, in access to and control over resources and other broader aspects, are characterized by duality. Specifically, the issue constitutes both spatial and temporal facets in Ethiopia. Despite national and all-inclusive legal frameworks that profess to provide equal rights to women and men in resource ownership, strong customary and cultural practices dictate the realities of women at the micro level, especially in rural areas. So, from a temporal perspective, rural women are immersed in numerous quagmires indicating highly precarious and unsteady prospects for equality with men. Nationally recognized constitutional rights are influenced by the spatial and diverse customs and beliefs, which in turn are subject to changes and improvements time-wise. The problems of these rural women range from the feminization of poverty to the feminization of agriculture, the feminization of immigration and so on.

The Central Statistical Authority classifies a *de jure* female-headed household (roughly constituting 20–25 percent) as a household where the land is owned and managed by a woman, such as in families headed by widows or by single or divorced women. On the other hand, a *de facto* female-headed household is a household where a woman is responsible for all aspects of managing the household and the farm due to the absence of a husband. One should treat these statistical figures with much skepticism. In fact, in Africa in general, William Cavendish realizes that analysis of rural households and resources is beset by inadequate data (1999). Still, however, as a result of war, sickness and death from HIV/AIDS and migration of men from rural areas to towns and cities, there are trends that signal the decreased role of men in agriculture and the 'feminization of agriculture'. Such factors in turn have increased the number of female-headed rural households (Food and Agriculture Organization 2000).

Ruth Meinzen-Dick *et al* argue that access to and control over resources 'include far more than titles and pieces of paper specifying 'ownership' of a defined piece of land or other resource. They encompass a diverse set of tenure rules and other aspects of access to and use of resources' (Ruth Meinzen-Dick *et al. 1997*: 1). The Secretary General's report of the United Nations underlined that although rural women may have *de jure* rights, they do not have *de facto* rights (2001: 6). Perhaps a common denominator among these variables might be the culturally dominant role of men in the long history of the country. Distinctively the ownership of and succession to land has historically been a fiercely protected

sphere of men. The question of land has been a burning issue leading to protracted peasant revolts. Based on the land question, the manner and nature of
warfare have been shaped, where 'whose face have you not disfigured? Whose
wife and child have you not captured?' ran rebels' song for a long time (Caulk
1978: 460). Generally in Africa women obtain rights to land through men, mainly
through their husbands or sons (Kabutha 1999: 9).

According to the results of this research study, one major problem of women
with access to land was their inability to efficiently and effectively use their land.
They are highly dependent on men's labor. What is widely known as 'ye equl',
which literarily translates to as equal share of the produce of the land, was practised in the research areas. 20 percent of the interviewees had an average family
size of 6 in which women were responsible for supporting the family, while 15
percent of the respondents constituted women-headed households. The extent
of the women's dependence on men's labor is such that in Humera area of Tigray
region women with access to big plots of land could not actually use their land.
The plots that they received were virgin plots full of acacia trees that needed a
community labor force to clear them and put to use. In Kalu area more than 63
percent of the women with access to land did not own oxen, an indispensable
component of agriculture in the region. A landless male farmer with a pair of
oxen can receive much of the produce of a plot of land if he works on the plot,
which actually belongs to a woman. Even if women entrust equal share arrangement to their relatives, any assistance received by the women had to be paid for.

The inability of women to enjoy the benefits of access to land results in a
paradoxical exclusion of women from agricultural resources. According to Charles
Gore, this includes 'restriction access to land resources and patterns of land
poverty; exclusion from access to productive inputs, high value crops and output
markets; and processes of land degradation.' Gore emphasized that 'in the past
in Africa, some people were poor because they were excluded from livelihood.
Now they are poor because they are excluded from livelihood and they are excluded from livelihood because they are poor' (Gore 1994:26,81). For Baden and
Milward (1995), it has become common in development circles to talk of the
'feminization of poverty'. The phrase implies that poverty is becoming a female
phenomenon, or that women are becoming poorer relative to men According to
Mayra Buvinic (1997) evidence of feminization of poverty is seen when women
are consistently found to be more impoverished than men based on their level of
well-being. However, based on the income-level definition of poverty, evidence
shows that the gap between the two sexes is decreasing in terms of well-being. In
Atsbi Wonberta of Tigray, the majority of women own plots of land requiring
up to 5 hours of walk from their residences. It was nearly impossible for women
farmers to maintain these travel schedules, especially during weeding seasons
when they have greater responsibilities. In these conditions, as witnessed in Kalu

area of this research, women were forced to rely on the labor of children as young as 7 years old.

For an agrarian society that suffers from chronic food insecurity like Ethiopia, understanding the link between access to land and actual benefits of land ownership is as essential as searching measures for alleviating the twin problems of food insecurity and poverty (Melmed-Sanjak & Lastarria-Cornhiel 1998: 5). The problems have wider impacts when women are most populous but with the least benefit and control over resources. This is particularly important due to its repercussions on children, the future of society. As Mayra Buvinic argues, women caught in a vicious circle of deprivation are unable to cope with too much work leading them to hand over child-care responsibilities to older daughters, who then must drop out of school. As a result, 'deprivation carries from one generation of women to the next, leading to the feminization of income poverty' (Buvinic 1997: 8).

Some gender analysts envision that just increasing women's access to land will revolutionalise agriculture by resolving food insecurity and other agrarian problems of developing countries like Ethiopia. For example, the recommendations of the Kigali Plan of Actions of 1998, among others, called for the adequate and secure rights of women to property ownership, and their independence from men in order to secure or enjoy their rights (United Nations 1998). Given what lies at the micro level within the structure of agrarian societies and cultural hindrances to women's effective ownership and use of land, this study is highly skeptical of such recommendations. We acknowledge that proper intervention in redressing the problem of resource inequality, environmental degradation and scarcity in the country should tackle the problem of rural women. The field works in Atsbi Wonberta, Kalu and Humera indicated that the dependence of women with access to land on men led to series of conflicts between landowners and laborers. In the three areas of this study, more than 65 percent of women reported that they had an average of four incidences of conflicts with men laborers who worked on their farm. Late start by male laborers (144) constituted the highest incidence of conflicts followed by breach of agreements (59) and high demand of produce (42). These problems arise because of the patriarchal structure of the societies and men's commanding influence in the political and social spheres.

Agricultural land in northern Ethiopia has been undergoing tremendous negative changes leading to a sharp decline in food productivity and vicious circle of chronic food insecurity. A mix of factors ranging from population pressure, farming system, overexploitation, government policies, land tenure and its associated problem of security for conservation, soil erosion, culture and knowledge of environmental conservation/protection and the like account for this. There also seems to be a link between productivity and management of agricultural land.

Consequently, agricultural land in the two research areas need well-organized and continuous land management systems. A comparative assessment of land owned by women and leased on to landless men and land owned and managed by male-headed households revealed a disparity in productivity. Rain distribution being a constant factor, a comparison of land productivity within a four-year period between the two land management modes showed an average decline of 12.4 kilo grams of produce per year of leased land. Paradoxically women's role in conservation and environmental protection is well documented.

The indispensability of land as a resource base and the need to reconcile the rhetorical call for increased access to and control over land resources constitute one of the major problems facing policy makers and rural development experts in Ethiopia Evidence from this and other research indicates that the majority of women were not the actual owners of their produce. While different paradigms within gender analysis recommend that gender mainstreaming and empowerment are keys to addressing the problem of women's control over resources, findings of this study shows that the prospects for empowering women in Ethiopia are grim. Nevertheless, empowerment is central to issues of rights and power to own land and its produce. Power here involves four possibilities: power over (controlling power over someone and something); power to (generative or productive power that creates new possibilities and actions without domination); power with (power generating a feeling that the whole is greater than the sum of individuals and action as a group is more effective; and power from within (a sense that there is strength in each and every individual) (Rowlands 1997).

The gender approaches of the two successive regimes in Ethiopia have been too weak to provide either a stimulus for reform or a challenge to the patriarchal structures of the agrarian society. Many respondents in this study believed that despite the positive changes and attempts by the incumbent Ethiopian People's Revolutionary Front (EPRDF) to address gender issues in resource ownership, women are far from influencing decisions at the local level. The composition of local decision-making organs in Tigray and Wello, where EPRDF has a strong root, showed increasing participation by women. Among the five villages in Atsbi Wonberta, women led two local administrative councils. In Humera, women had strong voices in the tight returnee communities. In Kalu, the influence of Islamic customs proved to be a serious challenge to increased political roles for women. I had the chance of participating in a meeting of two local administrative councils to discuss distribution of seeds and arbitration of conflicts arising out of land management between women owners and men laborers. The experience revealed that women's participation in local councils were directly correlated to the desire to address gender inequalities in the system. Informal discussions with men farmers indicated that they recognized women's need special attention in farm management and produce ownership. Yet, the same men were hesitant to give women special treatment at the expense of endangering customs and family decision-making. Unfortunately these issues are at the center of de facto land ownership and access to other resources and benefits such as extension services, credit and membership to farmers' organizations (United Nations 2001: 6).

Another finding of this study is that despite efforts to diversify the income of rural communities throughout the country there was still high dependence on incomes derived from land. One major aspect of income diversification projects has been the food-for-work (FFW) and cash-for-work (CFW) programs. These schemes are interchangeably called employment generation schemes (EGS), employment guarantee schemes (EGS) and so on. Such projects help to generate supplementary incomes for peasant farmers. Employment and income generation schemes have become important poverty mitigation strategies by government and non-government organizations in developing countries (The World Bank 1989: 39-66; Zetter 1996: 217; UNRISD 1995: 7; Nyamugasira 1995: 161-64; Hurley 1990). However, these programs have had implementation difficulties arising from overriding problem of deep-rooted poverty, governance deficiencies and drought and conflicts in most of developing countries.

According to the National Policy on Disaster and Preparedness Measure (NPDPM) in Ethiopia, such schemes aim to provide a means of income (in cash or in kind) to the most affected people in disaster affected areas; build up the assts of affected areas in order to improve their resilience to disaster; create conditions for eliminating the root causes of disaster and build up the infrastructures for future development and; reinforce work ethos of the affected population (NPDPM 1993: 22). Ethiopia's income and employment generating projects undertook micro-dam constructions, soil conservation, road constructions and reforestation. The financial, organizational and grass-root advantages of NGOs mobilized peasant farmers for intensive participation. Tigray and Wello areas have benefited from extensive and large-scale income and employment projects since the 1980s, and especially after 1991. One comprehensive study of 24 such projects in the country found them to induce people for 'extensive communal activities for the first time in many areas, and that farmers, necessarily cautious people, are at least open-minded and often positive about the benefits of the *physical works*, but will finally judge them by the test of time' (emphasis added, Solomon & Yeraswork, 1984:94). The contribution – material, financial and labor – of NGOs and the community in employment and income generating projects was in the ratio of 70:30. Whilst a number of NGOs' projects pay in the form of food - 3 kegs per person per day, few NGOs, like the Adigrat Catholic Secretariat in Eastern Tigray, paid cash. In the 1980s UNICEF undertook similar cash-for-work project in Ethiopia (Webb & Von Braun 1993).

Selections in such important employment and income generating projects mainly give priority to landless peasants. Interviews and discussions at three project sites, Haresaw, Debre Selam (Rubafelege) and Atsbi Endesilassie, and the payment distribution center at Atsbi Wonberta, in addition to supplementary interviews conducted for other projects in Irob and Saese Tsadamba of Tigray showed that women registered as owners of land could not participate in the projects. This was especially true in cases of fallow plots where women could not clear the plots and put them in use. On the other hand, landless male peasants working on women-owned plots, were selected to participate in FFW/CFW projects and could derive incomes from both sides. Cases like this indicate that selection criteria in project participation do not look beyond titular ownership of land towards examining the nature of the claims to access in the same way that calls for access to and ownership of resources fail short of dissecting who really controls the produce.

Rural Ethiopian women only have recourse to long and arduous mechanisms to realize equal control over agricultural land. These involve political and social aspects, which show limited improvements with time. At the international and regional levels, donors, non-governmental organizations and women advocates brought the issue to the macro policy level. A case in point is the formulation of a new Family Law in 2000 substituting the 1960 Family Law whereby the husband was recognized as the head of the family. The interest in women's participation as an integral part of any successful policy for tacking the problems of food insecurity and poverty is encouraging. However, while positive, the changes are too limited to bring real women's control over resources without impediments.

Another factor is the impact of environmental degradation and scarcity in aggravating the problem of land availability. Research reports and findings point to a declining role of land as resource and income base for rural households. They argue that since rural households are not able to support themselves exclusively on land-based activities, they seek additional income from different sources. Consequently, most rural households are undergoing significant income diversification. The strategy a household can adopt depends, among other factors, on access to productive resources such as land, capital, education and skills (United Nations, 2001). In studying peasant households in Ethiopia and Tanzania, Stephan Dercon and Pramila Krishana indicate the various productive resources available to a household: a plot of land, consumer goods for sale in local markets, crops for subsistence and/or cash. In addition, 'the household might engage in local crafts and trades, hire out its labor and keep livestock. The household might receive remittances from relatives away in town and help in a crisis from neighbors' (Dercon and Krishnan 1996: 850). These findings are worth noting, especially when 'diversification' come with negative implications. For example, when rural households encourage the trafficking of their young daughters for prostitution (Atsbi and Humera) or illegally cut trees for sale or increase forced child labour (as high as 27 cases in Kalu area of Wello), then the strategies need to be reconsidered thoroughly. Eventually, it appears that all strategies become double-edged swords.

Conclusion

The indispensability of land resources for the livelihood of millions of rural people in Africa is tremendous. Agrarian societies are facing increasing problems of environmental degradation and resource scarcity. Acute environmental degradation and resource scarcity are producing impacts that seriously challenge the capacity to provide enough agricultural land for an increasing world population with various needs. A mix of factors such as population increase, politico-economic policies, resource use management and approaches, soil erosion and other account for the intensity of the problem. African governments are faced with challenges in responding to demands for resource distribution amid acute scarcity. The overwhelming war and famine-ridden agrarian society of Ethiopia is a litmus test of the challenges. The livelihood of the great majority of rural women depends on access to and control over land resource, which in turn substantially influences access to other resources and assets. However, we find that women's actual control over land, despite constituting almost 50 per cent of the rural population, is deplorably poor.

Some gender analysts envision that just giving women access to land will revolutionalise agriculture by resolving food insecurity and other agrarian problems of developing countries like Ethiopia. Given what lies at the micro level within the structure of agrarian societies and the extent of women's status to effectively use ownership of land, this study is very skeptical of just calling for women's access to land resource. Increased calls for resource access and control should focus on feasibilities of extracting benefits from ownership of resources. Rhetorical calls just for the sake of granting titular ownership of resources amount to zero sum results. From the political dimensions, reforms and policy advocacy need to appreciate the conditions at the micro level and the structures of agrarian societies.

This study explored the trajectories of access to and control over resources by rural women in Ethiopia, with a focus on the feasibility and actual benefit of control over and use of land resource. It attempted to show that women's ownership of land and its products in Ethiopia is currently an illusion. Women do no actually own their resources!. The failure to bring about special and realistic considerations of women's conditions in land (re)distribution programs, conflict in the management of leased agricultural land, a decline in the productivity of leased land, inability to benefit from public projects, and an extensive and almost absolute dependence on agricultural land, as well as the corresponding challenges of income diversification constitute major themes that this research tried elucidate. Women's access to and control over resources, mainly agricultural land, needs to be problematised. Mainstream gender analysis should focus on critically questioning the pros and cons of addressing the role and status of women within access to and control over agricultural land. By way of conclusion, there is a need to redirect the attention from changing fashions to fashioning changes in shaping the almost conflictual gender relations to follow a conflictual-cooperative dimension in resource management and ownership.

References

Amare, Y. *et al.*, 2000, *Food Security and Resource Access: A Final Report on the Community Assessments in South Wello and Oromiya Zones of Amhara Region, Ethiopia*, Broadening Access and Strengthening Input Market Systems-Collaborative Research Support Program (BASISCRSP), January, Madison: The Land Tenure Center.

Baden, S. and Milward, K., 1995, *Gender and Poverty*, *BRIDGE Report*, No. 30, SIDA, January.

Bamberger, M., 2001, 'Integrating Gender into the PRSP: Key Issues and Lessons from Cambodia.' World Bank Gender and Development PREM Network, Washington DC.

Bevan, P. and Pankhurst, A., 1996, *Report on the Sociological Dimension of the Ethiopian Rural Economies Project*, Center for the Study of African Economies, Oxford University and Department of Sociology, Addis Ababa University.

Blackden, C. and Bhanu, C., 1999, 'Gender, Growth, and Poverty Reduction: Special Program of Assistance for Africa, 1998 Status Report on Poverty in Sub-Saharan Africa' *Technical Paper 428*. World Bank, Poverty Reduction and Social Development, Africa Region, Washington, DC.

Bredin, M., 2000, 'Great Scot.' *Geographical*, Vol. 72, No. 3.

Brown, L. R. *et al.*, 1997, 'Gender, Property Rights, and Natural Resources' *Discussion Paper*, Food Consumption and Nutrition Division International Food Policy Research Institute (FCND), No. 29.

Buvinic, M., 1997, 'Women in Poverty: A New Global Underclass' *Foreign Policy*, Fall.

Caulk, R., 1978, 'Armies as Predators: Soldiers and Peasants in Ethiopia, c 1850-1935' *International Journal of African Historical Studies*, Vol. 11.

Center for the Study of African Economies, 1999, 'Empirical Regularities in the Poverty-Environment Relationship of African Rural Households.' WPS, 99-21 September, Available online: http://www.economics.ox.ac.uk/CSAEadmin/workingpapers/1999

Central Statistics Authority, 1994, *Results of Population Census*, Addis Ababa.

Ciriacy-Wantrup, W., 1952, *Resource Conservation, Economics and Policies*, California: University of California Press.

Cohn, J., 1987, *Integrated Rural Development: The Ethiopian Experience and the Debates*, Uppsala: Scandinavian Institute of African Studies.

Cohn, M. and Anderson, P., 1999, 'Food security and conflict' *Social Research*. Vol. 66, no. 1, Spring.

Dercon, S. and Krishnan, P., 1996, 'Income portfolios in Rural Ethiopia and Tanzania: Choices and constraints,' *The Journal of Development Studies*, Vol. 32, no. 6.

Djene, A., 1990, *Environment, Politics and Famine in Ethiopia: A View from the Village*, Boulder and London: Lynne Rienner Publishers.

Duetch, J., 1996, 'The Environment on the Intelligence Agenda.' *Remarks to the World Affairs Council*, Los Angeles CA, July.

Fafchamps, M. and Quisumbing, A., 2000, 'Control and ownership of assets within rural Ethiopian households', *Working Paper*, Center for the Study of African Economies, Oxford: University of Oxford.

Food and Agricultural Organization, (nd) 'Gender and Food Security: Agriculture', Available online: http://www.fao.org/Gender/en/agri-e.htm.

Food and Agricultural Organization, 2000, 'Food and Agriculture in Ethiopia' Available online: http://www.fao.org/giews/english/basedocs/eth/ethpop1e.stm.

Food and Agriculture Organization, 2000. 'The Feminization of Agriculture,' Gender and Food Security, Available online: http://www.fao.org/Gender/en/agrib2-e.htm.

Gopal, G. and Salim, M., 1999, *Gender and Law: Eastern Africa Speaks*, Washington, DC.: The World Bank.

Gore, C., 1994, *Social Exclusion and Africa South of the Sahara: A Review of Literature*, ILO, Geneva.

Gray, L. and Kevane, M., 1999, 'Diminished Access, Diverted Exclusion: Women and Land Tenure in Sub-Saharan Africa', *African Studies Review*, Vol. 42, No.2.

Haddad, L., 1999, 'Women's Status: Levels, Determinants, Consequences for Malnutrition, Interventions, and Policy,' *Asian Development Review*, Vol. 17, Nos. 1-2.

Haile, T., 1988, 'Causes and Characters of Drought in Ethiopia,' *Ethiopian Journal of Agricultural Sciences.*, Vol. 10, No. 1-2.

Homer-Dixon, T., 1999, *Environment, Scarcity and Violence* Princeton, NJ.: Princeton University Press.

Hopkins, J, Levin, C. & Haddad, L., 1994, 'Women's income and household expenditure patterns: gender or flow? Evidence from Niger,' *American Journal of Agricultural Economics*, Vol. 76, No. 5, December.

Hughes, B., 1993, *International Features, Choices in the Search for a New World Order*, Boulder Colorado: Westview.

International Food Policy Research Institute, 2000, 'Gender and Intra-household Aspects of Food Policy Resource Allocation and Empowerment of Women in Rural Bangladesh,' *Project Brief.* No 1.

Johnson, C. *et al.*, 2000, 'Improving Household Food Security Institutions, Gender, and Integrated Approaches,' *Broadening Access and Strengthening Input Market Systems, Management Entity.* The Land Tenure Center, Madison, March.

Johnson-Welch, C., 1999, *Focusing on Women Works: Research on Improving Micronutrient Deficiencies through Food-based Interventions,* Washington DC: International Center for Research on Women.

Johnson-Welch, C., 2000, 'Gender and Household Food Security: A Lost Opportunity.' *Paper presented at the International Center for Research on Women, International Food and Nutrition Conference, October 8–10,* Tuskegee University, Washington DC.

Jones, G., 1987, *The Conservations of Ecosystems and Species,* New York: Croom Helm.

Kabutha, C., 1999, 'The Importance of Gender in Agricultural Policies, Resource Access and Human Nutrition,' *A Paper Presented to a Seminar on Agricultural Policy, Resource Access and Nutritional Outcomes,* Addis Ababa, November 3-5.

Katepa-Kalala, P., 1999, 'Mid-Decade Review Of The Implementation of The Beijing Platforms for Action in the African Region Assessment Report on: Evaluation Report on Women and Poverty, and the Economic Empowerment of Women,' *Sixth Regional Conference On Women,* Economic Commission for Africa, 22-26 November, Addis Ababa

Kebbede, G., 1992, *The state and development in Ethiopia,* Atlantic Highlands NJ: Humanities Press.

King, Y., 1983, 'Toward an Ecological Feminism and a Feminist Ecology' In Plant, J. (Ed), *Healing the Wounds: The Promise of Eco-feminism,* London: Green Print.

Komjathy, K. and Nichols, S., 2001, 'Principles for Equitable Gender Inclusion in Land Administration: FIG Guidelines on Women's Access to Land,' *New Technology for a New Century International Conference FIG Working Wee,* Seoul, 6–11 May.

Lanz, T., 1996, 'Environmental Degradation and Social Conflict in the Northern Highlands of Ethiopia: The Case of Tigray and Wello Provinces,' *Africa Today.* Vol. 43, no. 2.

Laswell, H. 1969, *Who Gets What, When, How,* London: Whittlesey House.

Levin, D., 1974, *Greater Ethiopia: The Evolution of a Multi-ethnic Society,* Chicago and London: The University of Chicago Press.

Markakis, J., 1987, *National and Class Conflict in the Horn of Africa,* Cambridge: Cambridge University Press.

McCann, J., 1991, 'Ethiopia' In Glantz, M., (ed) *Drought Follows the Plough: Cultivating Marginal Areas,* Cambridge: Cambridge University Press.

Meadows, D. *et al.*, 1979, *The Limits To Growth: A Report For The Club of Rome's Project on the Predicament of Mankind*, 2nd ed., New York: Universe.

Mearns, R., 1999, 'Access to Land in Rural India,' *Policy Issues and Options*, Washington DC: World Bank.

Meinzen-Dick, R. *et al.*, 1997, 'Gender, Property Rights, and Natural Resources,' *FCND Discussion Paper*, No. 29, Food Consumption and Nutrition Division International Food Policy Research, 7.

Melmed-Sanjak, J. and Lastarria-Cornhiel, S., 1998, 'Land access, off-farm income and capital access in relation to the reduction of rural poverty,' *Land Reform*, 1

Merchant, C., 1980, *The Death of Nature: Women, Ecology and the Scientific Revolution*, San Francisco: Harper & Row Publishers.

Merchant. C., 1995, *Earthcare: Women and the Environment*, New York: Routledge.

Molver, R., 1991, 'Environmentally Induced Conflicts? A Discussion based on Studies from the Horn of Africa,' *Bulletin of Peace Proposals*, Vol. 22, no. 2.

Myers, N., 1993, *Ultimate Security: The Environmental Basis of Political Stability*, New York: W. W. Norton and Company.

Novartis Foundation for Sustainable Development, 2000, 'Food Security for a Growing World Population: 200 Years After Malthus, Still an Unsolved Problem,' Available online: http://www.foundation.novartis.com/food_security_population.htm

Pankhurst, R., 1985, *The History of Famine and Epidemics in Ethiopia Prior to the Twentieth Century*, Relief and Rehabilitation Commission, Addis Ababa

Picket, J., 1991, *Economic Development in Ethiopia: Agriculture, the Market and the State*, OECD, France

Rahmato, D., 1985, *Agrarian Reform in Ethiopia*, New Jersey: Red Sea Press.

Rahmato, R., 1999, 'Environmental Change and Ecological Conflict in Ethiopia,' Unpublished paper, Forum for Social Studies, Addis Ababa, Ethiopia

Rowlands, J., 1997, *Questioning Empowerment. Working with Women in Honduras*, Oxford: Oxfam Publishing.

Steel, B., 1996, 'Thinking Globally and Acting Locally?' Environmental. Attitudes, Behaviour and Activism,' *Journal of Environmental Management*, 47.

Sturgeon, N., 1996, *Eco-feminist Natures: Race, Gender, Feminist Theory and Political Action*, New York: Routledge.

Tadele, F., 2001, 'Men in the Kitchen, Women in the Office? Working On Gender Issues in Ethiopia.' In Sweetman, C., (ed.) *Men's Involvement In Gender And Development Policy And Practice: Beyond Rhetoric*, Oxford: Oxfam Print Unit.

Tareke, G., 1991, Ethiopia: *Power and Protest, Peasant revolt in the Twentieth Century*, New York: Cambridge University Press.

Tareke, G., 1996, 'A History of Ethiopia,' *The American Historical Review*, Vol. 101, No. 1

The United Nations Development Fund for Women, (2001), 'Women's Land and Property Rights in Situations of Conflict and Reconstruction,' *1998 Inter-Regional Consultation*, Kigali, Rwanda.

The United Nations, 1998, Peace for Homes, Homes for Peace', *Inter-Regional Consultation on Women's Land and Property Rights in Situations of Conflict and Reconstruction. Kigali Plan of Action*, Kigali, Rwanda, February.

The United Nations, 2001, 'Advancement of Women Improvement of the Situation of Women in Rural Areas,' *Report of the Secretary-General*, Fifty-sixth session, Item 124 of the provisional agenda, General Assembly, New York

Thomas, D., 1990, 'Intra-household resource allocation: an inferential approach,' *Journal of Human Resources*, Vol. 25, no. 4, Fall.

Thomas, H., 1999, *Environment, Scarcity and Violence*, Princeton NJ: Princeton University Press.

Tvedt, T., ed., 1993, Conflicts in the Horn of Africa: human and ecological consequences of warfare, Uppsala: EPOS.

Udry, C., 1996, 'Gender, Agricultural Production, and the Theory of the Household,' *The Journal of Political Economy*, vol. 104, no. 5, Oct

United Nations Center For Human Settlements, 1999, *Women's Rights to Land, Housing And Property in Post Conflict Situations and During Reconstruction: A Global Overview, Series No. 9*, UN, Nairobi

United Nations, 1995, 'Platform for Action and the Beijing Declaration,' *Report of the Fourth World Conference on Women, Beijing, China, 4-15 September*, UN, New York.

Van Evera, S., 1997, *Guide to Methods for Students of Political Science*, Ithaca and London: Cornell University Press.

W -Semait, B., 1989, 'Ecological Stress and Political Conflict in Africa: The Case of Ethiopia,' In Hjort af Ornas, A. & Mohamed Salih, M., eds. *Ecology and Politics: Environmental Stress and Security in Africa*, Uppsala: Scandinavian Institute of African Studies,

Wallensteen, P., 1986, 'Food Crops as a Factor in Strategic Policy and Action' In Westing, A ., ed., *Global Resources and International Conflict: Environmental Factors in Strategic Policy and Action*, New York: Oxford University Press.

Webb, P. & Braun, V., 1994, *Famine and Food Security in Ethiopia: A Lesson for Africa,*. New Jersey: Red Sea Press Inc.

Wolde, M., 1984, *Rural Vulnerability to Famine in Ethiopia: 1958–1977*, Stosius Inc/ Advent Books Division.

World Bank, 2001, 'Question & Answer on Land Issues at the World Bank.' *Prepared for the 2001 Annual Meetings of the Boards of Governors World Bank Group and International Monetary Fund*, September 29–30, Washington, DC.

Yefru, W., 2000, 'The African Challenge to Philosophical Paradigm: The Need for a Paradigm Shift in the Social, Economic, and Political Development of Africa,' *Journal of Black Studies*. vol. 30, no. 3, January.

Young, J., 1997, *Peasant Revolution in Ethiopia: The Tigray People's Liberation Front, 1975–1991*, Cambridge: Cambridge University Press.

Young, J., nd, 'Regionalism and Democracy in Ethiopia.' *Third World Quarterly*, Vol. 19, No. 2

Zuckerman, E., 2001, 'Engendering Poverty Reduction Strategy Papers (PRSPs): Why it Reduces Poverty and the Rwanda Case,' *WIDER Development Conference on Debt Relief*, August 17–18, Helsinki.

6

Understanding Women's Experiences of Citizenship in Nigeria

Charmaine Pereira

Introduction

Citizenship, as the relationship of the individual to the state, has been reconstructed in feminist theorizing during the 1990s. Such work has analysed citizenship as plural and multi-layered, embodying the recognition of multiple identities and associated new claims for distributing and redistributing the rights and practices linked with citizenship (e.g. Yuval-Davis 1997; Young 1990). Whilst such work is useful for providing a general framework for understanding citizenship, there is a need to understand the realities of women's lives in specific African contexts and use this as a starting point for developing grounded theory on citizenship.

In Nigeria, for example, it is only relatively recently that women's status has been explicitly discussed at national levels by women's autonomous organizations in terms of *citizenship*. This is all the more paradoxical, given the heightened attention paid to certain categories of rights for women under military rule in the 1990s, such as reproductive rights, political rights and at the eve of the millennium, the right to freedom from gender based violence. Women's marginalisation from the national state has been largely instrumental in the recourse made by various categories of women's organizations to international discourses and frameworks of human rights. The prospects of a return to civilian rule and deepening processes of democratization of the state and society have no doubt facilitated what appears to be a re-articulation of human rights for women with discourses of citizenship. The articulation of rights discourses with discourses of citizenship for women is in itself worthy of greater research attention than it has so far received.

The multi-textured character of women's citizenship is effectively depicted below in a memorandum (Salihu et al., 2002:3) sent to a recently constituted Presidential Committee on Provisions and Practice of Citizenship and Rights in Nigeria:

> For women, whatever happens at the level of the domestic arena is in turn carried over to what is generally called the public space. The reason that this is significant is that women may experience the denial of their citizenship and fundamental human rights at any one, if not more, of these levels – family, community, private sector, state and so on. Hence it is necessary to go beyond the public space when we talk about women's citizenship and rights, to address the interconnected and interlocking character of women's lives as well as women's rights. Realising women's fundamental rights requires addressing women's unequal access to economic, political, social and cultural resources, which are located not only in formal, public arenas but also in private and semi-private places, households and communities. This is the paradox that lies at the heart of women's citizenship as well as public policy formulation and the political process today.

The sense in which women's experiences of citizenship are deeply steeped in experiences structured by gender inequality is also highlighted (Salihu et al., 2002:3):

> Gender inequality is thus embedded in the most fundamental ways of being citizens – in the socio-cultural, political, economic and religious dimensions. Redressing these inequalities requires a systematic, deliberate approach that addresses the fundamental causes and effects of unequal citizenship status. This means that in addition to addressing constitutional provisions or the lack of them, there is also a need to go beyond these, particularly when dis-cussing the application of such provisions. For Nigerian women to realize full citizenship status, much work needs to be done, in addition to reviewing and restructuring the 1999 Constitution. More specifically, this means creat-ing the enabling environment in which policies and institutional mechanisms can be developed that allow women to have access to the decision making structures and processes that affect their lives as citizens of Nigeria.

At heart, citizenship is a fundamentally contested notion, for women and for men, but the terrain on which such battles are fought and sometimes won, differs considerably for women compared to men. This chapter points to a range of scenarios in which there is a clear need for research into the gendered contesta-tions that take place over state or local citizenship. For example, women who have successfully contested and won entry into politics have been faced with concerted public denial of their right to contest (see Ibrahim and Salihu 2004).

This has been the case for women who contested in states in which their husbands were 'indigenes' as much as it has applied to women who contested in states where their fathers were 'indigenes'. The contradictions faced by married women in public life undermine the notion that citizenship is primarily about the relations between individuals and the state. Male contestants generally do not have their citizenship questioned on marital grounds.

In the wake of processes of constitutional review, women's citizenship in Nigeria has been the subject of considerable scrutiny and advocacy on the part of women's groups and others active in struggles for gender equity. Such struggles are taking place against a backdrop of widespread gender blindness and discrimination against women in legal and constitutional provisions as well as in social relations more generally. Yet gender sensitive research on citizenship is in its infancy. This essay highlights the ways in which the issues thrown up by advocacy on women's citizenship and existing writing in this area could be pursued in greater depth and breadth through a gendered research agenda.

There are three parts to the chapter. The first outlines some of the issues encompassing relations between states, civil society and citizens that form the backdrop to the focus on women's citizenship in Nigeria. These include themes such as federalism, laws and administrative practices that discriminate against women and the gendered effects of differing sources of citizenship. The second part of the chapter addresses the 1999 Constitution and advocacy around its review. Finally, I discuss women's citizenship as it is experienced in practice.

The State and Citizenship

What kind of state?

The excessive centralization of state power under military rule has left individual states weak and dependent on the federal government for resources and power. The current interest in federalism reflects a concern with the unity of the country and the consequences of its regimes of rule, in the aftermath of the Babangida (1985–1992) and Abacha (1993–1998) military regimes in particular. Earlier debates in the 1980s centred around ways of promoting greater local autonomy and equality of access to power and resources by federating units, in the context of considerable reduction in the powers of the federal government. This line of argument has been counterposed to the more recent focus on the creation of new states and local governments (Olukoshi and Agbu 1996).

Until the late 1980s, the state has been conceptualized in monolithic and unitary terms (Mama 1996). Ironically, it is the very machinations of military regimes in the realm of state configuration and reconfiguration that have contributed to the conception of the state as no longer given but subject to change (see Beckman 1996). Such change may take place at different levels of the state and to differing degrees; its existence highlights the significance of state practices in upholding or undermining state structures. Both practices and structures are embedded in the fundamentally contested nature of the post-colonial Nigerian state.

Elsewhere I have discussed the need to clarify and reconcile the current territorial basis of divisions of power – states and state creation – with the rights of citizens, many of whom (predominantly women) are not territorially bound (Pereira 2001). The proliferation of states has not addressed the problems that their introduction was meant to solve. Indeed, continued state creation has created new problems whilst intensifying old ones. The emphasis on 'indigeneity', and therefore on 'origins', is contradicted by the reality of the ever changing boundaries of one's 'state of origin'. Women experience diverse forms of discrimination as a result.

Discriminatory features of state processes and practices restrict the character of citizenship in diverse ways. One such arena is that of the existing laws in Nigeria that discriminate against women, thus constituting a significant area of limitation on the application of citizenship and fundamental rights. The law on domestic violence is clearly inadequate, particularly regarding wife battery. Domestic violence is currently classified under common assault, which downplays the seriousness of this crime. According to section 55 of the Penal Code, wife beating is allowed as long as it does not amount to 'grievous hurt'. As defined in section 241 of the Penal Code, 'grievous hurt' includes emasculation, permanent loss of sight, ability to hear or speak, facial disfigurement, deprivation of any member or joint, bone fracture or tooth dislocation (Imam 2000). This means that a man who beats his wife, short of exercising the injuries above, is acting within the law. One may very well ask how women's fundamental right to dignity is protected under such circumstances.

Section 353 of the Criminal Code makes an indecent assault on males punishable by 3 years imprisonment. A similar offence of indecent assault on females treats it as mere misdemeanour punishable by a maximum of 2 years imprisonment (section 360), clearly a discriminatory provision. Rape is yet another area in criminal law where women are discriminated against on the basis of marital status. Forced sexual intercourse, or marital rape, is not recognized as an offence. Sexual harassment is also not recognized as an offence, despite the fact that it is extremely widespread (Imam 2000). In view of all this, it is not surprising that women's organizations such as WRAPA (Women's Rights Advancement and Protection Alternative), that work on violence against women and the human rights of women, have advocated strongly that the legislature should hasten the process of repealing all laws discriminating against women.

In addition to discriminatory processes and practices that are directly located within state institutions, there are certain administrative practices that pervade state institutions, institutions elsewhere in the public sector and in the private sector; these also discriminate against women in a number of ways. It is clear that there is a multiplicity of practices and domains in which women are rendered second-class citizens. Discrimination against women on the basis of marital status is not prohibited in the Constitution or other Nigerian laws. Pregnant women who are not married continue to be targets in the civil service and in the private sector, being denied maternity leave because of their marital status. At the same time, qualified married women of childbearing age are often turned down by prospective employers on the grounds that, if employed, they would soon get pregnant and start asking for maternity leave. Taxation and revenue laws and policies discriminate against married women and women with children. Such women pay higher taxes than men because they have no automatic allowances for children, even if they are the only income earner in the household.

Breastfeeding mothers in the public sector, and often in the private sector too, lose part of their annual leave if they go on maternity leave. This is despite the fact that having a baby entails hard work and is in no way synonymous with having a holiday. Married women but not married men are prevented from joining the police. Women police officers but not their male counterparts require the written permission and approval of their prospective spouses before marrying. Women face restricted economic opportunities due to credit and loan conditions that are not illegal but are biased in favour of men. All of this points to the significance of the absence of a democratic culture in which women are recognized as full citizens in their own right. Such a culture needs to be fostered by government working in genuine partnership with civil society organizations and local communities.

Sources of citizenship

In federal polities such as Nigeria, citizenship is conferred at more than one level and experienced differentially at national and state levels. Nigeria's most recent Constitution, the 1999 Constitution, confers citizenship by birth via either parent or grandparent who 'belongs or belonged to a community indigenous to Nigeria' (s.25, 1a). Whilst this confers citizenship at a national level, women are expected to derive their state citizenship from a different source. Citizenship at the state level is defined in a masculinist way, in terms of the 'indigeneity' or 'state of origin' of one's father, but not one's mother. Gender activists have drawn attention to the ways in which the tension between these differing levels of citizenship has differing implications for women compared to men. Married women are often denied state citizenship when the 'state of origin' of their husbands is different from that of their fathers. Hence they lose indigeneity as defined through the father without gaining indigeneity as defined through their husbands. This experience is particularly contradictory in view of the constitutional call to 'encourage inter-marriage among persons from different places of origin, or of different religious, ethnic or linguistic association or ties' (s.15, 3c).

The contemporary conception of citizenship as defined by 'indigeneity' or 'state of origin' has consequences for its application. There is a huge gap between the promise of citizenship and its practice, which more often than not infringes on the fundamental human rights guaranteed to *all* citizens, female as well as male, under the 1999 Constitution. For women, these include rights such as freedom of movement, freedom from discrimination and freedom to acquire and own property. Married women are likely to have problems when seeking employment, scholarships, loans, land, admission to schools, in either their 'indigenous' states or in the states where their spouses are indigenous. When they seek access to such resources in the state where their husbands are indigenous, they are asked to apply for them in their indigenous states. The converse also applies.

Activists have pointed out that there is a need to treat citizenship at the national level separately from citizenship at the state level, in recognition of the different dynamics that operate at these levels in a federal polity. For example, Salihu et al., (2002) recommend that citizenship at the local level should be defined by residence and not by indigeneity. In other words, every Nigerian woman or man should have the right to reside anywhere in Nigeria and derive the benefits and resources accruable to any member of that society. This position has also been affirmed by other groupings such as the Citizens Forum for Constitutional Reform (CFCR). However, this option effectively aims at substituting *the* dominant source of citizenship – indigeneity – with another singular source, namely residence. No doubt, residence alone, if it were to be adopted as the basis for citizenship, would bring in its wake new problems for those people whose residence in a given locality fell short of the minimum period necessary to acquire full citizenship status.

What has not yet been fully taken on at the level of advocacy or research, is the question of whether or not it is possible or desirable for multiple sources of citizenship – birth, residence, indigeneity, marriage – to be equally recognised in practice. If yes, what kind of social and political changes would be required? In other words, how can the power relations that render some sources of citizenship more dominant than others in specific contexts, be addressed? What kind of administrative arrangements would be necessary to ensure equality in practice? Whilst it is beyond the scope of this essay to do justice to these questions, a closer look at the 1999 Constitution will point to some of the principal issues concerning women's citizenship that need to be engaged with more deeply, in advocacy as well as research.

Citizenship and the 1999 Constitution

The 1999 Constitution is in many ways a contradictory document, reflecting the authoritarian and arbitrary process that began with its formulation under the military regime of Sani Abacha (1993–1998), culminating with its imposition under the military transition of Abdulsalami Abubakar (1998–1999). True to form, the fundamental principle of equality is enshrined, at least in intent, in the 1999 Constitution. Section 17 provides that 'the State social order is founded on ideals of Freedom, Equality and Justice'. These principles can be said to be respected in those provisions that *do* recognize women's rights and protect against discrimination. Section 15.2 expressly prohibits discrimination on the grounds of origin, sex, religion, status, ethnic or linguistic association or ties. The basic principle of gender equality is therefore embodied in the fundamental objectives and principles of the 1999 Constitution. Furthermore, the right to freedom from discrimination (s.42) provides that no citizen of Nigeria of a particular community, ethnic group, place of origin, sex, religion or political opinion shall, by reason of being such a person, be subjected either expressly by, or in the practical application of any law, to any disabilities or restrictions to which citizens of Nigeria of any other community, ethnic group, place of origin, sex, religion or political opinion are not made subject.

At the same time, however, the Constitution is itself discriminatory and fails to protect women from discrimination in a number of ways. At least three major manifestations of this process can be identified. First, the language used is exclusively masculine. This applies as much to Chapter III on Citizenship as it does to Chapter IV on Fundamental Rights. The use of exclusively masculine language implies that the norm is masculine and therefore that women are not full citizens in their own right. Moreover, section 318 of Chapter VIII, Part IV, on interpretation of the Constitution, has no provision addressing this. Nowhere in the Constitution does it state clearly that references to the rights of male citizens apply also to female citizens (Imam 2000).

Secondly, the capacity to transfer citizenship is conferred on Nigerian men but not on Nigerian women. Section 26.2a provides for Nigerian men to confer citizenship by registration to their non-Nigerian wives but there is no such provision for Nigerian women. Thirdly, marriage confers adulthood on women but this is not the case for men. This provision is embedded in the section on renunciation of citizenship. Section 29.1 states that any citizen of full age who wishes to renounce their citizenship can do so. Section 29.4b goes on to state that married women are considered to be of 'full age', that is, fully adult. Since young girls are often married off as early as twelve years of age, this means that girls who are too young to vote may decide or be coerced into renouncing their citizenship.

There are also several areas in the Constitution that do not adequately protect the fundamental rights of women (Imam 2000). First, there is no definition of what constitutes discrimination against women. It has been argued by some that where the Constitution does not specifically provide protection on gender issues, the general safeguards against discrimination afforded to all citizens in the areas of governance, the economy, social order, health and education are enough to ensure that women's rights are protected. This does not take account of the fact that some of the discriminatory practices that are specifically targeted at women – harmful traditional practices, such as widowhood rites for example – are not addressed by so-called 'general' safeguards against discrimination.

Secondly, there is a need to redress the imbalances between women and men through extensive and specific measures implemented for this purpose. This is the case for several domains, notably education, politics and governance. The need for specific measures is recognized in international treaties such as the Convention on the Elimination of all forms of Discrimination Against Women (CEDAW), as well as in the African Charter Protocol. Nigeria ratified CEDAW in 1985 without reservations and is therefore committed to providing special measures to enhance gender equality and protect against discrimination against women. This should be reflected in constitutional provisions.

It is worth noting that the provisions intended to ensure equality before the law for all citizens of Nigeria (s.42.1b) have been used to resist or challenge any form of affirmative action or temporary special measures designed to redress inequality, whether gender based or otherwise. Section 42.1b states that no Nigerian citizens shall be accorded any privileges or advantages under any laws, executive or administrative actions where such privileges and advantages are not accorded to other communities, ethnic groups, places of origin, sex, religions or political opinions. This ignores the fact that certain categories of citizen, mostly men, are currently already privileged and therefore enjoy the material and ideological resources accompanying these privileges that are not accorded to other categories of citizen.

Paradoxically, affirmative action is considered acceptable when it does *not* target women! One such form of affirmative action is 'federal character', ostensibly aimed at redressing regional and ethnic disparities. Federal character has been described as necessary in order to promote national unity, and also to command national loyalty, thereby ensuring that there shall be no predominance of persons from a few States or from a few ethnic or other sectional groups in the Government or in any of its agencies (s.14.3). Federal character has also been described as necessary in order to recognize the diversity of people within its area of authority and the need to promote a sense of belonging and loyalty among all peoples of the federation (s.14.4). The reference to federal character in section 318, on interpretation, does not include gender differences or even state, ethnic and sectional differences, in its characterization of the diversity of people living in the country.

Advocacy initiatives around constitutional reform

The ongoing review of the 1999 Constitution has afforded an opportunity for advocacy concerning constitutional reform, on the part of several organizations. Three main initiatives are reviewed below: proposals by Nigerian women under the auspices of the National Centre for Women (sic) Development; the process

initiated by the Citizens' Forum for Constitutional Review (CFCR); and the memorandum on 'Women's Citizenship Rights in Nigeria'.

i) Proposals by Nigerian Women on the Review of the 1999 Constitution

Following the formation of the Presidential Technical Committee on the review
of the 1999 Constitution, women's organizations worked separately and collectively on the amendments and new provisions that they wanted to incorporate
into a review of the Constitution. The proposals were collated and synthesized
by the National Centre for Women Development under the leadership of Dr.
Timi Agari and submitted to the Presidential Technical Committee as a 'Memorandum Conveying Proposals by Nigerian Women for Amendments to the 1999
Constitution'. Documentation on the processes leading to the formulation of
the Memorandum is sadly lacking. A more comprehensive analysis of the processes, debates and challenges that formed the basis for the synthesis has yet to be
carried out.

Nevertheless, two things are notable about this development. The first is that
the diverse women's organizations were able to come together in the first place
and reach a common position regarding proposed changes. The second point
worth noting is that many of the women involved were also organizationally
linked to mainstream human rights groupings that were striving for greater
representation of women within their ranks and greater gender sensitivity in the
content of their work. One such coalition was the Citizens' Forum for
Constitutional Review (CFCR). Although the women's Memorandum suffered
from a lack of follow-up at the level of the Presidential Committee, women were
still able to draw on the proposals made in that Memorandum in their membership
of the Citizens' Forum and their engagement with its work.

ii) The Citizens' Forum for Constitutional Review (CFCR)

The Citizens' Forum is a coalition of over forty civil society organizations
'committed to a process led and participatory approach to constitutional reform
in Nigeria' (CFCR 2001: 1). The Forum has a nine-person National Steering
Committee, six zonal co-ordinators and state co-ordinators for the thirty-six states
of the Federation and Abuja. CFCR argues that the process of making the
constitution is as important as the final product. The following principles are
viewed as critical in guiding the constitution review process: inclusivity of all
voices and opinions; diversity regarding ethnicity, language, religion and gender;
participation of people at all levels; transparency and openness of the process;
autonomy of the review body, process and final document; accountability of the
review body to parliament and the people; and legitimacy through a national
referendum to test the draft constitution.

Nine critical areas were identified as forming the focus of CFCR's intervention
in constitutional review:

1. Citizenship and residency rights
2. Federalism (to address the over-concentration of powers at the centre)
3. Engendering the language and content of the Constitution
4. Fiscal federalism/resource control
5. Constitutionally entrenched independent commissions
6. Freedom of association and political parties
7. Social and economic rights
8. Access to justice and the rule of law
9. The role of the security sector

CFCR organized colloquia on all the themes above. Given the inter-related character of constitutional provisions, it is not only the colloquium on Citizenship and Residency Rights that is relevant for our purposes. The meetings brought together a range of actors that were working in the area: organizations in civil society, academics and practitioners from Nigeria and abroad, to share their knowledge and experience. Through the colloquia, the various sections of the Constitution were examined with a view to providing the basis for mobilization at State and Zonal levels, as well as the content for a model constitution.

The Citizens' Forum recommended the need for constitutional reform in two directions. The first concerns amendments to existing sections, addressing the following Fundamental Rights in Chapter IV of the 1999 Constitution:

- the right to freedom from discrimination (s.42)
- the need for affirmative action (addendum to s.42)
- the right to the dignity of the human person (s.34)
- the right to private and family life (s.37)

Much of the content of these amendments draws on the Women's Memorandum referred to earlier.

- Section 42 on the right to freedom from discrimination should be amended as follows: All persons are equal before and under the law in all spheres of politics, economic, social, cultural life and in every other respect and shall enjoy equal protection of the law.
- A proviso on affirmative action should be added to section 42: Notwithstanding anything in the Constitution, the state shall take affirmative action in favour of groups marginalized on the basis of gender, age, disability or any other reason created by history, tradition or culture, for the purpose of redressing imbalances which exist against them. At least 30 percent of all elective and appointive positions should be reserved for women.
- Section 34 on the right to the dignity of the human person should be strengthened. Subsection (a) should read: No person shall be subjected to torture or to inhuman or degrading treatment whatsoever; the subjection of any man,

woman or child to torture or degrading treatment on the basis of culture, custom, tradition or religion shall be prohibited.

- Subsection (d) should be added: No person shall be subjected to any law, culture, custom, tradition, religion or gender practice which undermines his or her dignity, welfare or interests.
- Section 37 on the right to private and family life should be considerably strengthened. The following subsections should be added:
    1. In recognition of the fundamental importance of reproduction to the continuity of family life, the state shall ensure that every pregnant woman shall have free access to pre-natal, perinatal and post-natal care.
    2. Men and women at the age of 18 years and above shall have the right to marry and found a family and are entitled to equal rights in marriage, during marriage and at its dissolution. The minimum age of marriage shall be 18 years.
    3. The National Assembly shall make appropriate laws for the protection of the rights of widows and widowers to inherit property of their deceased spouses and to enjoy parental rights over their children.
    4. Marriage shall be entered into with the free consent of the man and woman intending to marry.
    5. It is the right and duty of parents to care for and bring up their children, irrespective of marital status.
    6. Children may not be separated from their families or other persons entitled to bring them up against their own will or the will of their families except in accordance with the law.
    7. Male and female children shall have equal rights to inheritance.
    8. The rights in this section shall not be exercised in a manner inconsistent with any provisions of the Constitution.

The second direction in which the Citizens' Forum recommended constitutional reform is in the addition of new sections to Chapter IV on Fundamental Rights, which are to be made justiciable. These sections address the following themes:

- equality of sexes
- spousal rights
- the rights of mothers
- rights of the child
- the right to culture

The content of these sections is outlined below.

Equality of Sexes
1. Women shall be accorded full and equal dignity of the person with men.
2. The State shall provide the facilities and opportunities necessary to enhance the welfare of women to enable them to realize their full potential and advancement.

3. The State shall protect women and their rights, taking into account their unique status and natural maternal functions in society.
4. Women shall have the right to equal treatment with men and that right shall include opportunities in political, economic and social activities.
5. Without prejudice to article 42 of this Constitution, women shall have the right to affirmative action for the purpose of redressing the imbalances created by history, tradition or custom.
6. Laws, cultures or traditions which are against the dignity, welfare or interest of women or which undermine their status, are prohibited by this Constitution.

Spousal Rights
1. A spouse shall not be deprived of a reasonable provision out of the estate of a spouse, whether or not the spouse died having made a will.
2. The National Assembly shall, as soon as practicable after the coming into force of this Constitution, enact legislation regulating the property rights of spouses.
3. With a view to achieving the full realization of the rights referred to in subsection (2) of this Section:
   a. each spouse shall have equal access to property jointly acquired during marriage; and
   b. assets which are jointly acquired during marriage shall be distributed equitably between the spouses upon dissolution of the marriage.

Rights of Mothers
1. Special care shall be accorded to mothers during a reasonable period before and after childbirth; and during those periods, working mothers shall be accorded paid leave.
2. Facilities shall be provided for the care of children below school-going age to enable women to realize their full potential.
3. Women shall be guaranteed equal rights to training and promotion without any impediments from any person.

Rights of the Child
1. The National Assembly shall enact such laws as are necessary to ensure that:
   a. Every child has the right to the same measure of special care, assistance and maintenance as is necessary for its development from its natural parents, except where those parents have effectively surrendered their rights and responsibilities in respect of the child in accordance with law;
   b. Every child, whether or not born in wedlock, shall be entitled to reasonable provision out of the estate of its parents;
   c. Parents undertake their rights and obligation of care, maintenance and upbringing of their children in co-operation with such institutions as the

National Assembly may, by law, prescribe, in such manner that in all cases the interests of the child are paramount;

d.   Children and young persons receive special protection against exposure to physical and moral hazards; and

e.   The protection and advancement of the family as the unit of society should safeguard promotion of the interests of children.

2.   Every child has the right to be protected from engaging in work that constitutes a threat to his or her health, education and development.

3.   A child shall not be subjected to torture or other cruel or inhuman or degrading treatment or punishment.

4.   No child shall be deprived by any other person of medical treatment, education or any other social or economic benefit by reason only of religious or other beliefs.

5.   For the purposes of this article, 'child' means a person below the age of eighteen years.

Right to Culture

1.   Every person is entitled to enjoy, practice, profess, maintain and promote any culture, language, tradition or religion subject to the provisions of this Constitution.

2.   All customary practices which dehumanize or are injurious to the physical and mental well-being of a person are prohibited.

iii) 'Women's Citizenship Rights in Nigeria' – a Memorandum to the Presidential Committee on Provisions and Practice of Citizenship and Rights in Nigeria

In December 2001, a Presidential Committee was set up on 'Provisions and Practice of Citizenship and Rights in Nigeria'. Calls for memoranda were publicized in the media and a deadline set for February 2002. The terms of reference of the Committee were to:

i.   Examine the intent and implications of the constitutional provisions on citizenship and fundamental rights, and limitations on their application;

ii.   Identify sources of conflict between the constitutional provisions on citizenship and rights, and the issue of 'indigeneship', 'settler', 'host community' and 'native', etc.

iii. Advise on measures necessary to achieve a fair and just balance between the legal provisions and the practical application of the constitutional provisions of citizenship and rights.

iv.   Identify roles of governments, communities and leaders in eliminating conflicts arising from disputes over the issue, concept and practice of citizenship and enjoyment of rights as constitutionally provided.

From the terms of reference, it can be seen that one of the assumptions underlying the work of the Committee is that the constitutional provisions on citizenship are basically appropriate and that the problems lay primarily in the implementation of those provisions. Achieving a 'balance' between legal provisions and the practical application of constitutional provisions concerned with women's citizenship and rights, for example, assumes that there is a level playing field for women and men.

Among those to respond was an ad hoc group of five gender activists, at least two of whom identify themselves as feminist (including myself).[1] The memorandum (Salihu et al., 2002) highlighted three major areas of concern, pointing out in the process that there is no level playing field as far as women's and men's citizenship and rights are concerned. The first was that limitations on the *application of constitutional provisions* on women's citizenship and rights existed in the form of numerous administrative, legal and cultural practices. These amounted to violations of women's rights to dignity, as well as physical and mental wellbeing.

Secondly, the memorandum pointed out that constitutional reforms were required that not only addressed fundamental rights but also the very *conception of citizenship*. Citizenship for women was restricted due to discrimination within the Constitution itself as well as the lack of protection for women's rights within the Constitution. Finally, there was a need to change the *practice of citizenship* so that women could claim full citizenship status in their everyday lives. At the very least, this required eliminating violence against women; creating an enabling environment for women to participate in decision making; and developing institutional mechanisms and policies to promote women's rights.

The statement below summarises a number of the key issues that have been expressed in different ways in the differing advocacy initiatives discussed. The Memorandum on Women's Citizenship and Rights (Salihu et al., 2002:15) outlined the following principles as a basis for changes in the way citizenship is conceptualized, provided for and practised.

- The *rights* of citizenship are accompanied by *obligations* to the state. The obligations of citizens to the state can only be discharged appropriately when governments are seen to be legitimate and state institutions work effectively towards justice for all citizens, women and men.
- The *powers* of the state are accompanied by *duties* to citizens. These include duties to protect and promote the human rights of female and male citizens, and prevent the violation of citizens' rights, for women and for men.

For both principles to operate, it is necessary to establish an environment in which *people can participate in governance*, and *government is open to working in a participatory manner with people.*

The practice of citizenship

Whilst the principles underlying the rights of citizenship may be articulated in a normative manner, as evident from advocacy initiatives such as the Memorandum on Women's Citizenship Rights in Nigeria, these principles are belied by the actual practice of citizenship in everyday life. It is the very distance between principle and practice that spurs advocacy and which, ideally, should inform research. The general statement of the existence of discrepancy between principle and practice applies, in differing ways, to men as well as women. My focus in this section is on some of the ways in which the practice of citizenship in contemporary Nigeria is specific to particular categories of women.

Customary laws

The denial of women's citizenship frequently occurs through the assertion of group rights, such as rights to 'culture', in ways that involve varying degrees of violence directed at women. At the same time, 'cultural' practices are generally spoken about as intrinsically unchanging and as essential to the sense of identity of a group of people. Mainstream representations of such practices tend to ignore shifting historical and political contexts, just as they ignore historical examples of women's pre-eminence in the exercise of power, and therefore deny the possibility of change in the face of continuity. The ways in which 'custom', 'tradition' and/or 'culture' have been used specifically against women, have been documented under the rubric of harmful traditional practices. However, the linkage between such practices and women's experiences of citizenship is not often made.

Women's right to dignity is often violated through practices that are justified as 'customary'. Under many customary laws, wives are expected to undergo very harsh and degrading rites at widowhood and are often subjected to ritual periods of isolation. Discriminatory socio-cultural practices such as male preference, child marriage, forced marriage, female genital mutilation, wife beating and other harmful practices limit the possibilities for women to realize constitutional provisions on citizenship and fundamental rights. More work is needed on the construction of customary laws and their role in the practice of violence. There is a clear need for research to analyze the ways in which customary laws are produced, reproduced as well as modified, with a view to sustaining those that combine social justice with gender equity.

Women's access to credit is blocked usually as a consequence of discriminatory customary laws concerning women's right to own property. Male supremacist structures of authority, whether in kinship structures or 'traditional' rulers, often act to marginalize women systematically from access to and control over land. The significance of such access and control is located in the relationship between land rights, property rights and the sustainability of livelihoods. Without land or property rights, women are unable to provide collateral for bank loans or formal credit schemes. This undermines their ability to sustain livelihoods that are not, in themselves, dependent on land usage. Questions such as land distribution and its relationship to land use and the possibility of establishing tenure security for all within the context of gender equality are critical for advocacy as well as research.

The application of criminal law in Sharia

In November 1999, Ahmed Sani Yerima, Governor of Zamfara State, inaugurated the extension of Sharia to include criminal law in the State of Zamfara. Sharia in Nigeria had previously been applied only in the domain of personal law, that is in matters relating to marriage, divorce, child custody, maintenance, inheritance and the like. The practice of Sharia had never previously utilized the *hudud*, i.e. criminal punishment such as caning, amputations and so on. The event was a turning point in Nigeria's political and legal history. The contradictions in the 1999 Constitution, the politicization of religion and the demise of the justice system at a time when 'democracy' was expected to bring about improvements in the quality of life (however defined) for citizens are some of the critical features leading to this state of affairs.

Controversy has continued to shroud the Sharia which has since spread on a state-by-state basis, taking differing forms in different states. By December 2001, Sharia in its use of criminal law had been legally established in the States of Zamfara, Sokoto, Niger, Kebbi, Kano, Katsina, Jigawa, Borno, Yobe, Bauchi, Kaduna and Gombe. Plans were afoot to extend Sharia similarly in Kwara, Oyo, Lagos, Ogun, Osun, Taraba, Adamawa, Plateau, Nasarawa and Kogi States. This statement was made by the President of the Supreme Council for Sharia in Nigeria (SCSN), Dr. Ibrahim Datti Ahmad, at a meeting of the Council in Gusau, Zamfara State capital, in December 2001 (Babalola 2001).

Religious laws, as well as customary laws, have often been used to violate women and deny them their citizenship rights. Whilst punishments such as amputations, flogging and the threat of death by stoning may be used against men as well as women, women are more likely to be criminalized in circumstances involving sexual relations. Muslim men have succeeded in using provisions intended to protect women, in pursuit of the criminalisation of certain categories of Muslim women (Iman 2001).

The most notorious case in the year 2001 concerned Safiyatu Hussaini of Tungar Tudu, a village in a remote part of the Gwadabawa Council area of Sokoto State, who was sentenced to death for adultery in October 2001. She had been raped three times by a man called Yakubu Abubakar. The attacks took place after she had separated from her husband and she subsequently fell pregnant (Uguru 2001). She left Tungar Tudu for her mother's village but was caught by the police and brought back to Gwadabawa. Her pregnancy was used against her and Safiya was charged with adultery.

Yakubu denied any responsibility for Safiya's pregnancy, refused to contribute to her daughter's naming ceremony and was later discharged for lack of evidence by the judge when the case went to a Sharia court in Gwadabawa, Sokoto State. Safiya, on the other hand, was tried and found guilty by the same court; the penalty was stoning to death. Her sentence was widely condemned by human rights groups across Nigeria and abroad. A Sharia Appeal Court in Sokoto granted her a reprieve at the end of November 2001. The appellate court granted her a stay of execution of the death sentence until her grounds for appeal were heard (*ThisDay* 2001).

Safiyatu's conviction did not go unresisted. Women's groups such as INCRESE (International Center for Reproductive Health and Sexual Rights) strongly condemned the sentencing of Safiyatu to death. Dorothy Akan'Ova, the Executive Director, pointed out that according to the Sharia, Safiya, as a divorcee, should not have been charged with adultery but with fornication. The punishment for the latter was 100 strokes of the cane as opposed to death by stoning. Moreover, the judge, having discharged the man named by Safiya as responsible for her pregnancy, Yakubu, had no basis for charging her 'as she could not have committed adultery by herself' (Alofetekun 2001).

Human rights groups and NGOs in Nigeria took part in the "Safiya Must Not Die Campaign", co-ordinated by Abiola Afolabi, the co-ordinator of WARDC (Women Advocates Research and Documentation Centre). Abiola pointed to the controversial unfolding of events culminating in the extension of Sharia to include criminal law in northern states of the country. Whilst President Olusegun Obasanjo had described the extension of Sharia as politically motivated, the then Attorney-General of the Federation, Chief Bola Ige, had pronounced the development as constitutional (Anaba 2001).

Women also organized in religious groups, across religious lines. The women's wing of the Pentecostal Fellowship of Nigeria (PFN), under the auspices of Social Security Outreach (SSO), took a letter of protest to the Alausa Secretariat, seat of the Lagos State Government. Women carried placards with messages such as "SSO women say no to Safiyatu's death", "Tinubu, don't let them kill Safiyatu", "Motherhood says spare Safiyatu", "Women say no to Safiyatu's death". Led by their president, Grace Onyekwene, the women in a letter addressed to Governor Bola Tinubu, asked for his intervention:

> We may not be able to reach the governor of Sokoto State, but we can reach you our governor, and we know you can reach the governor of Sokoto.
> .....Our motive is straightforward. We want our daughter pardoned and her life spared. We do not want Nigeria (sic) motherhood stoned to death. (Ogunmodede 2001).

On Monday 25 March 2002, Safiya Husseini was discharged and acquitted after the Sharia Court of Appeal overturned the Gwadabawa Upper Sharia Court ruling. One of the main reasons for her acquittal was that Sharia law could not be applied retrospectively: the law took effect in Sokoto State on 31 December 2001 whereas Safiya was charged with adultery on 23 December 2000. Other reasons were technical, such as not establishing the date, time and location of the offence; not ascertaining Safiya's sanity or whether she understood the term *zina* (Arabic for adultery); not informing her of her right to appeal; not accepting the withdrawal of her confession and so on (Bello and Abdulsalami 2002). Ultimately, however, the substantive charge of being criminalized for pregnancy out of marriage was not addressed.

Activists working on Safiya's case in Sokoto State found at least four other women incarcerated in jail, in similar circumstances to Safiya, awaiting death sentences. Their cases were unknown to the wider world and unreported. And whilst the judgement on Safiya's appeal was still pending in March 2002, a Sharia court in Bakori, Katsina State, sentenced another woman, Amina Lawal Kurami, to death by stoning after finding her guilty of adultery. The man charged with her, Yahaya Mohammed, was discharged after he denied the allegation (Asemota and Uzendu 2002).

Violence against women

Perhaps the clearest example of the devalued status of women's citizenship is the widespread existence of alarmingly high levels of violence against women in Nigeria, in new as well as old forms. Violence against women represents one of the largest obstacles to realising female citizens' rights to life (s.33) and to dignity of the human person (s.34). Women, often those living in poverty but not poor women alone, suffer all kinds of assaults and violence. These may occur simply because they are women or because they attempt to assert their fundamental rights as citizens, whether politically, economically or socially. Such conflict – gender conflict – is not generally recognized as a serious form of conflict, simply because the violence rarely involves large numbers at any one time and because its intensity may be relatively low in a number of cases. Yet women are attacked, maimed, raped and killed on a daily basis. As the Legislative Advocacy Coalition on Violence Against Women put it: 'Violence Against Women must be treated as a national crisis. There can be neither justice, development nor democracy if Violence Against Women is seen as acceptable' (LACVAW 2001a: 41).

The generalized tolerance of high levels of woman abuse, by the state as well as by the society at large, constitutes one of the greatest challenges to women realising full citizenship status. As long as women are unable to exercise control over their minds and bodies, and as long as women cannot claim rights to dignity in the way that they are treated by other people, they cannot claim full citizenship status. Salihu et al., (2002:17) make it clear that '[t]he responsibility for eradicating violence against women lies with all members of Nigerian society, including the state, civil society organizations, community leaders and members.'

The authors propose the following measures to remove obstacles to women's full citizenship status, in the form of violence against women. The proposed measures, in their view, could be achieved through interdepartmental collaboration and co-ordination of state institutions, as well as collaborative initiatives between the state, civil society organizations and grassroots communities (Salihu et al. 2002:17–18).

- Government should prohibit all forms of cultural, administrative and legal practices that constitute and perpetuate violence against women.
- Government, civil society organizations and the society at large should work towards the eradication of all forms of cultural, administrative and legal practices that constitute and perpetuate violence against women.
- Government, civil society organizations and the society at large should work towards the support of cultural beliefs that enhance the dignity of women.
- Government should support initiatives to transform cultural beliefs in line with the constitutional commitment to freedom, equality and justice for all citizens, including women and girls.
- Government should be open to legislative advocacy on violence against women. Legislation, backed by vigorous public enlightenment campaigns, should abolish abuses of the rights of women and girls.
- There should be an automatic incorporation of international treaties and conventions, such as CEDAW (the Convention on the Elimination of All forms of Discrimination Against Women) once Nigeria ratifies them.

The increasing salience of women's organizing around particular features of woman abuse is evident from the formation of two coalitions on violence against women in the same year, 2001. The National Coalition on Violence Against Women was formed in January 2001 and officially launched on 13 March 2001. Set up by 12 founding organizations, the main goals of the Coalition are to increase awareness of all forms of violence against women and to campaign for its eradication. The National Coalition carries out its work through research, advocacy and the provision of support to female survivors of violence (see LACVAW 2001a: 43–44).

At the end of January 2001, the Legislative Advocacy Coalition on Violence Against Women (LACVAW) was formed after a conference of stakeholders active in pursuing a legislative agenda on issues of concern to women. The focus of the meeting was violence against women in all its forms. The conference, convened by the International Human Rights Law Group,[2] had two main aims. The first was to harmonise the efforts of NGOs that were proposing Bills at the State and National Assemblies on issues such as domestic violence, inheritance rights, harmful traditional practices and so on. The second aim was to multiply the efforts of such groups by encouraging and supporting the formation of collaborative networks. The conference brought together women and men from

fifty-five civil society organizations, the federal executive, the legislature, the
judiciary and international human rights groups (LACVAW 2001a).

The following points of consensus emerged in the resolutions. The first
concerned the formation of a Coalition. Participants agreed that there was a
need to form a Coalition that would take responsibility for initiating a process
that would result in the enactment of a National Bill on Violence Against Women.
Such a Bill would be comprehensive, as opposed to addressing a singular
manifestation of woman abuse, in order to serve as a reference point for women
in all parts of the federation. Implicitly, if not explicitly, the Bill acknowledges
the significance of social cleavages such as class, 'tradition' and religion in rendering
some categories of women more vulnerable to violence. Whilst foregrounding
legislation, LACVAW acknowledges that:

> The formulation of laws alone is not enough to eliminate Violence Against
> Women. We must accept to transform our cultural beliefs, prohibit and
> eradicate all forms of cultural, administrative and legal practices that constitute
> and perpetuate Violence Against Women (LACVAW 2001b: 1).

Getting a Bill enacted is viewed as only the starting point for a longer-term process
of monitoring its subsequent implementation. Accordingly, the work of the
Coalition includes community advocacy, sensitization and mobilization. A second
stakeholders' meeting was held at the end of February 2002 to review the draft
Bill. By 20 March 2002, the finalized Bill entitled 'Violence Against Women
(Prevention, Protection and Prohibition) Act 2002' was sent to the sponsor, Hon.
Florence Aya, the Chairperson of the House of Representatives Committee on
Women Affairs and Youth Development, for onward submission to the House
of Representatives in the National Assembly.

Citizenship and ethno-religious conflict

The erasure of women's citizenship through the masculinist way in which
'indigeneity' has been constructed has a number of repercussions. There is an
intimate relationship between 'indigeneity' and ethnicity, each of these terms resting
as they do, on a territorial base. Apparent differences between 'settlers' and 'hosts'
are critical in justifying unequal treatment of the two groups, whether this concerns land rights, political rights, economic rights and so on. Uncovering the
extent of discrimination as well as privilege vis-à-vis women's (not only men's)
access to resources, key social structures and institutions – employment, education, political office, marriage, property ownership – is likely to reveal a more
complex scenario than is often envisaged. At the same time, the differences that
are said to exist between groups are often premised on the assumption that the
groups may be *identified* as different in the first place. An uncovering of the extent
of intermarriage that is likely to have taken place between groups living in close
proximity, however hostile they are to one another, may well pose the question of

how distinct from one another the 'settlers' and 'hosts' truly are. Recognizing that there are multiple sources of citizenship entails reconstructing ethnicity in terms that are inclusive, as opposed to being exclusive, of women.

Our understanding of conflicts arising between so-called 'settlers' and 'hosts', such as the Ife–Modakeke clashes in the South West, the Tiv–Jukun conflicts in central Nigeria, to name a few, needs to take account of the gendered configuration of the respective groups. During situations of communal conflict, women are often faced with having to choose between the families they were born into and the families they have married into. At the same time, during communal conflicts, women may be under special threat of gender-based violence, such as sexual assault or rape, on the part of members of the 'enemy' group. When it comes to peacemaking, women are rarely involved in official discussions or negotiations concerning the resolution of conflicts, despite being the ones who are predominantly faced with the task of caring for community members and picking up the pieces after periods of conflict.

Social and economic rights

Organisations such as Gender and Development Action (GADA), the Citizens' Forum for Constitutional Review and the activists setting out the memorandum on Women's Citizenship and Rights have all addressed the question of social and economic rights for citizens, particularly women. Salihu et al. (2002) argue that for women to attain full citizenship status, it is necessary that they have access to the full range of fundamental human rights, including social, economic and cultural rights in addition to civil and political rights. It is in the denial of social, economic and cultural rights as well as political rights that women have most often experienced diminished citizenship status. Hence, the authors argue, improving the status of women's citizenship and implementing women's rights requires the development of appropriate institutional mechanisms and policies.

Salihu et al. (2002) also draw attention to the extent of poverty in the country and the fact that the poorest of the poor are women. The authors argue that national budgetary votes must be able to answer the question: What percentage of public spending in every sector is geared towards addressing women's concerns? Answering this question will require a high degree of co-operation among government agencies such as the Ministry of Finance, the agency responsible for audits and the Federal Office of Statistics. The authors also argue that government should allocate sufficient funds for the implementation of the National Policy on Women. The arguments for gender budgeting are increasingly being voiced, even if the capacity to carry out such work will yet need to be built.

The realization of social and economic rights requires policy formulation and implementation to be carried out in a participatory manner with members of civil society organizations and communities (see NWSN 1998). The continued need for gender-disaggregated data in all social and economic sectors has been highlighted by several actors. The Federal Office of Statistics began its efforts in this direction in 1996. This initiative needs to be sustained and harmonized across state institutions. State institutions need to be able to work more efficiently and effectively in order to protect and promote the fundamental rights of female as well as male citizens, and to this end, gender sensitive capacity building for state officials is required. At the same time, the capacity for women's organizations to engage the state with regard to policy formulation, implementation and so on is fundamental. The pan-African women's organization ABANTU for Development has carried out research and training aimed at building the capacity of women's organizations to engage with policy (ABANTU 1997).

One of the recommendations of the Citizens' Forum for Constitutional Review was that a constitutionally entrenched Gender and Social Justice Commission should be set up to replace the Federal Character Commission. The Gender and Social Justice Commission should be independent of the Executive and funded from the consolidated fund. Membership should reflect gender balance and other diversities such as age, ethnicity, religion, marital status and disability. Members should be appointed through a process that is competitive, open and transparent. The functions of the Commission would be to:

- Promote gender equity and ensure the establishment of social justice in all spheres of life.
- Ensure that all discriminatory laws, policies and practices that are in conflict with basic principles of equality and social justice should be repealed.
- Monitor the observance of social and economic rights.
- Monitor all appointments to ensure that they reflect the principle of gender balance.
- Monitor the implementation of social and economic rights.

Concluding Remarks

Women's experiences indicate that their citizenship is treated as being of secondary or devalued status relative to men's citizenship, a likely consequence of the subordinated status of most categories of women. This chapter has highlighted how many of the most fundamental ways of being citizens are steeped in gender inequality – citizenship for women is more often experienced in the denial of rights than their realization. The effects have been to exclude most women from formalized, state-centred modes of recognising 'belonging', and the access as well as entitlement to resources, to structures and processes of decision making, that flow from such recognition.

The classic conception of citizenship as the (unmediated) relationship between the individual and the state is destabilized once women's experiences of citizenship are placed in the foreground and made the subject of analysis. Women's citizenship, more often than men's citizenship, is mediated by processes within families, communities and civil society, in addition to the injustices inherent within the institutions and processes of the state itself. The situation is compounded by divergent sources of citizenship at national and state levels, in the contemporary federal polity.

The recognition that the practice of citizenship is not synonymous with its ideal requires a concerted examination of the realities of women's lives in specific contexts. This essay has outlined women's experiences in diverse yet overlapping areas such as customary laws, the application of criminal law in Sharia, violence against women, ethno-religious conflict, social and economic rights. From this, it is clear that the contested character of citizenship for women is often fought on distinctly different terrain from that of male contestations.

Developing grounded theory that recognises the plural and multi-layered texture of citizenship will require a contextualised understanding of the realities of women's lives and experiences. At the same time, recognition of women's activism and analysis of the issues highlighted by the varied spheres of struggle around women's citizenship points to areas that could fruitfully be pursued further in a gendered research agenda.

Notes

1 These were Amina Salihu, Nkoyo Toyo, Charmaine Pereira, Ime Udom and Chinonye Obiagwu.

2 Now known as Global Rights.

References

ABANTU, 1997, *Strengthening NGO Capacities for Engaging with Politics* ABANTU Publications.

Alofetekun, A., 2001, 'NGO Flays Sharia Judge over Verdict', *The Guardian on Sunday*, 28 October, p.5.

Anaba, I., 2001 'Sharia: Rights groups urge FG, Sokoto govt. to save condemned woman', *Vanguard*, 8 November, p.4.

Asemota, A. and Uzendu, M., 2002, 'Another woman to die by stoning', *Daily Champion*, 25 March, pp.1-2.

Babalola, A., 2001, 'Where Sharia meets politics', *The Comet*, 2 December, p.27.

Beckman, B., 1996, 'The Free Fall of the Nigerian State.' Paper presented at workshop on The State of Nigeria, St. Peter's College, Oxford, 30 May 1996.

Bello, H. and Abdulsalami, A., 2002, 'Safiya's Acquittal: Judgement will strengthen Sharia – Yadudu', *Daily Trust*, 26 March, pp.1-2.

CFCR, 2001, 'Position of the CFCR on the Review of the 1999 Constitution of the Federal Republic of Nigeria' Citizens' Forum for Constitutional Reform, Lagos.

Ibrahim, J. and Salihu, A., eds., 2004, *Women, Marginalisation and Politics in Nigeria,* Lagos: Joe-Tolalu & Associates.

Imam, A., 2000, 'International Instruments and Legislation for the Advance of the Rights of Women' Paper presented at the Conference on International and Regional Human Rights Instruments, National Human Rights Commission, Abuja, 2 November.

Iman, 2001, 'Citizen Bariya: Between Sharia and Justice' *ThisDay,* February 18.

LACVAW, 2001a, *Report of the Interim Working Group of the Coalition on Legislative Advocacy to Eliminate Violence Against Women* Abuja, August 2001 Legislative Advocacy Coalition on Violence Against Women.

LACVAW, 2001b, Communique of the Stakeholders' Conference on Legislative Advocacy and Violence Against Women, organized by the International Human Rights Law Group, Nigeria at the Chelsea Hotel, Abuja, 31 January–2 February.

Mama, A., 1996, *Women's Studies and Studies of Women in Africa During the 1990s,* Working Paper Series 5/96, CODESRIA, Dakar.

NWSN, 1998, 'Press Statement: Towards a National Gender Policy' Network for Women's Studies in Nigeria, November 1998

Ogunmodede, B., 2001, 'Death sentence: Group seeks reprieve for Safiyatu', *The Comet,* 4 December, p.5.

Olukoshi, A. and Agbu, O., 1996, 'The Deepening Crisis of Nigerian Federalism and the Future of the Nation-State', In A. Olukoshi and L. Laakso, eds., *Challenges to the Nation-State in Africa* Nordic Africa Institute, Uppsala/ Institute of Development Studies, University of Helsinki.

Pereira, C., 2001, 'Culture, Gender and Constitutional Restructuring in Nigeria' In J. Oloka-Onyango, ed., *Constitutionalism in Africa* Kampala: Fountain Pub.

Salihu, A., Toyo, N., Pereira, C., Udom, I. and Obiagwu, C., 2002, Memorandum to the Presidential Committee on Provisions and Practice of Citizenship and Rights in Nigeria: Women's Citizenship Rights in Nigeria

ThisDay 2001, 'Safiya and Sharia', 4 December, p.15.

Uguru, O., 'Travails of Convict Safiyatu', *The Comet,* 24 November, pp.8-9.

Young, I., 1990, *Justice and the Politics of Difference* Oxford: Princeton University Press.

Yuval-Davis, N., 1997, *Gender & Nation,* London: Sage.

7

Interrogating Sexual Identities and Sex Work: A Study on Constructed Identities Among Female Sex Workers in Kampala

Richard Ssewakiryanga

Introduction

> We have arrived in the sexual tower of Babel where a world of past silences has to be breached (Plummer 1996).

This quote from the work of Plummer very tellingly energises scholars to ask new questions about sexuality and its meaning in the current discourse on gender and work. Recognisably, the subject of sexuality has moved the domain of knowledge production away from psychologists and psychiatrists (Freud 1993) to the social sciences. Hitherto, knowledge of sexuality was anchored within the totalising discourse of the 'pure sciences' and based on the idea of a monolithic meaning of sexuality derived from a universal biological determinant. Consequently, sexuality was perceived as an inherent energy accounting for all human behaviour. The heterosexual married couple was the ideal. Any deviations from that required scientific explanations. Today the ideal of the heterosexual couple has been complicated by the emerging sexual behaviours driven, in part, by the triumph of capitalism and reconstitution of communities into providers of labour power. In this new context, sexuality has become increasingly contested, commercialised and commodified.

This study is concerned with mapping the complex terrain of commercialised sexuality – commonly known as sex work. The study forms part of an interrogation of identity politics focusing on issues of representation and its impacts on the configuration of sex work in a post-colonial city. These questions acquire increased importance since the symbols and icons that line the world of sexuality are in themselves living cultural products and processes that shape our understanding of what sex work is, at least in Africa.

In most writings on prostitution, the opening statement invokes a canonical given with the famous cliché of prostitution as *'one of the oldest professions in our history'* (White 1980; Bakwesigha 1982). Such a cliché implies a common understanding of the nature of prostitution, the only debate being in the ascription a moral marker on it as 'good' or 'bad'. I want to emphasise here that this study is not anchored on the moral dichotomy of the good and bad things about prostitution. Instead, it intends to unravel and foreground questions about how identities are formed, negotiated and recreated within the realm of prostitution and new issues needing attention in our engagement of the larger intellectual project on gender and work.

The identity category, prostitute, is one of the most contestable areas in the discussion of labour issues globally. In nearly all countries of the world, prostitution exists in one form or the other. Authors have indicated that in some countries like the United States up to $40 million is spent daily on prostitution. In Birmingham, a British city, up to 800 women are engaged in prostitution, with one million people working in prostitution-related businesses like massage parlours, saunas, escort agencies and on the streets (Pateman 1988). Paradoxically in a country like United States, cities spend up to 7.5 million dollars per year on prostitution control (http://www.bayswan.org/stats.html). These kinds of complex situations are important to unpack if only to understand why today's most liberal form of capitalism still considers prostitution a double tragedy.

In the intellectual world, there is increasing scholarly and activist work on the pros and cons of prostitution. Medieval scholars stand out prominently in the quest for knowledge about prostitution when it is named as the oldest kind of trade in human bodies. References in the Holy Book of Christianity, the Bible, are a case in point (St. John 8:3 and St. Matthew 21:31). These biblical utterances valorised and complicated the place of prostitution in ancient society and Christian morality, since the prostitute was both criminalised and condoned by the same society. Many laws of different countries continue to exhibit similar ambiguity towards prostitution. In British law, it is the acts associated with prostitution (like loitering, soliciting for sex publicly and earning from 'immoral means') that constitute a crime, not the act of exchanging sex for money (Davidson 1996). Versions of this law exist in different parts of former British colonies. In Uganda, the same vagueness exists in the law books against prostitution.

Critical concerns that still mar the understanding and legal response to prostitution could be traced to the conception of the trade itself. An everyday definition of a prostitute suggests that it is a person who engages in sex for money. This definition however, falls short in pointing to other critical parameters like - the duration of relationship, mode of exchange, nature of exchange and a host of other issues that compound prostitution. This has made the curbing of prostitution difficult, with myopic sections of the law like being 'idle' and 'disorderly' are invoked to charge women who are viewed as prostitutes. This in itself shows the frustration of the law and the patriarchal domination and oppression that still define the morality of the world we live in. Nevertheless, the debate on prostitution still rages on and now needs to be taken into new horizons if we are to 'move out of the ghetto in a methodological way', to borrow Mbembe's (1999) phrase.

One other dimension that still informs our knowledge production in post-colonial Africa is the ways urbanisation and the organisation of labour impacted on the African continent. It is argued that the advent of urbanisation and the reconfiguration of labour processes in African societies made prostitution possible and a necessary evil accompanying the vulgar capitalism that came with colonisation (White 1980). The 'detribalised' urban worker was catered for in all aspects but their sexual needs. In this case, the women who only existed in the informal urban setting served the sexual needs of the heterosexual male. It is also mentioned that for the colonial urban worker in very harsh conditions, the prostitute offered a place for solace on their day off and possibly the only opportunity to sleep in a *real bed* (Nelson 1987). This was the kind of knowledge that was produced on colonial discourses on prostitution in East Africa although little is known about how these new relational paradigms shaped the labour discourse – if they ever did.

Arguably, in present day Uganda, there are no more restrictions on the movement of male workers who only access *real beds* in the city through sleeping with prostitutes. This then means that the parameters around which prostitution was mobilised, along with its past dynamics, have changed. It also highlights the fact that the dominant discourse that shaped the relationship between male wageworkers and female sex workers criminalised the female while viewing male behaviour as a necessary evil of the patriarchal colonial capitalist system. Today, the women and men who exchange sex for money can no longer be described accurately through some crude method of women serving men in a dark corner of the city or the illegitimate beer brewer offering 'a bed' to the legitimate but sexually starved colonial worker. The terrain of prostitution is now more complicated and interspersed with the complexities of urban living and urban survival. Economic problems seem to be the overriding factor, given the increase of women entering the body marketplace. However, it may be too reductionist to argue that material concerns are the only reason driving human action. Can we then read other contending discourses besides economics in the study of prostitution?

What this study has done therefore is interrogate the different identity questions on prostitution while reflecting on the dominant discourses and the resultant complications. For instance, feminist thinkers express bewilderment at how prostitution can be treated within the framework of feminist politics. For radical feminists, prostitution is the ambiguous embodiment of male oppression that reduces women to merchandise with which men affirm their patriarchal rights of access to women bodies (Shrage 1990; Pateman 1988). Yet this argument is complicated by the fact that exchange of sex for money does not always occur within a coercive space. Additionally, distinctions between 'free choice' prostitutes and 'forced prostitute' need to be clearly articulated. The forced prostitute is usually a child prostitute or the vulnerable woman captured to become a sex slave and is an issue of great concern in the East Asian countries where the highest statistics of sex tourism in the world. 'Free choice' prostitution is still an area of great controversy. This is so because of the complexity that arises in the interpretation of the contours of power and how they operate within this arena.

Consequently, the nexus between sex work and identity questions in Uganda is an important area of inquiry in gender scholarship because of the limited attention it has received and its significance in everyday work experiences. In Uganda, two studies have been conducted in this area (Bakwesigha 1982; Southall and Gutkind 1957). Bakwesigha's study uses data from the 1970s and is anchored within a sociological perspective. It labours to assemble statistics but does not actually clarify to the reader the different power complexities at play. The Southall study is anchored within the colonial patronising mode of knowledge that does not see any agency in the African subjects. My study therefore borrows from discourse analysis popularised by Foucault (1977 and 1978) in understanding the nuances encountered within the world of prostitution.

The Problematique

Prostitution has always taken place in the 'illegal realm'. It is sometimes regarded as the nameless trade where men and women buy sell and the services of the most contestable parts of the human being – the sexualised body. In order to understand the different facets of prostitution we also have to understand the social meaning of the body and the different ways in which power constructs the body as both a *labouring* body and a *sexual* body.

One influential writer in this area is Michel Foucault who has written various works on the subject of sexuality. His work has been very instrumental in making the body a favoured subject of analysis in Sociology, Anthropology and Philosophy (Gatens 1992). One of his major arguments is that the symbolic meanings we attach to the body are not inherent in the body but are invoked through the different activities that bodies engage in as social beings (Foucault 1978). Moore (1994) has also argued that the body is never finished and never perfectly socialised and adapts to different situations and challenges. It is used for work, a site of enjoyment and a medium for the perpetuation of other bodies.

Prostitution refuses to fit neatly in our understanding of what work is or is not. One reason for this is that the body is both the site of work in prostitution and also a site of power struggles and identity politics. In prostitution, sex becomes the commodity and the body the marketplace. People pay and sell to step out of the complex web of rules and regulations that non-commercial sexuality accords them. Prostitutes are condemned by religion, laws are made against it and feminists' viewpoints are made to stand on their heads in debates about prostitution. At one point the prostitute is seen as the tragic frontline casualty and at the other point she is the self-serving collaborator betraying her sisters (Davidson 1996:180).

Through other kinds of logic, the prostitute, unlike the married woman, may be considered capable of exercising a great deal of power and control over her sexuality. She can refuse men sexual access and also exists on the fringes of patriarchal control. Indeed, it can be argued that in contracting sexual services, the prostitute is resisting patriarchy and refusing one-man ownership over her body, thus challenging the stereotypical notions of power. Similarly, men have many ambivalent attitudes about prostitution. In some instances, the very men who complain about commercialised sex are often the ones who may be going out to seek the prostitute's companionship.

In Uganda, prostitution was complicated by the arrival of a Victorian middle class and religious morality that accompanied the entire colonial project. Workers who were moved from rural areas were kept in the city without their families while single women existed on the fringes of the cities. These two conditions facilitated the development of different kinds of sexual liaisons (Obbo 1980; Nelson 1987; White 1980). Contemporary Uganda has witnessed rising costs of living, but the city continues to be seen to possess various opportunities for work, some of which subsumes the confluence between work and sex. In this paper, we explore the different facets that can help paint a picture – with a context – about the nature of prostitution in Kampala City. The following questions guide this research: How does one conceptualise the notion of identity and prostitution? What are the different ways in which identity articulates itself in sex work? In the emergent identities in sex work, what are the implications for patriarchal domination? What kinds of issues emerge for a better conceptualisation of gender and work?

Theoretical perspectives on sex work and the body

While anchored within a theoretical framework popularised by Foucault (1978) on sexuality and identity formation, this work is linked to different theoretical formulations by feminists and sociologists about prostitution (Sunstein 1990; Pateman 1988; Weeks and Holland 1996). Foucault's original contribution follows the intellectual fallacy of 1960s Freudian psychoanalysis arguing that sexuality is an inner human quality generated by our childhood and producing particular forms of adult behaviours (Freud 1933). Sexuality was reconstructed around the image of the dominant male phallus. Variations in sexuality were deviations from the masculine sexuality needing redemption and understanding within the masculine perspective. Foucault's contribution to this debate was to deconstruct this popular belief with the argument that sexualities are constantly produced, changed and modified and hence the nature of sexual discourse and experience also changes.

An explicit example of this perspective on sexuality comes from Theweleit. In his 1987 book, he writes that, '[I] f intercourse has always and everywhere felt, meant, and been the same, if a kiss is just a kiss, a sigh just a sigh, then it does not matter whether you are Roman or Barbarian, ancient or modern, 5 or 55, in love or just earning a living' (1987:73). Here, Theweleit illustrates the fallacy of universal assumptions, claiming that any Freudian biological pre-determinist approach to sexuality would not get to the real history of sexuality in any context. This point is well illustrated in the genealogy that Foucault maps out in his analysis of sexuality in ancient Greek narratives (Foucault 1985).

To locate this discourse within the discussion on sexuality and the female body, I briefly sketch out two ideological perspectives in feminist scholarship about the body and sexuality. Some feminists have argued that women need to affirm and celebrate the capacity of the female body, especially the capacity to recreate as well as nurture human beings. This school of thought presents the body more as a biological entity that is *ahistorical* in its characteristics and its capacities (Gatens 1992). Hence people are seen as essentially male or female without an assessment of the power that constructs these body dichotomies.

Another school of thought refuses body dichotomies of male/female and claims a history for the body. Within this perspective, understanding of the body and sexuality incorporates the different ways in which the environment and other typical activities of the body vary historically and create its capacities, desires and actual material form (Foucault 1978). For example, the body of a domestic worker or housewife and the body of a female athlete do not have the same capacities. Each has different capacities as well as different desires and demands in order to accomplish its work. Consequently, biological similarities cannot account for the specificity of these two bodies even though they are both female (Gatens 1992). When applied to the study of prostitution, sexual difference is not just reified. Rather, the ways in which typical spheres construct and recreate particular kinds of bodies to perform particular kinds of tasks is also explained. In this case then, the body is not only seen as sexual, but as *sexual within a context*.

A formulation that historicises the body exposes the different ways in which power constructs bodies and urges us to challenge *power* and not the *bodies* per se. It is also important to note that sexuality and the body are integrally connected to conceptions of femininity and masculinity and all these are constitutive of our individuality and sense of identity (Pateman 1988). Consequently, when sex becomes a commodity, so will bodies and selves.

It is often easy to see prostitution as oppression of women by men – as if men and women are rigid categories that can be easily identified and their oppression easily mapped out. Further, this formulation gives us the chance to look at some of the ways in which bodies in prostitution also map out their own contours of power so that they cannot be analysed by focusing on monolithic entities like male or female. In the next section I link this debate to the issue of sexual identities.

Sexual Identities and Sex Work

Identity becomes an issue when it is in crisis (Shotter 1993)

The crisis of identity occurs when things we assumed to be fixed, coherent and stable are displaced by the experience of doubt and uncertainty. Foucault introduces this angle when he points out, in a number of influential works on sexuality, discourse, power and subjectivity, that identity is bound up with the workings of power (Foucault 1978, 1985 & 1986). He suggests that identities are not 'pregivens', neutral, unified and fixed, but products of a normalisation strategy regulated and 'carefully fabricates' the individual. This normalisation strategy – which he calls discipline – has the ultimate goal of eliminating all kinds of social and psychological irregularities and producing useful-docile bodies and minds.

Foucault extends this perspective to the understanding of sex, when he argues that the prevailing sexual discourse at anyone time shapes how different people influence or encounter sexuality. In our understanding of sex work and identities, we therefore need to explore the different notions of normalisation that go on in Kampala. These range from the social construction of the prostitute, the representation of the prostitute and the ways in which prostitutes subvert the different social icons that society and sex work inscribes on them.

Giddens (1991) writing on self-identity offers some useful tips in the argument that self-identity has to be routinely created and sustained in the reflexive activities of an individual. Who to be? What to be? How to act? These are questions that must be asked in the formation of ones identity. In this way, identity incorporates choices we make based on questioning, answering and continually ordering the narratives that shape our lives. Giddens adds that, the more tradition (as a normalising strategy) loses its ability to provide a secure and a stable sense of identity, the more individuals negotiate lifestyle choices and attach importance to these choices. When thrown into doubt, concern with lifestyle makes the individual question those relevant routinised habits, especially those most closely integrated with self identity (Giddens, quoted in Heaphy 1996).

How then can these formulations be useful for understanding sex work? The fact that identities here are not seen as a given and static entity is a very important element of our understanding of sex work today. Different lifestyle choices evoke instability of identity and make the case for a pluralistic view of the prostitute. One cannot just confer her with a monolithic identity of deviance. The findings of this study indicate that the sex worker is faced with different choices and narratives, some involving innovative strategies that subvert the normalisation processes of society. He/she travels and lives through different identities, invoking different logics in different contexts. Sometimes, the prostitute has to emphasise her femininity and 'availability' and at other times, she has to 'wear' the identity of the 'sophisticated woman'.

Another category that needs to be theoretically cleared before we employ it as an intellectual travelling companion in this study is the concept of sex work as used by different writers. Sex work is sometimes taken as the 'politically correct' term to use for prostitution. It has been used to make a distinction between paid and consensual relationships between sexual partners. It is a term that is employed to try and locate sex within the realm of work. Yet, despite the naming, the category still suffers ambiguity and fluidity. Some feminist scholars and labour activists have shunned this distinction by arguing that marital sex should also be seen as a type of sex work (Delpy and Leonard 1992). Other influential thinkers in this school of thought include Simone de Beauvoir (a pioneer feminist) and Friedrich Engels (a renowned Marxists writer). The following citations of both writers will be useful to illustrate their points of view:

Simone de Beauvoir writes that, 'for both, the sexual act is a service, one hired for life by one man, the other has several clients who pay her by the piece. The one protected by one male against all others, the other defended by all against the exclusive tyranny of each' (1974: 619).

Engels asserts that '[M]arriage of convenience turns often enough into crassest prostitution-sometimes of both partners, but far more commonly of the women, who only differs from the ordinary courtesan in that she does not let her body on piecework as a wage worker but still sells it once and for all into slavery' (1985:102).

In both cases, de Beauvoir and Engels consider sex as work for both the prostitute and wife in a home because in each case, the woman is *selling* herself to a man.

This debate has been taken up by contemporary feminists like Pateman in her influential work entitled *Sexual Contract*. In this book, Pateman argues that prostitution has to be understood within the whole rubric of the sexual contract, especially since, in some instances, prostitutes undertake sex work in order to earn money, as in any other job chosen by women. However, she is quick to add that we should not therefore just equate prostitution to other forms of labour where the contract is between the men and workers. Prostitution can be differentiated from other forms of labour because it is exclusively a contract between men and women. It is conducted in the context of the exercise of male-right to sex and is therefore one of the ways in which 'men have always ensured that they have access to women bodies' (Pateman 1988:194). Connell (1987) has also contributed to this discussion by pointing out that sex work takes place in the context of interpersonal balance of power and unequal access to resources favouring one partner against the other. These resources, Connell says, may include money, physical strength and sexual attractiveness or even the capacity to deploy anger or love.

While the debate on sex work continues a view from the practitioners may be useful at this point. In the Manifesto for Sex Workers of Calcutta, they note under the sub-heading *why do women come to prostitution?*

> Women take up prostitution for the same reason as they may take up any other livelihood options available to them. Our stories are not fundamentally different from the labourer from Bihar who pulls a rickshaw in Calcutta, or the worker from Calcutta who works part time in a factory in Bombay. Some of us get sold into the industry. After being bonded to the madam who has bought us for some years we gain a degree of independence within the sex industry. A whole of us end up in the sex trade after going through many experiences in life – often unwillingly, without understanding all the implications of being a prostitute fully (http://wwww.bayswan.org/manifest.htlm).

One notes from this discussion that the history of prostitution and work is one that is marred with many contradictions and complexities. It also tied in with the history of sexuality, social control and capitalist exchange relations, which increasingly commodify everything. Consequently, I find that taking a stance on either to use the term sex worker or prostitute is a complex and futile position. I will therefore want to use the terms interchangeably in this study, in order to allow for a break in the terminology monotony but also to make the political statement that a discussion of prostitution cannot be separated from a discussion of work. Trying to only name the trade prostitution and not see it as any other thing is hiding away from the practical reality of prostitution, since prostitution is not so much the sexual service but the return, or rewards that the persons who engages in it gets.

In conclusion, therefore, a lot can be said about the disciplinary factions that make up the world of scholarship on sex work. However, I will put the debate to rest if only because I have borrowed a few intellectual signposts that will help to mould the rest of this paper into a useful contribution to the debate. In the presentation of findings I will keep returning to some authors to draw energy and intellectual morale for arguments presented. I will only make one point that binds most of the pieces in this section together; that an intellectual engagement with prostitution cannot operate without subverting the normalising strategies of social sciences. In the quest to understand the notion 'sex work', we need to work on the basic assumptions that create the knowledge of sexuality that we hold and use throughout our processes of knowledge production. As it will become evident in the sections that follow, the generation of knowledge in this work depends on innovations rather than inscriptions of the paradigms of traditional social science research.

Methodological Issues

I open this section with a caveat that this paper in some ways grapples with the question of research ethics, often presented as a personal and moral concern for the individual researchers. At the outset, let me submit that, focusing on ethics can also be a way of de-emphasising and downplaying the power relations that structure every aspect of research. 'Ethics talk' can be a way of separating and 'purifying' one area of thought from another. By showing that ethical debate cannot be separated from questions of power, this study recognises the paradox that research cannot be justified - in and of itself - as an ethical practice because all social research *is* an engagement with power. Let me also add that the way individuals operate in sex work raises difficult methodological, ethical and philosophical questions, not only in the research process, but also in the evaluation of what the individuals are prepared to reveal about this most intimate part of their lives.

The Sampling Process

Thirty-one (31) women who are self-professed sex workers were interviewed for this study. Ten of these were contacted through one of the sex workers who agreed to work with the research team – this group was coded as Speke Hotel Group. The rest were contacted through a Local Council (LC) leader in one of the locations of the study coded as the Kisenyi group.

Sampling for the Speke Hotel Group

We contacted the main sex worker who worked with us one evening before the fieldwork commenced in a Kampala pub known as Rock Garden Café. Through a confidant who is a bouncer at the Café and also works in one of the sports clubs I go to, it was possible to establish contact with this key informant. I brought up the topic of sex work with the bouncer during one of our conversations and he offered to show me one of the girls who was 'good-natured' and would be helpful. We arranged a meeting through the club bouncer to talk to the key informant. At that meeting I introduced myself and told her about the objectives of the study but realised that she was reluctant to continue that conversation on the first day. We therefore talked about social life generally in order to build enough rapport. I gave some more explanations about the kind of work I was doing but without asking for any particular help. She was fascinated by the idea that a man was 'just interested in learning about sex workers'. We arranged a second meeting for the following day to allow both of us to think through this first encounter.

From the bouncer I learnt that she crosschecked my information and asked if I was a genuine person or she was being used or spied on. After the bouncer convinced her, she accepted to come on the second day. I found out that this key informant was studying in one of the business schools in Kampala. She accepted to be part of the study if she was going to be paid for the time she would spend doing the work. We agreed on the mode and amount of payment. Her task was to identify some of her friends who would be willing to talk to the study team. She mentioned that she could identify them but it may be better that we meet them during the day or on Sundays when they are relatively free. She suggested that her residence would be the meeting place. Through her we managed to talk to nine (9) girls who all confirmed that they were sex workers. In order to ensure that we talked to operating sex workers, I always insisted that our main contact identify her friends during the evenings when we are in the bar. I would then follow up the meeting during the days suggested by the respondent.

Sampling for the Kisenyi Group

Sampling for the Kisenyi Group was through a secretary of the Women Local Council in the area whom we had worked with on a previous study in the area. During that study on poverty we did an analysis of the livelihood options of a prostitute and drew a livelihood analysis diagram using participatory methods. When we asked a few questions on the subject of sex work, the LC official promised to be helpful when we come to do a specific study on sex work. When we returned for this study, she identified about 25 women who were sex workers, but we could not interview all of them for various reasons. Some were not available during the interview times and 3 of them refused to be part of the study.

Sampling of Locations

Kisenyi is part of the Central business district area of Kampala City long associated with sex work. In the early sixties, it was known for bringing together many immigrants from different parts of East Africa. The people in Kisenyi still talk of the Tanzanian women known as the Baziba who were very popular among men because they were considered very beautiful[1]. Most of those working in the biggest market in the area lived in Kisenyi. In addition, prostitution has been politicised in the public sphere discourse of the area. For example, during the Constituent Assembly Elections in Uganda, one of the contestants for the election who is a half-caste was referred to as *mwana wa malaya (child of a prostitute)*. We were told that because of this metaphor being used on the candidate he was able to win overwhelming support in Kisenyi because all the women in Kisenyi said *we are all malayas so we shall give our son.*[2] The councillor has since then been an ardent supporter for sex workers rights and, in one of the dissemination exercises in a study we had done earlier, he specifically asked us not to use the word prostitute in our work but sex work.[3] These informed our decision to choose Kisenyi for this study.

Speke Hotel Area/Rock Garden Café is located in an area that could be taken as the *Red Light District* of Kampala, next to one of the popular and oldest hotels in Kampala, Speke Hotel. Sex workers line the streets around this café and the hotels in the neighbourhood, including Sheraton Hotel (a five-star hotel), Grand Imperial Hotel, Speke Hotel, Nile Hotel and Mosa Courts Apartments (high-class apartments). These are the best hotels in Uganda used by nearly all the expatriates that first come to Kampala. Mostly middle class Ugandans can afford to drink in this area where a bottle of beer goes for 1500–2000 shillings compared to 1000–1200 shillings in other places. It therefore attracts a richer clientele than other parts of Kampala.

Data Collection methods

In order to get data on a complex topic like prostitution, it is necessary to engage with the respondents' lived experiences and perspectives as well as the feelings and perspectives of other persons. I therefore used ethnographic research methods for data collection, emphasising the longer interviews and unstructured questioning as well as observation of the spaces where the different key informants were. The first self-professed prostitute who connected us to her friends was one of the key informants in this study. Through long-term engagement with her in the research process, she was able to reveal a lot of inside information that could not be easily accessed by working with tools like questionnaires. We were able to even hold focus group discussions – not structured in any conventional way – on tables in different bars where we worked. Though the women gave us their names they said they did not want them used in the report.

Many of the women in Speke Hotel area offered to first write a script about their lives, as a basis for discussion. Although some of the scripts were not easily readable, we worked with them and acknowledged their efforts as very important. We also worked with a short interview guide for the women in Kisenyi because they could not have long interviews with us. This is because some of them worked during the day and our 'transport refund'[4] was not enough for the long interviews which we wanted to carry out with them'.

We did not have any structured interviews with any men but talked to some of the men who have interacted with the world of prostitution. We talked to male bar attendants and security guards at the different drinking locations. Policemen were reluctant to participate in the research due, in part, to a big Uganda Government inquiry into police conduct concurrently taking place at the time of this research. As one of the policemen we approached put it: 'how do we know that you are not Ssebutinde staff trying to find out how we handle these sex workers'. [5]

Problems Encountered during the Research

Studying sex work is a challenging and interesting topic. One has to start by grappling with one's personal biases. In the first place I found that some of the questions we started off asking were sometimes offensive to the women whom we interviewed. So, we had to learn to ask questions in a non-offensive way and we had to be patient with the respondents.

We also had to find ways of working through some of the research biases that the respondents had. Sometimes the respondents started off talking about their problems and they were wondering if we worked for Non Governmental Organisations that could provide 'credit' for them. These kinds of respondents preferred to portray themselves as a suffering lot. After learning that we were not only interested in their problems but also about heir daily coping mechanisms, they changed the direction of their answers to reveal the different ways in which they worked.

Interview times for this research were awkward. We had to always work late into the night. Some of the respondents felt safer talking after 10:00 p.m. We also sometime had to cope with the wrath some of the women had against the state. For example some of the women wanted to know why men go out with prostitutes and yet they are married, or why the Government does not want to legalise sex work yet so many men in Government go out with prostitutes. To these questions we had no answers and therefore all we did was to sometimes stimulate a debate and that meant that we ended up using a lot of time. We also had to spend a lot of money because we usually met in bars and we had to buy some drinks.

The methodologies used for this study could not be standardised to our satisfaction because we found that there were different perspectives we could not get at easily using some of the tools we are trained to use in social research. We therefore had to be as innovative as possible. In addition, because we often had late interviews without immediate recording, we had resort to recollections and, where possible, crosschecking information, but this was not always possible.

The Routes and Roots of the Trade

The story of the trade in sex in Kampala City cannot be divorced from the story of the rise and development of Kampala City. One of the detailed studies in the colonial scholarly tradition on urban living comes from the work of Southall and Gutkind. In *Townsmen in the Making*, they give an account of Kampala's development, pointing out that the object of the study was 'not to discredit the unfortunate, but to reveal the unhealthy features of urban development at their growing points before they become widespread (1957:19). This shows the patriarchal and patronising principle that informed the production of knowledge on urban places. Indeed, for Southall *et al*, urban development only involved and affected 'townsmen', not 'townswomen'. This is despite references to women in some of the observation scenes and indications of the central part they played in the waragi trade and the immunity they enjoyed from the Buganda Police because some of them were related to the Kingdom. These dynamics, one may argue, could have brought in more interesting analysis of some of the notions of identity in the urban setting and how the context influences people's mobilisation of identity.

However works like the Southall study were instrumental in informing the colonial policy on 'free' developing communities in the city. These places were seen as deviant spots and therefore in need to be sanitised because they were in themselves creations of the failed strong hand of the colonial law on urban centres. They also recorded some of the issues of prostitution in Kisenyi and Mulago. One of the opening statements made in this study reveals the long held perception of Kisenyi as a haven for sex work: 'Every variety of sexual relationships is found in Kisenyi, from relatively durable concubinage to blatant prostitution for cash payment. Kisenyi is always full of good-time girls who hang around beer bars waiting to be bought drinks' (79). The quotation is accompanied with some detailed accounts of the ways in which different women and men were involved in sex work in Kisenyi.

To date, Kisenyi remains mostly the same, with just a few cases of out-migration by men and women since the end of colonialism. One elderly woman in Kisenyi who accepted a short interview about the changes that she saw in the area had this to say:

> Today the high-class men do not come here for sex. In our days all the African men who were big shots in Government would have a girl in Kisenyi. We had the Baziba who were very beautiful and very 'clean' women and the men liked them a lot. But when the bazungu went at independence then the high-class men stayed up so they could drink from those bars where the bazungu used to go.[6]

Obbo (1980) has analysed some of these changes and their effects on women who migrated to Kampala City in the post independence period in Uganda. From the work of Southall and Obbo one realises that sex work in Kampala City is historically related to the changes in the urbanisation process. In the next section we focus on how some of the demographic characteristics of the interviewees helped to restructure their identity positions. This focus on the demographic is not just a description of characteristics. It aims to show how self-identity is created through a negotiation with different normalising strategies of the individual.

Demographics as Sites of Identity Construction

Age and Identity

When does one become a man or a woman? This is a question that not only related to the age as a demographic factor, but also relates to age a defining factor in prostitution. In the short survey of the 21 respondents in Kisenyi we found most of them (80 per cent) were below 30 years of age. Of these, about 38 per cent were below 20 years. This is an important indication that mostly young women are involved in sex trade. The ten respondents who offered life histories had an average age of 18 years. When we discussed the issue of age and its importance in the construction of the self-identity of the sex workers, one of the respondents had the following to say:

> As young girls if you have dropped out of school or your family does not have money to pay for your school fees, sometimes you find that you have no choice but to quickly find an occupation that you can do while you are young. I did start off as a house-girl but all the boys in the family I was working for - even their father wanted to sleep with me and they were only paying me 10,000/= per month. I met a young woman who was staying near our shop and I noticed that she was always very smart and yet she was always at home through out the morning. So one day I asked her if she could help me and find a better job but she just laughed and said I should just wash her clothes. I did this for sometime and I found she had very nice trousers and shoes and I asked her again and one night she told me we should go together. That first night I earned 25,000/= shillings and I was fascinated by the idea that I could actually double my salary in a night. I realised I had to use this body before I grow old![7]

Age for the women was seen as part of the critical points for a person who intends to be a sex worker. Indeed the women said that in some instances one has to look younger than one is - because 'men like young women... we do not even mention that one has ever had a baby otherwise the man may think that wagwaamu da (you are already spent)'.[8]

I am reminded of Giddens's (1991) argument that self-identity in what he calls 'high modernity' is sculptured from a complex plurality of choices and reordering of narratives. The narrative of age in this scheme of the prostitute's identity seems to be one that is reordered with contradictions and divergent choices. For the customer looking for the 'experienced' woman then age becomes a lucrative identity and yet for those who are out to explore the young and innocent, age loses its currency. It is important therefore to recognise the role of age on the level of self and representative identity. Age offers a discursive space for the articulation and reproduction of different identities for the sex worker in which dominant definitions of feminine presented are made explicit and sometimes contested.

Educated Identities

Western education is one of the invasions brought by colonialism. Education is supposed to be mode by which 'civilisation' and 'modernity' is delivered (Alan 1990; Ashcroft *et al* 1995:425). Education as a technology of colonialist subjectification works by universalising values embedded in the English while representing the colonised as the inferior and uncivilised. The educated person can talk authoritatively and therefore access different kinds of spaces and mobilise different identities. Higher education improves wages and social status of people. For the sex worker, knowledge of the English language was not only a marker of success but a reaffirmation a sophisticated sex worker identity and gateway to success in the trade.

Most of the women we interviewed in this study said they had limited education. This meant that they had gone to school for a few years and did not speak very good English. Majority of the women in Kisenyi (57 per cent) reported that they had attended only primary school. There were a few women who had never attended any school. Education was an important factor because many of them cited the 'end of being at school' as a very decisive factor in the their becoming sex workers. Below are some quotations from different women on education and how it shaped their lives:

Respondent 1:

Yes, I used to go to Bwala Primary School and stopped in Primary 6. Things became very expensive and my parents could not afford school fees. I stayed at home for four years and I got a boy friend who made me pregnant and then he refused to take responsibility of the baby... I suffered and struggled until I gave birth. My child is now seven years and she goes to school.

Respondent 2:

I used to go to school up to primary five but I found school boring and I was ageing (she was getting to 13 years) so I dropped out.

Respondent 3:

Yes I have attended school and I am still in school in one of the schools in Kampala. (*she refused to mention the school and the class*). But I had to drop out

because my parents could not pay. But because I know I cannot be on the
streets all my life, I go to school and I pay for myself.

Respondent 4:

I stopped in senior one. My father passed away when I was still very young
and my mother got married to another man who helped to pay the school
fees. He also died when I was in senior one and my mother become sickly.
So I had to stop school so that my sisters and brothers could continue.

The quotations above point to the different ways in which education was very
instrumental in influencing these respondents' decisions to opt for sex work. In
addition, there was the he reality that their parents could not cater for their daily
needs when they dropped out of school.

Women also talked about the importance of education in sex work. As one
of the women put it:

If you are educated there are chances of getting a good man. Those girls who
know a lot of English easily get men. That is why some of the girls come from
Makerere to work with us here because they know that if they 'add' their English
to sex work they can make a lot of money on the streets. That is why there is a lot
of competition now.[9]

Fulfilling a client's needs did not just entail having a good body but also being
able to communicate in a way that ensures the camouflaging of the identity of
the illiterate street girl. The women mentioned that sometimes men are attracted
to women because they can speak 'good' English. One of the women brought
out the perspective that one can deny her identity as a prostitute and therefore is
able to negotiate a higher fee if she can portray herself as *a good girl who 'does not do
these things for money' but just has a small problem.* Again one notices the mobility and
fluidity of identities in sex work intertwining the discursive strategy of being an
educated person. The women involved have learnt to *live* these multiple identities
as everyday strategies of their investment in sex work. Education was therefore
related more to the representative identity that the prostitute mobilises.

While age is a marker of self-identity as shown in the previous section, education was an icon, a defining factor that gets thrown into the body market place
through the employment of language and speech. Indeed in the whole schemata
of the use of English, one sees the ways in which language is a fundamental site
for identity construction and therefore is a potent instrument for cultural control
but in this case for entering the post colonial body market. The English language
here displaces the native languages of the sex workers which are then constituted
as impurities. English becomes the standard while other languages are variants
(Ashcroft *et al*, 1995).

Place and the Identity Question

The place subject is supposed to be able to throw light upon subjectivity itself (Ashcroft *et al*, 1995). It is important to think of place conceptually because the relationship between the self and place where the self is located can increase our understanding of the notion of identity. The naming of a space as urban gives it a discursive productivity and a history and process of social construction is embedded on it. For the sex worker, the space where the trade can be carried out is a not only a visual construct. It is also a space that enables alternative lifestyles. The sex workers in this study came from different parts of the country. For example, 38 per cent of the respondents in Kisenyi were from the western parts of Uganda. Another 38 per cent came from southern Uganda; about 20 per cent from the central districts and 5 per cent from the eastern parts of the country. Some of the respondents from the south mentioned that they came from as far as Rwanda.

The wide regional representation of these sex workers was significant for other reasons. Some of them noted that some men even go on to ask them where they come from before they can buy their services. The women noted that these were usually men who looking for women from specific tribes because of the imaginations they held about the sexual prowess of certain ethnic groups. In a group discussion the women mentioned that the Banyarwanda and the Banyankole were seen as women with better bodies than most of the other girls.[10]

Respondents in Kisenyi noted that currently the ethnic mix is mostly Ugandan and as one respondent mentioned, there were many more people from different East African countries in Kisenyi in the sixties and early seventies. They noted that the eighties and beyond were marked with political upheavals and economic hardships and therefore it was mostly women from within the country who migrated to Kisenyi. The Speke Hotel Group also mentioned that in other locations like Kasanga there are many more women from different countries. One of them had this to say:

> The Banyarwanda, Barundi and the women from Zaire usually opt to stay in places like Kasanga. This is because here the community does not care a lot about the girls and most of the people in the slums around work in bars where these girls go so they do not want to antagonise them. After all, they are the ones who make business boom. When some of the women from these neighbouring countries come to Kampala, they hire a room and they stay there for about one or two months and they live in group of four or five afterwards they go back to their countries. These girls speak many languages like – French, English, Germany and very good Kiswahili so the white men like them a lot.[11]

From the above quote it is evident that origin for the women in sex work was not limited to Uganda only. We had a chance to talk to one of the girls who said she comes from Rwanda and she said that, *Uganda today has got a lot of white men who come to do work for many Government projects in the country and we come to give them company*. In this kind of migration, the anticipation of the kind of clientele that is available in the certain place is a very crucial factor. We shall return to the point of clientele later. Many of the girls also mentioned that they came from rural areas. We did not have a question on the rural-urban divide but the metaphor 'coming from the village' was very prominent in the speech of the different women we interviewed.

It is important to point out that the use of these three kinds of demographic characteristics is not so much to stay true the traditional social sciences – of knowing the demographic structures - but to actually interrogate their contribution to the production of the identity of the sex worker. One notes that sex workers' representation and self-identities are negotiated within other demographic discourses. This section therefore attempts to elaborate that age, education and place provide different iconographic energies to the construction of the identity of the sex worker. In the next section I go on to present the different *sites* where multiple identities are played out. I discuss how these different factors shape and are reshaped by the existence of sex work.

Space, Sex and Identities

In this section, I engage in an interrogation of the role of spaces in the constitution of the identities employed by the sex worker. It is important first to start with a theoretical exposé if only to rejuvenate the spirit that informs my analysis. Harvey (1990) argues that the capitalist mode of production is one where material practices and processes of social reproduction are always changing and with that comes the attendant changes in the meanings of spaces. In the progress of capitalist consumption and production our conceptual apparatuses and representations of space and time change, with material consequences for the ordering of daily life. The invasion of the capitalist mode of production on the space we call Africa today is a case in point for this study.

The case of the Ugandan urban experience is anchored within the paradigm fetishised by the colonialist that the African was a temporary wageworker at the risk of being 'detribalised' (Cooper 1996). This was then turned into the vision of the African - turned industrial man after colonialism - living with his wife and children in the modern society. Around this conception came the problems that we see throughout the urban experience. When the above two fetishes failed, a patriarchal and gendered imagery of African labour followed. The colonialist became obsessed with prescribing a social reproduction of a space where the African wage labourer would be joined by his wife and the wife's role prescribed as *reproducer of labour*. The African woman was relocated to the informal urban locale or customary structures to ensure masculine domination over her in the urban space reconstructed by colonial powers.

Obbo captures the attendant spatial and social reproduction of identities that occurred through time. She writes that once 'the migrants have arrived in the towns, they make pragmatic attempts to relate to the urban conditions that they encounter, as individuals, as members of ethnic communities, and as representatives of social groupings and classes (including religious organisations), or just as women' (1980:101). In the urban setting, new meanings can be found for older embodiments of space while ancient spaces are appropriated in very modern ways, sometimes subverting the original logic prescribed for the urban space (Harvey 1990).

In this regard, we recognise that the pace occupied by sex work is constructed around the western capitalist mode of production discourse. This discourse celebrates the male libido whose erotic explorations are fulfilled as part of the accumulation of resources and exploitation of the female body. In the next section I give some of the recorded descriptions of the different spaces and the attendant discourses that surround these spaces.

The Homes of Sex Work

The slum has always been a sexualised and 'free' space where anything can be done. There are therefore a variety of activities and opportunities in slum areas. Southall *et al* describe Kisenyi as undergoing 'free urban development', explaining that: 'free here means free from fully effective regulation of the building and settlement' (1957:19). In Kisenyi, as in many other slums, *effective regulation* of the sex worker is also not possible. The women in this study mentioned that the reason they choose slums for places of abode is because 'no one peeps into your life'. One is thus able mobilise identities in a way that is not possible in other locations where government regulatory apparatus is used to 'poke' into people's businesses. The slums are therefore important spaces for the sex worker in urban areas because of the *laissez faire* identity. They also make economic sense for the struggling sex worker who needs cheap accommodation and minimal attention. Many of the women in this study would either live in the slum or work in the slum. Even for those who chose to work in the high-class parts of the city, the slum was always an important place of abode.

Sex workers in Kisenyi generally worked from their homes, although some had makeshift brothels, which they operated from. One of them described how the brothels functioned:

Usually, an official on the LC in this area owns the house. So he takes care of any law enforcers who may want to disturb us. We pay him some five thousand shillings per day and he gives you a room where you meet your customers. I come here from around 10:00 am in the morning and sometimes I go on until the evening. The owner provides a bed; some water, and soap. Business is good here and one just has to decide how long you are ready to work each day.[12]

Another kind of brothel mentioned by the respondents is the 'lodge'. These have proliferated the Kampala urban space, and depend mostly on 'short time' customers ready to pay the rate equivalent to that charged for a full night's accommodation. They serve a more upper class clientele, generally middle class males who want a decent place away from the eyes of the public.[13] It was mentioned in the group discussions that some lodges are located in decent neighbourhoods, which do not have any inscriptions of sex work on them.

Places of Operation

From the previous discussion, we notice that homes of sex work only involve those spaces where service provision is carried out. From the respondents, we found that the various locations preferred by different clients determine the sex workers' 'point of soliciting'.[14] When a question was asked about places of operation we had various responses, although three major categories could be discerned. Some women solicited sex on the streets, dance halls and bars even when they operated from different places. A respondent's narrative of her daily routine during the week is useful at this point:

After I put my house in order, I start off at around 5:00 p.m. and I go to one bar in the middle of town where I play some pool up to around 7:30 p.m. Sometimes I get lucky and get a customer during that period. But, if I do not get one I chat with the bar boys and any patrons in the bar. At 7:30 p.m. I walk along Nile Avenue to see if there is any customers passing by. If there are no customers coming my way I go to Rock Garden Café or Speke Hotel. I go to the toilets and make up my face in the Ladies and sometimes change my dress, because in the day I wear trousers and in the evening the men want to see your legs so you have to expose them. I then move on to the streets up to about 10:30 p.m. Usually I get a customer for a short time before 10:00 p.m. If I do not get one I then go to a bar in Kansanga where many white men drink till late. I stay there until I get someone for the night.[15]

This narrative was very telling for us because it made us understand how sex workers negotiate different identities to fit in different contexts. Most of the girls mentioned that operating in those different contexts required having friends who work in the bars or hotels that can allow the women use a table for drinking while waiting for customers. Some sex workers also pointed out that important as it is, moving around is easier for those who have worked long enough to make many friends in the city as well as escape bullying by other girls. Newcomers to the business mentioned that they needed to first operate from one place before going out to other places.

Some respondents highlighted how the days of the week determined a sex worker's mode of operation. One girl had this to say:

> On weekends there are many people around, so the clubs and the bars are very popular. Men get drunk as early as 7:00 p.m. and want sexual services after that. On weekdays it is a bit complicated and sometimes the most lucrative places are the streets because the men want to have some quick sex and then go home. So one has to keep thinking about where to go.[16]

Apparently, a number of strategic decisions have to be made for one to be able to get the most out of sex work.

Additionally, the importance of foreigners in boosting sex trade was highlighted. The women in this study mentioned that when there are many 'foreign guests' in town, especially white men, their business booms. Many women remembered when a contingent of American troops en route Rwanda during the aftermath of the 1995 genocide came to Uganda. Those who were sex workers at the time said that they made a lot of money. Other respondents also mentioned that at times when there are conferences with foreign delegates – these are very lucrative times. A newspaper article in the Sunday Monitor captures the essence of the moment when it describes the life of sex workers in Durban. The author writes:

> From experience, major conferences, never mind what kind, offer a considerable upswing income. Last year's Commonwealth Heads of State conference, also held in Durban, saw her averaging R 500 (USD 5) a day. There was no way she was going to miss out on the 13th International AIDS Conference. AIDS or no AIDS, survival was the game. Better to die of AIDS than of starvation, she thinks. (Commey 2000)

Though written with an air of chauvinism the article did point to some of the gains that international conferences offer to sex work. However, the author portrays prostitutes as if they never think of AIDS but only their survival, an issue that is inconsistent with the findings of this study.

Some respondents also pointed out that they go upcountry or outside Uganda for sex work. However, they were quick to add that they only do this if there they know they will make money from other towns. In fact, one of our respondents felt that most towns in Uganda are not 'good for business' because, in most places, there are local women who usually charge very little money compared to the Kampala based women. Some of the outside 'markets' for Ugandan sex workers was Kenya, although portrayed to have recently become less lucrative. Our key respondent for the Speke Hotel group had a story to tell us about her trip to Dubai:

I saved money for a ticket and pocket money to go to Dubai for about eight months. A woman who had been to Dubai before convinced me to think of going to Dubai. We got visas and I bought my ticket and we went. In Dubai we started off in a small hotel where we both stayed. But I did not like the life in Dubai at all. We were going out with mostly Pakistan and Indian men who were very low class workers. They gave us a few dinars, which were equivalent to about 6,000 Uganda shillings. It was so disappointing to me. In Kampala that is money paid by taxi conductors and I do not go out with such men! It was so difficult even to make enough money for one to survive in Dubai. The men preferred prostitutes from Russia because they were white women. The Arabs were also very queer men. They would buy you and only have anal sex. I am not used to that and it was very uncomfortable. After two weeks I became desperate and I wanted to move on. The other disappointing thing was that the women we found in Dubai had sold their passports to some black market people and they were very hostile and intimidated me to give them my passport. I refused and they wanted to beat me. I had to change my hotel after and when I realised it was getting more dangerous, I booked my flight and came back to Uganda. I think in Uganda I am better off.[17]

Sex workers do not imagine success only at home. They also migrate for work to other countries. In this narrative it was clear that it is not very simple for the sex worker to break into other worlds. These kinds of trips are fuelled by the imagination and success stories that the women have been fed with. Most of the women believed they would go to Dubai, have sex with some 'Oil Sheikh' and come back to Uganda driving a sleek car with a lot of money to invest in business. This was mentioned many times by some of the younger girls. Many of the girls were also trying to find ways of travelling to foreign countries like Britain and the Scandinavian countries. One of the women mentioned that her colleagues had become successful because she was working in a Strip-Tease bar in Copenhagen, Denmark - she was saving money to join her.

The Price Tag

Early studies on Kampala suggest that sex for money has been around for some-time. Southall *et al* (1957) pointed out the different rates and modalities applied by Baziba women in charging for sex in Kisenyi. Gutkind (Southall *et al*, 1957) also reports that the phenomenon of charging men money for sex was prevalent in Mulago. Obbo (1980) introduces another angle when she analysed how women in Namuwongo, another low-income community, manipulated the men in their lives to get money from them. One of our respondents indicated an ambiguity around money and relationships. She mentioned that money was one thing that needed careful negotiation. All the respondents mentioned a variable price for sexual services based on customers' presentation. A respondent had this to say:

> Some of the men want straight sex so they ask you up-front how much you want and they 'go with you' and you pay. In that case you only have to ask if it is 'short time' and 'transnight'. If he looks smart and a presentable gentleman you then ask for 10,000/= -15,000/= for short time and about 30,000-50,000/= for transnight. If you have already worked and you can afford to 'miss him' you can play around with him, go and dance, drink beer and then disappear when he is drunk and you go home. If the man is an amateur you may decide to push the price higher. If it is a muzungu you charge in dollars usually between $20-50 depending on how he looks. Very few bazungu want short time. Sometimes, you find that it is a guy who always comes back to you so you give him the price he is comfortable with. Sometimes you like the character of the man so you do not charge him a lot so he can keep coming back. Other times he can be a filthy guy but also with a lot of money so you give him a high price and go with him. There are many things that one has to consider in this business.[18]

Incomes earned from prostitution do not appear in the statistics on prostitution. However, for women involved in prostitution, these incomes offer a competitive and viable work option to some of the work in other professions. Respondents pointed out that they are able to invest their money in other businesses, pay for brothers and sisters in schools and carry out a variety of livelihood support activities spent 'responsibly'.

From a theoretical perspective, I am reminded of Appadurai's (1986) thesis regarding the artificiality of the divide between commodities and gifts. In one sense, it is 'Ugandan custom', in sex work, that the man who takes out a lady pays the bills while expecting 'something' [read sexual favour] in return for this generosity. Yet, girls do not always want to 'pay back' in the ways that men would want to be paid back. Clearly many of relationships in Uganda are understood and mediated through the medium of money, but how much coercive power does this social category – money – have? Does control of money define the shape of the relationships? How does sex work reshape understanding of commodities? Can we then talk about the materiality of relationships and sociality of things? In this case, is money only a material resource that shapes the social world of prostitution or is there a social element that is fulfilled in the exchange of money in relationships (Ssewakiryanga and Mills, 1995)? If the sex worker engages in sex work to fulfil material needs, could we argue that men buy sex to fulfil a socially anchored need – the expression of male domination and satisfaction of the male ego? Answering these kinds of questions will help us understand the confusing tangle of things, emotions and power that make up everyday experiences of sexual relationships in the area of work.

The Commodity – The Body

The body-as-used, the body I am, is a social body that has taken meanings rather than conferred them (Connell, 1987:83).

Connell's point above provides us with a very important tool to analyse how identities are deployed within the world of sex work. It shows how the different elements of our social practice act as significant markers of our bodies. Connell indicates the inadequacy of using the body as a biologically determined entity since social processes essentially mark bodies and therefore allows different uses of the body. Moore (1987) also makes another point when she borrows Bourdieu's phrase that 'bodies take metaphors seriously'. Consequently, living bodies give substance to the social distinctions and differences that underpin social relations. If one is to link this to the representation of bodies in sex work, one realises that the body of the sex worker is an important part in the construction of what sex work is. The body of the sex worker is adorned, pierced and oiled to live to the patriarchal ideology of the feminine.

Nearly all the girls we talked to mentioned that it was important to keep ones body 'in shape', 'clean' and try to wear 'something sexy'. All these were telling metaphors because they were anchored within a knowledge base that celebrated certain elements of femininity. One of the girls had this to say when interviewed about what they wear and how appearance counts in this trade:

Our bazungu [white men] customers like slender and dark girls. The fat girls do not get a lot of market among the whites. The black men have varied tastes but some of them look only for fat girls. One has to be careful about how you look if you are targeting the guys with good money then you have to work on yourself very well. We also have to dress well, you have to know what is the latest style and try and get it. The good thing is that Owino market[19] now has a good variety of clothes. Some of the shops in town also have good and cheap clothes - one has to always be on the look out. Of course the short skirts are very popular and so are the bikini-like dresses, so we have to look for those ones also. For the hair, braids are the best because they are cheap to maintain and one does not have to keep worrying about combing after every customer.[20]

It appears then that many ideologies and discourses are mobilised in determining how sex workers treat their bodies. Some of these markers can be traced back to how the black woman has been represented by colonial history. A case in point is the history of Sarah Bartman, the slave woman billed the 'Hottentot Venus', whose naked body is still displayed after her death in the Musee d'Histoire Naturelle in Paris. Studied by many scientists, her nude body and large buttocks is admired by a large audience in Europe as the icon of colonial African women's sexuality. The quote below illustrates the paradox of images held within the colonial world and surviving today. 'African men were assumed to be virile, to have huge penises, and to be obsessed with despoiling the European women, while the African women were assumed to be insatiable mistresses of seduction, a disposition which rendered them well suited for the provision of sexual services (Mama 1997: 68).

We still need to seriously ponder the extent to which these images have been deconstructed. However, what we see here is that sex workers live to some society images of femininity that also contribute to the perpetuation of sex trade. Another important element is how these women negotiate their body politics, which is essentially anchored with the 'politics of dress'. The women have got to look and imagine themselves as modern even if the second hand market is the only place of solace. They buy these clothes because the magazines, the TV, the videos all sanction certain images as modern, sophisticated and sexual. One of the women mentioned that they use JIK detergent to bleach themselves since the 'brown girl' is one of the identities in vogue.[21] Let me move into the area of representation and try to establish the connections.

Representing Sex Work

One of the elements that this research investigated is how sex workers are represented both in speech and in writing. In order to give this section meaning I take recourse in some of the works that critic the very notion of what we use as an essential paradigm of gender studies today. Here I am inspired by the following words of MacKinnon:

> Post-Lacan, actually post-Foucault, it has become customary to affirm that sexuality is socially constructed. Seldom specified is what, social, it is constructed of, far less who does the constructing or how, when, or where. When Capitalism is the favoured social construct, sexuality is shaped and controlled and exploited and repressed by capitalism; not, capitalism creates sexuality as we know it ... 'Constructed' seems to mean influenced by, directed, channelled, like a highway constructs traffic patterns. Not: Why cars? Who is driving? Where's everybody going? What makes mobility matter? Who can own a car? Are these accidents not very accidental (MacKinnon 1990: 212)?

The media, mostly print media, is very instrumental, in creating the identity of the prostitute. A very recent phenomenon in Uganda provides a case in point. In September 2000, Uganda witnessed massive arrests of sex workers off the streets by the Police. They were sent to Luzira Maximum Security Prison on charges of being 'idle and disorderly'. It beats one to understand the logic of that phrase but it seems an uncontested notion of the post-colonial law in Uganda. What was interesting however was how the prostitutes were photographed or drawn in cartoons. The front pages of the daily paper the *New Vision* and the *Monitor* all chose the photos of the sex workers boarding a very high lorry to Luzira. The photos all gave a detailed rear view of the most skimpy dressed sex workers. The cartoons that followed were even more intriguing and mostly eroticised the image of the sex worker so as to speak the language of male domination.[22]

In his work on cartoons, Mbembe (1997) called this representation the 'image as a figure of speech'. He argues that the pictographic sign does not solely belong to the field of seeing but is in itself a figure of speech. This speech is expressed as a mode of describing, narrating and representing reality as well as a particular strategy of persuasion and even violence (Mbembe 1997: 152). This is a useful tool for engaging the different articles that came out after the arrest of prostitutes. Some people supported sex work. Others felt it was an immoral act. Some take it to be a part of the strategies towards eradication of poverty in people's livelihoods. However, each of these views would be accompanied by a picture that will allow the 'male gaze' to function as an act of male domination and even violence.[23]

This representation is a normalising strategy, which intends to demonise, eroticise and fantasise prostitution as an object of sexuality. This opaque violence (to borrow Mbembe's term) in figurative expression through cartoons for public consumption affirms and recreates an imagined identity of the sex worker. An analysis of these cartoons is material for another study. However, I need to point out that one needs to read a number of discourses at play in these cartoons. What is seen – the visible cartoon – and what is not seen are both important figures of speech. In these cartoons, patriarchal social reality is transformed into a sign, which the public uses to decipher the erotic world of sex work. The 'invisible' evoked by the cartoons or the 'imagined visible' are not just two sides of the same coin, but are both played out as part of the same sexual and erotic identity of the sex worker.

Sex Work and the State

Here, I locate the discussion of sex work and the state in a framework that links identity politics to notions of the state. Identity politics in relation to sexuality is a problematic category. Different experiences and political desires of certain groups reconstruct what is known as identity politics. An analysis of identities can focus on the subject – that is the issues that a certain groups intend to put forward. It can also focus on the *form* that the identity politics tends to take (Wendy 1995). I consider both to be equally critical to the analysis of sex work, and will therefore examine *issues* and *form* for a contextual understanding sex work and its

There is always the danger of turning identity politics into 'injury politics', with claims and counter claims about a phenomenon like sex work. However, it is important to note that the quest for moral claims usually get handed over to the state authorities like the police and the justice system. This implies that a new legitimisation is endowed on these state structures (Valverde 1999). The state structures therefore take it upon themselves to decide and to take action on any issues of conflict between the state and sex workers. This not only empowers the sexist police and prison apparatus but also robs identity politics of its revolution- ary potential.

The state's violence against prostitution is one way of constructing different identities of the prostitute. In this regard, the sex workers' challenge of state hegemonies can be regarded as 'resistance identities'. These are identities that the prostitutes deploy in order to survive through situations where they get in con- tact with state agents. The police have always been the chief agents in the regula- tion and disciplining of prostitutes. Before we get into the insights provided by the different prostitutes on this issue I want to revisit the notion of the body and how bodies resistant and are controlled. In his analysis of Foucault's notion of power, Patton (1998) notes that adult pleasures are separated in two categories - the normal and the pathological. This he says is one of the pedagogic controls of the experience of modernity. In this schema, the female body is connected to the realm of reproduction and childbirth and these become the 'taken for granted' in orderings and classifications of the female body. Nevertheless, in this construc- tion, sexuality is always fabricated upon an active body and therefore resistance always accompanies the deployment of sexuality.

The police are always a real and feared arm of government for prostitutes in Kampala. Many respondents in Kisenyi identified their worst days in relation to arrests by police. One of the women had this to say:

> The police arrested me one day and the policeman gave me three options: give him all the money I had worked for, sleep with him or take me to the police. My money was hidden in two places in my bag and under my shoe. So I gave him – 10,000 shillings from my bag and then he said that I am a crook and he knew I am hiding some money in my shoe. I then had no choice but to give him the money in my shoe. It seems he had ever ar- rested somebody else who hid money in the shoe. So he took all my 30,000 shillings I had made that night. I was very frustrated. I just took a cab and went home crying.[24]

Thus, law enforcers use their power not only to discipline women, but also to extort money for their own personal gain and affirm patriarchal control. Some women noted that sometimes when they stand near guarded places, the security agents are useful allies. For a fee, they help sex workers escape the wrath of the police. However, in other instances, the women did have a lot of problems with the police who sometimes become very violent and beat them up. One woman had this to say:

> One day we were standing with my friend in our spot and then a small car with a muzungu and a policeman inside stopped and, as they jumped out, the policeman started by slapping me and said bring the dollars! Bring the dollars! I had no clue what he was talking about but it seems the muzungu had been robbed and he could not identify the girl who robbed him. They took us to a police station and we had to spend the night in jail. The next day I sent one of the policemen to a friend who came and I had to promise to give my friend my TV as mortgage so that I could find money for bail. Life on the streets can sometimes be very tough.[25]

In Kampala, the most spectacular swoop was the massive arrest of 60 sex workers from different streets and nightclubs in the city by the Police and Local Defence Units personnel in September 2000. The culprits were charged and taken to Luzira prison. There were mixed reactions to this from different places. Some people called it a hypocritical response to the issue of prostitution inn the city. The Chairperson of an organisation known as Federation of Women Business Industry Organisation and Agriculture contributed money towards the prostitutes' bail.[26] The sex workers vowed to go back to their businesses and even offered 'half price' to their customers to make up for the 'times of scarcity' when they were in jail.[27]

This incident exposes the confusion in the state's attitude to prostitution in Uganda. Whereas the law seems to criminalise prostitution, the state's law organs were completely confused about how to handle the sex workers. Many newspaper articles challenged criminalising prostitution without any thought about the identity of the clients. They regarded this outlook as very problematic and a reinforcement of the sexual domination that favours men in heterosexual liaisons. It appeared, from this incident, that the state was reacting to what we have termed 'injury politics' – with some people feeling that sex work was injuring their self-esteem as people and therefore the sex workers had to stop. The state in this case reproduced the violence against the sex workers, through invoking the power of the legal discourse of being idle and disorderly.

Other significant reactions to the incident included one from the Vice President (who is a woman) who was quoted as having argued that no one should talk about sex work without talking about how to find alternative survival strategies for the women.[28] She argued that women sex workers do not enjoy sex but do it in order to survive and provide money for their children. The Vice President thus revealed the complexity of the demarcation between pleasure and work and the plight of prostitution. She was arguing from an alternative discourse that did not just view sex outside marriage as very evil and sexual services as deviant behaviour. It became apparent from the reactions to her utterance, that many members of the public wanted to stay true to the discourse that mutes the voice of the sex worker. However, what was also interesting to note that the radio stations also cashed in on this event and quickly moved into inviting self-professed prostitutes to the radio stations so that they can offer their views.

A recurring discourse here is the insistence that prostitutes were forced into sex work. Very few people considered it as a deliberate alternative choice by the sex worker. Interestingly, one respondent who 'feels comfortable with this work' attributed this to 'the kind of talk that many people wanted to hear'. Consequently, within the public culture discourse, sex work was still an ambivalent issue. The sexual act was still seen to function within a heterosexual conjugal union and the sex worker was a deviant. The public was thus concerned with thinking of 'alternative' ways of stopping sex workers. By implication, the solution lay in controlling the women, with nothing serious being said about the male clients. The men seemed to be invisible, even as customers. The only clue available to the public was that the men are 'powerful' and 'respectable' people. In the public debate the men's voice was muted; only heard when condemning the girls and seeking a redemptive strategy to close off the deviant behaviour. This in itself is a reductionist approach that offers a universalist solution without a critical analysis of the different aspects that interplay in sex work.

Concluding Remarks

Based on current narratives of struggle and play of identities in sex work, it seems the polemics around prostitution will continue. There are debates about who gains from prostitution, whether prostitution is sex work, how much the men gain, whether there is a political economy of prostitution and whether sexuality should ever be liberated. While all these are still being played out, this study is a rejoinder to the continuing debate in the conceptualisation of sex and work. The conviction to take the bold step and investigate the question of sex work is in itself a political position that warns against reliance on hearsay and fabricated moral prescriptivism to answer complex questions that surround the area of sex work. Even with 'tongue in the cheek' caveats slapped on this narrative, I will try and point out some treads we can use to give some pattern and colour to this complex question.

For or Against Sex Work?

In order to make myself clearer I need to emphasize what this study is NOT about. Many times authors who write either in the newspapers or in academic publications want to get to the question of *why do women enter the world of sex work?* I do not think this is the most important question in trying to understand sex work. The reasons for entering a 'profession' is just one part of the story, and I think this perspective is located within the narrow focus that prostitution is a problem for women only. Asking the question why men buy sex is also important but may also polarise the debate and it becomes 'the knowing woman trying to find out what the pathological man is doing'. What I intend to do in this work therefore, is to move the debate into a realm that asks questions of the ways in which bodies are *disciplined* by different social systems and how new identities emerge in this process. The fact that there are emergences of new identities does not provide all the answers but helps us to look at the nuances that get covered up in the patriarchal sexual domination that women involved in sex work have to negotiate on an everyday basis.

The only moral I would like to associate with is contained in an analogy by Shrage (1990). The analogy is that: if a person decides to eat cat and dog meat, is the most important question whether eating dog or cat meat is 'really' healthy or unhealthy? Or whether it is 'really' like eating chicken or beef? What may be the most important point is that if one includes dogs' meat in ones diet, the person upsets others and therefore does damage to both themselves and to others. Hence the issue I am raising in this work is that 'objective reality' (if the dog meat is 'really' healthy) is not the most important but the 'social reality' (you and others are affected by your eating dog's meat) in which we live. Hence the argument here is not that unconventional behaviour is okay, but that, within the unconventional behaviour, we need to ask the harder questions of how it is played out in society. In there, lies the answer of the different ways in which capitalist domination articulates itself with the realm of sexuality. In that way we then get to the questions of the different elements of power that structure our identity and hence our relative position in society. Identity helps one to locate their position on the social compass, thereby getting one step further in deciding which direction one wants to take. This is the intellectual project that this paper tries to achieve.

Sexuality is one of the areas that have undergone a critical and yet frustrating engagement in feminist and gender work. Feminism gave us the energy to critic sexuality in the famous pronouncement of the 'personal is political'. Put another way, that the sexual is political'. What this meant was that we cannot keep engaging debates about sexuality as part of the private sphere which we know is marred with different shades of domination. This opening up has meant that even in the conceptualisation of other parts of the feminine experience one cannot run away from engaging with the most oppressive locale for many women in the world. As we question sex and work, there are unresolved questions about the nature of sexuality itself. Heterosexuality has already been earmarked as having undue oppression because of the ways in which it appropriates domestic work as no work and also uses sex work as a mode of oppression. Yet for many and mostly the developing world feminists, the role of heterosexuality is seen as central to the continuation of society's affirmation of other experiences of emancipation.

This study is anchored within this very large and ongoing debate in which I decided to take the narrow focus of 'wondering about' identities and sex work. We have made snapshots at the different parts of what sex work is – the place, the bodies involved, the spaces they occupy, their representation and the ways in which other hegemonic sites interface with the sex worker. There are other parts that have been deliberately left out, for example - the role of men – because one needs a theorisation of masculinities in order to arrive at some systematic knowledge production process in this area. This study cannot therefore end with a moral tone but rather with an affirmation that sex work as an experience of the advent of capitalist economies is in itself a very complex trade, the emancipatory sites within it are only limited and confined within the dominant site of male domination. Hence, to think of deconstructing sex work further, we should go on to engage the nature of capitalism and how it has been managed in the post-colonies; how it has become both a vehicle of emancipation and also oppression through its different shades of perpetuating patriarchy. I dare say that prostitution is not an aberration but it is a consequence of well-established beliefs and values that form part of the foundation of our lives – we need to redirect our guns to those beliefs and values!

Notes

1   Information given by the LC I councillor who worked with us as a guide on this study. For purposes of this study we shall refer to her as the Guide. Studies by Southall and Obbo attest to some of these facts. See for example, Southall A. W et al. (1957) *Townsmen in the Making: Kampala and its suburbs;* and Obbo Christine (1980): *African Women: Their Struggle for Economic Independence.*

2   Information from the Guide.

3   This was during the dissemination exercise for a on poverty assessment in Kampala. One of the activities we had to do was to take back the finding in a public meeting where the leaders from the area would be given a chance to comments

4   This refers to the small incentive fee of 5,000 shillings, which we had to give to each of the women.

5   Ssebutinde was the name of the Judge who headed the inquiry into the police. The particular policeman who said this was a friend because he came from the village neighbouring the secondary school I went to. But he was very sceptical about my involvement in this kind of study and was convinced that I had sinister motives. After sometime we also reanalysed our objectives

and were convinced that a police perspective would be another interesting study of it own.

6 Interview with elderly woman in Kisenyi May 2000

7 Interview with a woman staying in Kabalagala and working in the Rock Garden Café area.

8 This is a metaphor that suggests that some one had slept with so many men and therefore her body is spent. It is also interesting to note that in some other instances experience was said to be a very good investment because some men wanted 'experienced' women.

9 Interview with a woman from Kisenyi – May 2000

10 Group discussion in Rock Garden Café – June 2000

11 Interview with women in Rock Garden Café – June 2000.

12 Interview with a woman in Kisenyi May 2000

13 This issue was mentioned by a barman in Kabalagala

14 To use a working place language I have called this section Front Office to describe a space where the client first goes before being attended to.

15 Interview with a woman in Rock Garden Café – May 2000

16 Interview with a woman in Capital Pub – June 2000

17 Interview with women in Al's Bar Kansanga – April 2000

18 Interview with women in Gourmet Bar near Ange Noir Discotheque – June 2000

19 Owino market is one of the biggest markets in Kampala and is located in the central business area of the city near Kisenyi community.

20 Interview with a woman in Rock Garden Café – June 2000

21 Interview with woman in the Kisenyi – May 2000

22 See Sunday Vision of October 8th 2000, p. 14 and *Monitor* of September 11th 2000 in appendix I.

23 See for example cartoon in the *New Vision* of October 16, 2000 in appendix II.

24 Interview with women in Rock Garden Café – June 2000

25 Interview with women in Kisenyi – June 2000

26 See *The Monitor* September 30, 2000

27 See The Monitor October 1st 2000

28 See *Sunday Vision* article by John Eremu entitled: *VP Defends Prostitution*, October 15, 2000 and cartoon on October 16, 2000 in *New Vision*

References

Appadurai, A., ed, 1986, *The Social Life of Things: Commodities in the cultural perspective*, New York: Cambridge University Press.

Ashcroft, B. *et al*, eds, 1995, *The Post-Colonial Studies Reader*, New York: Routledge.

Bakwesigha, C., 1982, *Profiles of Urban Prostitution: A Case study from Uganda*, Nairobi: Kenya Literature Bureau.

Bishop, A., 1990, Western Mathematics: The Secret Weapon of Cultural Imperialism, *Race and Class,* No. 32, Vol. 2

Brown, W., 1995, *States of Injury: Power and Freedom in the Late Modernity,* Princeton: Princeton University Press.

Connell, R., 1987, *Gender and Power: Society, the Person and Sexual Politics*, California: Stanford University Press.

Cooper, F., 1996, *Decolonisation and African Society: The Labour Question in French and British Africa*, Cambridge: Cambridge University Press.

Davidson, O., 1996, 'Prostitution and the Contours of Control' in Weeks, J. & Holland, J., eds., *Sexual Cultures: Communities, Values and Intimacy*, Macmillan, London de Beauvoir, S., 1974, The Second Sex, New York: Vintage Press.

Delphy C. & Leonard D., 1992, *Familiar Exploitation: A new analysis of marriage in contemporary western society*, Oxford: Polity Press.

Engels, F., 1985, *The Origin of the Family, Private Property and the State*, New York: Penguin.

Ericcson, L., 1980, 'Charges Against Prostitution: An Attempt at a Philosophical Assessment', *Ethic,* 90, pp.335-66

Foucault, M., 1977, *Discipline and Punish,* Hammondsworth: Penguin

Foucault, M., 1978, *The History of Sexuality, Vol. 1*, Hammondsworth: Penguin

Foucault, M., 1985, *The Use of Pleasure*, Hammondsworth: Penguin

Foucault, M., 1986, *The Care of Self,* Hammondsworth: Penguin

Freud, S., 1933, *Female Sexuality*, Standard Edition, Vol. 21, London: Hogarth.

Gatens, M., 1992, 'Power, Bodies and Difference' in Barrett, M. and Phillips, A., eds, *Destabilizing Theory: Contemporary Feminist Debates*, Stanford: Stanford University Press.

Giddens, A., 1991, *Modernity and Self Identity*, Cambridge: Polity Press.

Harvey, D., 1990, *The Condition of Post-Modernity: An Inquiry into the Origins of Cultural Change*, Oxford: Blackwells.

Heaphy, B., 1996, 'Medicalisation and Identity Formation: Identity and Strategy in the Context of AIDS and HIV', in Weeks, J. & Holland, J., eds., *Sexual Cultures: Communities, Values and Intimacy*, London: Macmillan.

http://www.bayswan.org/manifest.htmlh

http://www.bayswan.org/stats.htmlh

MacKinnon, C., 1990, Sexuality, Pornography, and Method: 'Pleasure Under Patriarchy' in Sustein, C.,ed., *Feminism and Political Theory*, Chicago: University of Chicago Press.

Mbembe, A., 1997, 'The 'Thing'and its Doubles in Cameroonian Cartoons', in Barber, K., ed, *Readings in African Popular Culture*, Oxford: James Currey.

Mbembe, A., 1999, 'Getting Out of the Ghetto: The Challenge of Internationalisation', *CODESRIA Bulletin*, No. 3&4, Dakar: CODESRIA

Moore, H., 1994, *A Passion for Difference: Essays in Anthropology and Gender*, Indianapolis: Indiana University Press.

Nelson, N., 1987, 'Selling her Kiosk: Kikuyu Notion of Sexuality and Sex for Sale in Mathare Valley Kenya' in Caplan, P. (ed.), *The Cultural Construction of Sexuality*, London: Routledge.

New Jerusalem Bible

Obbo, C., 1980, *African Women: Their Struggle for Economic Independence*, London: Zed Press.

Pateman, C., 1988, *The Sexual Contract,* Cambridge: Polity Press.

Patton, P., 1998, 'Foucault's Subject of Power', in Moss, J., ed., *The Later Foucault*, London: Sage Publications.

Plummer, K., 1996, 'Intimate Citizenship and the Culture of Sexual Story Telling' in Weeks, J. & Holland, J., eds., *Sexual Cultures: Communities, Values and Intimacy*, London: Macmillan.

Shotter, J., 1993, *Cultural Politics of Everyday Life*, Buckingham: Open University Press.

Shrage, L., 1990, 'Should Feminist Oppose Prostitution?' in Sustein, C., ed, *Feminism and Political Theory*, Chicago: University of Chicago Press.

Ssewakiryanga, R. & Mills, D., 1995, 'Vegetarianus Economicus. The Relationship of Commodities, Masculinities and HIV Transmission Amongst Young People in Uganda', Paper presented at IXth International Conference on AIDS and STDs in Africa (ICASA) in Kampala: 10 14 December 1995.

Sunstein, C., ed, 1990, *Feminism and Political Theory*, Chicago: University of Chicago Press.

Theweleit, K., 1987, *Male Fantasies Vol.1: Women, Floods, Bodies, History*, Minnesota: University of Minnesota Press.

Valverde, M., 1999, 'Identity Politics and the Law in United States', *Feminist Studies*, Summer.

Weeks, J. & Holland, J., eds., 1996, *Sexual Cultures: Communities, Values and Intimacy*, London: Macmillan.

White, L., 1980, 'Women Domestic Labour in Colonial Kenya: Prostitution in Kenya 1905–1950', *African Studies*, Boston University Paper 30.

8

Globalisation, Trade and Gender –
The Key Concerns

Grace Ongile

Introduction

Globalisation, one of the most debated issues of the late twentieth century and new millennium, has been described as a process of internationalisation, growing interdependence and less important national boundaries. Simply stated, a globalised world supposedly behaves as a single market. The process of globalisation is complex, creating risks and opportunities with asymmetric impact on different groups.

For gender relations, this impact has been manifold and complicated. Available literature suggests that African women are being further isolated and disempowered by globalisation and the trade and financial policies associated with it. As African economies in particular try to grapple with the challenges of globalisation, it is necessary to sharpen our knowledge of the general gender implications of globalisation as well as specific benefits of trade liberalisation.

This chapter attempts to raise the key concerns on globalisation, trade and gender. After the introduction: Section 2 briefly explains the concept of globalisation. Gender and globalisation is discussed in section 3. Section 4 focuses on gender dimensions of trade liberalisation. A brief discussion of gender implications of World Trade Organisation (WTO) agreements is discussed in section 5. The chapter gives examples of ongoing work on international trade and gender in section 6. We also point out areas where future research is required to enhance our knowledge in globalisation, trade and gender and also to strengthen the capacity of policy makers in trade negotiation and implementation. Finally section 7 raises key areas of concern, particularly for research, WTO agenda from a gender perspective, capacity building and advocacy.

What is Globalisation?

Globalisation refers to the growing interaction of countries in world trade, foreign direct investment and capital markets. It is characterised by increases in flows of trade, capital, and information as well as mobility of individuals across borders. It is multidimensional, affecting economic, cultural, environmental and other social relations between governments and nations. The globalisation process has been enhanced by technological advances in transport and communications, and a rapid liberalisation and deregulation of trade and capital flows at national and international levels.

Globalisation is also about international financial crises. It encapsulates the fear of workers in developed countries losing their jobs to lower cost countries. It reflects concerns by workers in developing countries that decisions affecting their lives are made in international corporations' offices far away from them. Globalisation involves opportunities as well as risks. The risks must be addressed at national and international levels to ensure that globalisation works for all.

However, whether we approach it from an opportunity or risk stance, the fact that poverty remains the greatest challenge in sub-Saharan Africa is a central consideration. Consequently, we must ask how Africa can reposition itself to take full advantage of globalisation by accelerating growth and reducing poverty. Empirical research has consistently shown that no country with closed and inward looking policies can achieve or sustain high growth rates. Hence, the issue of Africa's share in the world trade cannot be ignored. According to the International Monetary Fund (IMF 2001), 'Africa's share in the world trade has dwindled, foreign direct investment in most countries has remained at very low levels, and the income gap relative to advanced countries has widened'.

Some scholars argue that Africa's integration into the world economy must be driven by its major goals of faster economic growth and development, and poverty reduction. To achieve these, implementing strong and comprehensive domestic policies to consolidate macroeconomic stability becomes paramount. These would ensure human resource development; improve basic infrastructure; spur agricultural development; promote a good banking system and improve Africa's trade performance. They would also guarantee good governance and bolster regional integration and increased economic co-operation thereby strengthening Africa's bargaining power within the global trading system. Others argue that a comprehensive reform agenda is not enough. Major institutional reforms are often necessary. In particular, limiting the role of the state to the delivery essential public services while promoting a dynamic private sector is crucial. Similarly a liberal and transparent regulatory framework and partnership between public and private sectors, including the civil society, should be promoted.

While debate on the economic dimensions and impact of globalisation continues, there appears to be a consensus that the process of globalisation has been accompanied by growing inequalities among and within nations. Women have been particularly badly hit since most of the world's cheap unskilled labour is female.

Gender and Globalisation

As discussed above, globalisation is a complex process creating risks and opportunities and uneven impact for different groups. Literature on gender and globalisation indicate that globalisation's impact on gender relations has been manifold and complicated. Through globalisation, the state has been weakened and fragmented. The patriarchal assumptions underlying power structures of the nation state have further marginalised women. Additionally, the fragmentation of power has led to the emergence of new social groupings able to present their claims internationally.

Trade liberalisation is an important part of globalisation since it seeks to create fair competition for economies at different levels of development by reducing tariff and non-tariff barriers. We cannot however ignore longstanding imbalances within and between nations, men and women that have translated into uneven patterns of growth and heightened inequality. Women in particular have unequal access to resources and face different constraints from those faced by men. Women may therefore not be able to benefit from trade liberalisation and are more likely to suffer from the adjustment costs of trade reform and economic restructuring.

Empirical research reveals that while women have not been able to utilise growth opportunities resulting from trade liberalisation in countries like Pakistan, they successfully entered the garment industry for export in a country like Bangladesh. Whereas these employment opportunities result in increased income for the women, the work conditions, benefits and rights of workers remain key issues of concern. A study on 'The Effects of the East Asian Crisis on Employment of Men and Women: The Philippine Case' found that during the East Asian crisis, male unemployment got worse than female unemployment because of the bigger decline in the tradable and industrial sectors. Female unemployment increased more slowly than male unemployment since the relatively female-intensive service sector was not hard hit. In short, the crisis created more 'idleness' for men due to unemployment and shorter working hours; and longer work hours for women compared to men.

Three points are worth noting from the above example. First, labour markets are not gender-neutral: markets embody social and cultural norms and practices. Secondly, macroeconomic and trade theories do not recognise important issues concerning the reproductive economy, that is, unpaid work hours in social reproduction and its implications. Lastly, during constrained macro-economic periods, families and households become major de facto safety nets. This is mainly due to the inability of the state to provide safety nets. Gender neutrality cannot be assumed since it is women who bear the main responsibility of maintaining the household (Lim 2000).

Available literature suggests that African women are being further isolated and disempowered by globalisation and its associated trade and financial policies. Yet, some scholars argue that technological and communications aspects of globalisation have improved women's long standing organisational methods, enhancing their skills and strengths in campaigning and communicating globally. This may not be true for many sub-Saharan African countries where even basic needs are still unmet. Similarly, globalisation process has achieved mixed results in reproductive technology. On the one hand women have a greater choice and freedom with respect to reproduction. However, this has been accompanied by various health problems. Consequently, clearer understanding of gender implications of globalisation and benefits of trade liberalisation is needed as African economies grapple with the twin challenges.

Gender Dimensions of Trade Liberalisation

The most important gender-specific topics relevant to trade agreement and free trade are 'food, water, health and education, access to ownership and control of income and resources' (Williams 2002). The following issues have been identified as important in the discussion of women's roles and concerns about globalisation and the impact of trade liberalisation:

- Women's undervalued and unrecognised labour in social reproduction and how this influences the market.
- Constraints faced by women, which may hinder them from benefiting from trade liberalisation.
- Rules and practices that promote import liberalisation and export promotion and the implications of such agreements on men and women.

In attempting to understand the gender dimensions of trade liberalisation scholars have looked at the issue from two premises:

- Trade liberalisation policy may intensify existing gender inequalities that worsen women's economic and social status. Trade liberalisation brings different costs, benefits and opportunities to men and women, and this gender difference is found across all economic and social categories.
- Existing gender inequalities can also undermine the effectiveness of trade policy thus affecting the implementation of the policy. The impact of trade liberalisation is mediated by gender relations and gendered social, economic and political structures.

Gender and trade have a two-way relationship. While trade has gender impacts, gender biases and inequalities can also influence trade policy outcomes. Due to the different constraints faced by men and women, women's inability to respond appropriately may limit their chances of taking advantage of new opportunities. Similarly, trade liberalisation may exacerbate existing gender inequalities thereby worsening women's economic and social status. For instance:

- Trade liberalisation may even lead to reduction of women's access to and control of resources like land particularly when there is a switch from subsistence to cash crop production for export;
- Trade liberalisation policies leading to increased employment of women without considering complementary measures like day-care will increase work burden of women; and
- Trade liberalisation may reinforce gender segregation and gender-typing of occupations and 'women's jobs' may have lower pay and be less secure than 'men's jobs'.

Despite scanty and inconclusive work on the impact of trade liberalisation on women, a review of the literature indicates that, for some countries, trade liberalisation and export promotion seem to have led to a feminisation of the labour force. It has not stimulated an expansion of female-intensive export-oriented manufacturing industries for most of sub-Saharan Africa countries.

However, the picture is not unilaterally negative. For instance, in some cases, new trans-national (TNC) export industries have provided women with employment at competitive or higher wages than other forms of local employment, giving women a sense of freedom and greater autonomy. Yet, evidence also shows that such production based on cheap female labour, under extremely arduous working conditions, is exploitative and ultimately damaging to women and their families. Preliminary evidence from Kenya and Uganda suggest a trend towards feminisation of horticulture (for French beans and flowers). The interplay between existing gender inequalities and trade policies result in a number of broader areas of gender-differentiated impact of the operation of the trade system: These include the following adopted from Williams (2001):

Trade-Induced Fiscal Adjustment and Gender

- Decreased tax revenues from the liberalisation of imports adversely impact fiscal deficits resulting in cutbacks in government spending on social programs special programs geared towards girls and women.
- Introduction of mechanisms such as privatisation and commercialisation of services, which are necessary correlates of trade liberalisation, often shift the burden of social reproduction to the household sectors.

Trade-Induced Employment Effects and Gender

- Feminisation of the labour market and or the informalisation of work (subcontracting, homework etc).

Destruction of Internal Markets

- Increase imports of products such as vegetable, meat, milk and milk products, which in some countries, are the domains of women.
- Threats to craft and dressmaking from machined produced import substitutes and increase cross border trade in second-hand cloths.

The above analysis clearly indicates that refining the analytical and policy framework of gender and trade is critical. A gender analysis approach to trade policy and trade liberalisation will need to identify key mechanisms through which trade liberalisation impact men and women differently. It will also need to emphasise gender differentiated roles, gender based constraints, women's time allocation, access to and control of resources, impact of increased export expansion, feminisation of jobs versus comparative advantage, rights and working conditions of workers and collection and analysis of gender disaggregated data. Due to the important role of gender relations in influencing the outcome of macro level trade policies, further research focusing on trade and gender will have to critically understand the following issues:

a. what trade policy is all about,
b. gender implications of WTO and other agreements,
c. gender relations in the African context,
d. trade policy's impact on existing gender realities and vice versa,
e. other policies affecting trade policies,
f. directional shifts in trade policy and the implications of such shifts for gender equity,
g. poverty reduction and sustainable development.

Appropriate trade policy reforms ensuring that women's interests are more fully taken into account at the design stage have to be put in place. The neglect of gender implications of reform process is difficult to justify or sustain if the African continent is to effectively and efficiently address the challenges faced. Moreover, a clearer understanding of gender implications on WTO agreements is a priority.

Gender Implications on WTO Agreements

Agreement on Agriculture (AOA)[1]

Agriculture continues to play an important role in sub-Saharan African economies. African women have always been highly represented in farming activities, providing most of the labour force producing food for local consumption and agricultural commodities for export. Three critical areas of concern emerge from the debate on agricultural liberalisation from a gender perspective: food security, food sovereignty and sustainable livelihood. The issue of food security is closely linked to the loss of domestic agricultural production and its implications for nutrition. The loss of sustainable livelihood is intertwined with import penetration and the loss of preference in the international agricultural markets (Williams 2002).

The reduction of domestic support to agriculture is likely to negatively affect small-scale farmers, particularly women, who have been relying on government infrastructural and storage support for their outputs. Furthermore, privatisation and transformation of land to cash crop or export agriculture has implications on food security and livelihoods. A study[2] conducted in Kenya on adoption of tea suggested that constraints on female tea labour are an obstacle to adopting tea, improving tea yields, and combining expansion in tea production with expansion in food production. Furthermore, women farmers in male-headed households very often do not directly receive any proceeds from the sale of export crops. The key point to note is that because of their different roles and responsibilities, men and women are likely to respond differently to economic reforms. The response to these changes depends on the rules and norms of market institutions as well as the structure of households and farms. Therefore, gender based distortions which influence market responses to the new incentives cannot be ignored. From both an efficiency and equity perspective, successful policy formulation has to address the specificity of women's contribution and the constraints they face. Both of these can inhibit their supply response in the cash crop sector.

Trade Related Intellectual Property Rights (TRIPS)[3]

Discussions on the implications of TRIPS agreement on gender have been focused in the following areas among others: public health with emphasis on HIV/AIDS, agriculture and implications on biodiversity, seeds genetic resources, traditional or indigenous knowledge. These in turn have implications for food security, nutrition, livelihoods and technological transfer. Research needs to focus more sharply on the gender implications of TRIPS on agriculture, reproductive health, technological transfer and privatisation and monopolisation and transfer of traditional knowledge in healthcare, medicines and agriculture.

The General Agreement on Trade and Services (GATS)[4]

The liberalisation of the services sector is an area of critical concern since women tend to dominate the services sector particularly health and education sectors. Discussions point towards the impact and access and availability of public services such as health, education, and natural resources such as water and energy. Areas of concern include: governments ability to regulate the quality of health care, clean water supply, education; stiff competition from high labour supply internationally; employment creation and conditions of work, and wages and income levels for men and women.

Trade Related Investment Measures (TRIMS)[5]

TRIMS raise concern about protection of local industries and the extent to which least developed countries are likely to respond to the needs of various foreign investments given their weak infrastructure and industrial base. The key gender concerns raised in the discussion of investment and trade liberalisation include: employment in the export manufacturing, health and working conditions, growth potential of small and medium sized firms. They are also questions around government's ability to regulate foreign investment to spur development, size and scope of foreign investors and governments ability to protect local producers and markets. In particular, it is noted that women are concentrated in small and medium enterprises raising high possibilities of government's abandonment of gender mainstreaming and equity programs or policies in favour of foreign firms. In sum, gender-based biases and constraints need to play an important role in the formulation of trade negotiations and trade policy. More focused research on gender implications of WTO agreements is also required. Furthermore, trade policy should be examined in the context of other macro-level policies in order to act as an instrument for promoting gender equality, eradicating poverty, raising the living standards of people and contributing towards sustainable human and economic development.

Ongoing Work on International Trade and Gender

International organisations such as UNIFEM, UNCTAD and UNRISD, CIDA, IDRC and others have devoted special attention to the analysis of trade policies and how they impact on men and women differently. In particular, UNIFEM has tried to unravel the mysteries of trade-agreements and incorporate a gender perspective to trade policies. UNCTAD has shown commitment by treating gender as a cross-sectional issue while developing important and useful analytical tools to clarify the links between sustainable development and international trade (Evers 2002). UNCTAD has also highlighted the effects of globalisation, especially issues of weakened capacity of national governments to achieve gender equity objectives.

Research organisations in the North and South have also addressed the issue of gender and trade liberalisation. Each year since 1994, CODESRIA organises a Gender Institute, which brings together some 12 to 15 researchers. During the first few years, the institute's main objective was to promote gender awareness. The Institute has subsequently been organised around specific themes to promote the strengthening of gender analysis in African social science research. One of the themes selected for the 2002 Gender Institute is 'Globalisation, Gender and

Trade'. The Economic and Social Research Foundation (ESRF) based in Tanzania is co-ordinating a research project on 'International Trade and Gender in East Africa'. This research aims to improve the ability of East African governments (Kenya, Uganda and Tanzania) to adopt a gender perspective in their analysis of international trade agenda, both in their negotiations and lobbying within the WTO, and with other trading partners. The research will provide insights into how gender inequalities may be intensified, reduced or newly created in East Africa, as a result of the changing international trade regime and the region's adherence to WTO rules. It analyses the how gendered structures of production and decision-making, and gender bias in access to resources might constrain the expansion of exports and/or reduce the potential benefits of trade liberalisation to the region. Specifically, the objectives of this research are to:

i)   chart the trade policy process and trade policy regime in Kenya, Tanzania and Uganda from a gender perspective;
ii) produce 'Gender Aware Country Economic Reports;
iii) investigate the following sectors: Fisheries, Floriculture, Garments and Coffee. The first two sectors were comparable across the three countries and one sector coffee in Uganda is not comparable across countries;
iv) to identify and disseminate policy implications of the research to all existing and potential actors in the trade process in Kenya, Tanzania and Uganda.

The study uses an analytical macro-meso-micro framework. A unique feature of this research is the integration of a gender perspective into the analysis and its interest in explaining the *actual* mechanics of economic and social transformation brought about by changes in the trade regime.

Despite ongoing work in this area, a lot of work still needs to be done as is spelt out in the next section. There is need to emphasise the value of strengthening the link between research and advocacy. Alliances and networks exploring issues of trade and gender include Women Working Worldwide (WWW), International Gender and Trade Network, Europe (IGTN), North America Gender and Trade Network-US, International Gender and Trade Network Secretariat, Centre of Concern, Gender and Trade Network in Africa (GENTA), Development Alternative with Women for a New Era (DAWN), Informal working group on Gender and Trade (IWGGT), Gender and Economic Reforms in Africa (GERA). These alliances and networks contribute towards electronic discussions and knowledge sharing among members.

Key Challenges

The following four broad areas have been identified as necessary to help us understand and implement policies on trade and gender:

 i)   Research
 ii) Understanding WTO agenda from a gender perspective
 iii) Capacity building
 iv) Advocacy

i) Build a solid knowledge base on the gender impact of trade policies, agreements and bodies by promoting qualitative and quantitative research and studies on:
 a. what trade policy is all about,
 b. gender implications of WTO and other agreements,
 c. gender relations in the African context,
 d. trade policy's impact on existing gender realities and vice versa,
 e. other policies affecting trade policies,
 f. directional shifts in trade policy and the implications of such shifts for gender equity,
 g. poverty reduction and sustainable development.

- Research requires a comprehensive framework that
  i) tracks how the effects in specific sectors percolate through the rest of the market economy and
  ii) analyses how the effects in the market economy influence and are influenced by behaviour in the unpaid household economy where women are the main workers.
- Refine the analytical and policy framework of trade and gender and strengthen the tools of analysis for the integration of gender perspective into trade policy.
- Close collaboration of research institutes, universities and national and international organisations, NGOs, Civil Society and policy makers addressing trade and gender issues.
- More acceptance and recognition of research work conducted by African scholars on the gender impact of trade policies.

ii) Understanding two agenda from a gender perspective
- Need to understand the most important items on the WTO agenda from a gender perspective i.e agreements on Agriculture (AOA), General Agreement in trade and Services (GATS), Trade Related Intellectual Property Rights Agreement (TRIPS), Trade Related Investment Measures (TRIMS) and a gender approach to treatment of labour in the global economy.

iii) Capacity building

- There is need to improve the capacity of developing countries to participate more actively in the WTO and benefit from new trade rules and Globalisation in general.
- Build the capacity of researchers on trade and gender to understand all the important agreements relevant to the African sub-continent i.e Cotonou, US Africa Growth and Opportunity Act (AGOA)
- Strengthen the capacity of Africa's regional Groupings such as ECOWAS, SADC, COMESA and EAC to integrate and analyse and accept the importance of gender in their work.
- Strengthen the capacity of ACBF funded projects on trade to integrate gender analysis.
- Increased training for researchers and policy makers on globalisation, gender and trade.
- Enhance skills and build capacity of a variety of stakeholders, including NGOs, national women's movements and policy makers to understand the gender implications of trade policies, agreements and bodies.

iv) Advocacy

- Build and strengthen strategic alliances among NGOs, researchers and policy makers.
- Support advocacy efforts for mainstreaming a gender sensitive perspective in trade policies, agreements and bodies.

Notes

1 'This agreement allows countries which have been using measures for import restraint and domestic subsidy to retain protection for their agricultural sector during the implementation period while those countries that are not using protective measures are prohibited from doing so' (Gender and Trade Network in Africa, 2001).

2 Ongile G. (1999), 'Gender and Agricultural Supply Responses to Structural Adjustment Programmes. A Case Study of Smallholder Tea Producers in Kericho, Kenya' Research Report No 109, Nordic African Institute, Uppsala.

3 'This agreement allows the patenting of biological organisms, including parts of animals and plants, altered plants and animals as well as genes and cell-lines. This agreement therefore allows companies to strengthen their monopoly over new agricultural and pharmaceutical products. Under TRIPS the inventor is granted a patent as the sole owner of a new product or technology for a

period of 20 years even in categories like medicine and agricultural products (Gender and Trade Network in Africa, 2001).

4 This agreement seeks to provide a set of rules on how countries should trade in activities whose output is not in tangible goods (non-tradable sector) and covers a wide spectrum of services such as telecommunications, tourism, water, electricity, banking, health, education, transportation and professional services). GATS require every government to treat services and service suppliers of other WTO members no less favourable than its own like services and service suppliers' GENTA, 2001. Simply put, this agreement provides a framework for negotiations on liberalisation of the services sector.

5 'TRIMS are concerned with the liberalisation of foreign investment conditions. Under the TRIMS Agreement, WTO member states commit themselves to treat foreign enterprises under the same terms and conditions as their domestic enterprises. Member countries also commit themselves to the reduction of all quantitative restrictions on imported goods, including tariffs and non-tariff barriers' (Gender and Trade Network in Africa 2001).

References

Elson, D. Evers, B. and Ongile G., 1998, 'International Trade and Gender in East Africa', A proposal submitted to International Development Research Centre (IDRC) Eastern and Southern Africa Regional Office, Nairobi

Elson, D., 1994, 'Micro, Meso, Macro: Gender and Economic analysis in the Context of Policy Reform' in Bakker, I., ed., *The Strategic Silence: Gender and Economic Policy*, London and Ottawa: Zed Books and North-South Institute.

Evers, B., 2002, *Gender, International Trade and the Trade Policy Review Mechanism: Conceptual Reference Points for UNCTAD*, Development Studies Programme, Manchester:University of Manchester.

Fontana, M. Susan, J. and Masika, R., 1998, *Global Trade Expansion and Liberalisation: Gender Issues and Impacts*, Report Commissioned by the Department for International Development, UK

Gender and Trade Network, 2001, *Trade Liberalisation: Impacts on African Women*, A paper prepared for the International Gender and Trade Network, Cape Town, South Africa, August.

Goetz, A., 1995, 'Macro-Meso-Micro Linkages: Understanding gendered institutional structures and practices', Paper presented to SAGA Workshop on Gender and Economic Reform in Africa, Ottawa, 1-3 October.

Haxton, E. & Olsson, C., eds, 1999, *Gender Focus on the WTO*, Global Publications Foundation, International Coalition for Development Action, Uppsala, Sweden

International Monetary Fund, IMF, 2001, *Finance and Development*, Volume 38, No. 4. December.

IWGGT, 1998, *Briefing Statement on Gender and Trade, Some Conceptual and Policy Links*, Paper for the Second Ministerial Meeting of the WTO, Geneva, May 18-20.

Hale, A., ed., 1998, *Trade Myths and Gender Reality: Trade Liberalisation and Women's Lives*, Global Publications Foundation, International coalition for Development Action.

Joekes, S., 1987, *Women in the World Economy*, An INSTRAW Study, New York: Oxford University Press.

Joekes, S., 1995, *Trade-Related Employment for Women in Industry and Services in Developing Countries*, United Nations Fourth World Conference on Women Occasional Paper, No. 5, UNRISD, Geneva.

Joekes, S., 1999, 'A Gender-analytical perspective on Trade and Sustainable Development', in UNCTAD, *Trade, Sustainable Development and Gender*, United Nations, Geneva and New York.

Joekes, S. and Ann W., 1994, *Women and the New Trade Agenda*, UNIFEM, New York.

Lim, Y., 2002, 'The Effects of the East Asian Crisis on the Employment of Women and Men: The Philippine Case' in *World Development*, Vol. 28, No. 7.

Ongile, G., 1999, *Gender and Agricultural Supply Responses to Structural Adjustment Programmes. A Case Study of Smallholder Tea Producers in Kericho, Kenya*, Research Report No 109, Uppsala: Nordic African Institute.

Oyijide, T., 1998, 'Using Trade and Industrial Policies to Foster African Development: Some Perspectives on Issues and Modalities', *Journal of African Economics* Vol. 7. Supplement, June.

UNRISD, 2000, *Visible Hands: Taking Responsibility for Social Development*, Geneva: UNRISD.

UNIFEM, 2000, *Progress of World's Women 2000*, New York: UNIFEM.

Williams, M., 2001, 'Gender and Trade in the International Economy: A Brief Overview', paper presented at the Seminar on 'Financing for Development: New Tendencies, New Exclusions and New Strategies for Women in the Region,' REPEM-DAWN, Cartagena de Indias, Colombia.

Williams, M., 2002, Public Hearing on the Issues of 'Globalisation and Gender', International Gender and Trade Network, Development Alternatives with Women for a New Era (DAWN) and the Centre for Concern, to the Enquete-Commission of the German Parliament, *Globalisation of the World Economy: Challenges and Responses*, 18 February 2002, Reichstage Building Plenary Area, Berlin.

9

Globalisation and the Feminisation of Poverty: A South African Perspective on Expansion, Inequality and Identity Crises

Manthiba Phalane

Introduction

The raging debate among African intellectuals regarding the implications of globalisation has tended to centre around two major positions, with the point of dispute being the (in)appropriateness of the globalisation agenda. Hence globalisation represents an agenda that has both advocates and critics (Hamelink 1999; Hendricks 1999). A lot has been said, done and published on globalisation and the feminisation of poverty, but as with most economic and social issues, the gender aspects of globalisation have largely been kept at the margins (Pape 2000). Consequently the meaning of globalisation depends on the 'eyes of the beholder' (Genge 2002).

South Africa has been undergoing a process of fundamental economic transformation as a result of policies promoting integration into the global economy. Women are bearing the brunt of the costs of this transformation. They are caught in a cycle of vulnerability which starts with their retrenchment from full-time employment. This form of globalised economic logic of neo-liberalism is costing working class women precious ground won over many years.

Globalisation is manifested today through three main neo-liberal policy measures: privatisation, deregulation of trade, and financial liberalisation. These forms of neo-liberal reforms have been evidenced by the overall withdrawal of the government from its roles of sovereign decision making, providing essential public services, developing and implementing policies aimed at promoting equity, and ensuring adequate public protection for economically, socially, and politically vulnerable populations (Guttal 2000). These trends are accompanied by an increase in the role and power of the private sector, and a surrender of most economic transactions to the market in the belief that free and unfettered markets will somehow lead to the most efficient allocation of resources and eventually result in economic equality.

The current trends of globalisation, economic reforms, the World Bank's policy of encouraging the privatisation of public services, and the global cut in social spending are only a few of the determining factors which decrease women's participation in the workforce and increase their poverty. Women are most vulnerable in the workforce and retrenchment continues to affect them more and long before their male counterparts.

The globalisation/gender interface and the feminisation of poverty

Globalisation trends and related policies are often thought to be gender-neutral, that is they have similar impact on men and women. However a closer look at the way they affect people reveals significant gender differentiated impacts (Lebakeng & Phalane 2001). Globalisation is an unfortunate phenomenon because the affirmation of differences in identities should open up endless vistas for the creation of true solidarity between otherwise diverse communities. As currently patterned, it has actually ushered in a non-conducive environment as it encourages inequality and reciprocity. Moreover it is unfortunate because it breeds a great deal of resistance and disdain.

The effects of globalisation are so profound that the stark reality in South Africa reflects the continued marginalisation of women in public life. Capitalism has always been a vicious circle with a small minority in the world controlling the resources and the majority living in poverty and destitution. However globalisation is a systematic process whereby the standard of living of poor people is made even worse. The majority of casualties of globalisation are women. This is a worldwide phenomenon driven by business interest, as opposed to a policy-led process where ordinary people can give input, hold governments accountable, and collectively shape their future (Fairshare 2001).

The greatest challenge of tracing and fully understanding the ways in which globalisation affects women is the absence of sex-disaggregated indicators and data in key sectors such as agricultural production and employment, services, and the informal sector. While independent researchers and institutions such as UNIFEM are gathering information and showing how women are affected by current globalised economic trends, many of the indicators and methods used to monitor these trends are in and of themselves not gender sensitive (Mehta 2001).

In reality the employment experience of women under globalisation is uneven and contradictory, often reflecting the polarisation stressed at the Beijing Conference of 1995, as the 'feminisation of poverty' rather that of 'work'. When we further unpack these processes, we find women represent 40 percent of the global workforce, yet they hold less than 3 percent of top executive jobs. In a study issued to mark International Women's day, the United Nations Labour

Agency pointed out that women account for one percent of trade union leaders although 40 percent of trade union members are women (ILO 1998).

These crises have dented the confidence in the integration of global markets and have pointed to some of the shortcomings in the international and institutional environment. The gains of globalisation have not been equitably distributed and the gap between men and women, rich and poor is widening. Even the Finance Minister in South Africa, Trevor Manuel, has conceded that globalisation has brought increased uncertainty and the world appears to be inadequately prepared to deal with the risk and equitably share the opportunities.

One of these shortcomings is gender stereotyping particularly when it comes to jobs. Workplace settings are a reflection of values and priorities of those in power. Men, in their egocentric preoccupation with harbouring traditional thoughts about women, choose to recognise, accept and cultivate the talents and skills of female workers in a manner inconsistent with how they treat most of their male workers. Certain activities or jobs are labelled as men's. This globalised situation indicates that the cards will always be stacked against women without connections in the workplace (Purvis 1995). In most instances gender stereotyping disadvantages women economically and socially, blocking them from a range of opportunities including access to more skilled and high paying forms of employment.

The impact of economic globalisation on women needs to be assessed in light of women's multiple roles as productive and reproductive labour in their families as well as their contribution towards overall community cohesion and welfare, and maintenance the social fabric. On the same level, increases in the prices of food, fuel and essential services such as water and electricity place extra burdens on females in low-income households. Women are usually responsible for managing food and water consumption including ensuring the overall health and welfare of their families. Because of this deep-rooted difference in gender roles and socio cultural expectations, the impact of globalisation is felt differently by females and males. While economic class, race and culture are also extremely important factors in determining the nature and extent of impacts, by and large, the very same policies and trends are likely to have quite different implications for both sexes (Kehler 2000).

The burden of impoverishment and marginalisation that results from the global integration process affects men and women differently (Mehta 2001). To understand this aspect of globalisation one must see it from the basic premise that women are situated differentially in the capitalist reproduction process. In South Africa the most disturbing feature of globalisation is that different aspects of poverty such as deprivation, powerlessness and vulnerability have gender dimensions (Phalane & Lebakeng 2002).

Among the latter are the rise of female participation in low return, urban informal sector activities. This trend is part of the evidence for the feminisation of poverty. Consideration of poverty often neglects differentials between men and women in terms of their access to income, resources and services (BRIDGE, 2001). In addition the greater insecurity and lower earning capacity in the informal sector is another reason for the feminisation of poverty. Women are employed in lesser skilled occupations and predominate in the informal sectors and service sector as domestic workers. Their levels of formal education and training are lower and if categorised as professionals, they are predominantly found in the 'feminised professions', for example teaching and nursing (Finnemore & Cunningham 1995).

Globalisation has not affected all countries or regions in the same way, and the country's internal preparedness is critical in how it can take advantage of or be completely overrun by globalisation. Because of differing levels of modernisation, industrialisation and technological capacity, regions and even areas within South Africa have felt the impact of globalisation quite differently.

Research indicates that the structural adjustment policies of the World Bank and the IMF affect women much more deeply than men. A critical one is the under-investment in women. Many parents are reluctant to invest their resources in their daughters with the understanding that sooner rather than later they would be married off to other families (Phalane & Lebakeng 2002). On the other hand, when basic education becomes privatised, or families cannot afford the rising cost of education, it is more often girls than boys who drop out of school because of the belief that boys need formal education more than girls to prepare them for their future social roles. This has further implications for the type of employment that women are able to find when they move into the wage labour market (Sandrasagra 2000).

It is against this background that we delineate the changed labour market context under globalisation and situate women in it. With lower levels of education, women will tend to be concentrated in the lower rungs of the labour market and in jobs that require less formal training or education. The replacement of manual labour with machines and new technology usually displaces more women than men since women have a large education gap to cross compared with men in the same class in order to learn how to use new technologies (Guttal 2000).

When combined with current economic changes this means that women's class, race and gender-based access to resources and opportunities perpetuate inequality and poverty and at the same time decrease women's socio-economic status. This further explains why rural women are the poorest of the poor in the South African context, oppressed by national and international injustices and family systems as well (Phalane 2001). Their lack of access to resources and basic services includes unequal rights in family structures as well as unequal access to family resources such as land and livestock. It is not a cliché but literally true to say that African rural women are not only poorer in society as a whole but also in their own families. Their level and kind of poverty and inequality is experienced differently and more intensely than that of men and the why socio-economic changes impact on them (Kehler 2001).

Sandrasagra (2000) noted that the opportunities created by the process of globalisation have opened clear avenues for development, but in some cases its benefits have not been equitably distributed, thereby impeding efforts to promote the advancement of women, particularly those living in poverty. Globalisation is market integration—how men, women, rich, poor benefit depends on their relative position in the market (Kiff & Kandirikirira 2002). Competition is a key factor resulting in winners and losers, where those with resources and technology dictate the rules of the game. The poor and women start from a disadvantaged position because they lack resources and technology, so they are the most likely losers. The majority of the poor in South Africa are women.

Gendering Globalisation: Some Implications for Development

The political and cultural dimensions of globalisation have had contradictory social effects on women as workers and as activists. The challenge is to shape policies and processes so that they promote improved living standards and increased gender equality. Further monitoring and policy research on the impact of globalisation is necessary because globalisation is leading to increased inequalities between men and women. Despite new initiatives and commitments, the sad reality is that the situation of the world's women is progressively deteriorating due to globalisation.

The link between gender equality and development means that marginalisation of women must be stopped along with the continued feminisation of poverty. The advancement of women cannot be achieved by passing legislation. Legislation existing on paper is only one side of the story, since rights must be put into practice. As a consequences social development on the national scale must be strengthened and a climate conducive to development must be created.

Problems of inclusion stem from the fact that women are very differently positioned in relation to the markets in different parts of the world. In certain places where they are socially excluded from leaving their homes, the challenge is to find ways for women to participate. This does not advocate the feminisation of the workplace or globalisation, it does not have to be masculine either. Instead, globalised equity policies should include an all inclusive gender and centralised management systems.

If policy makers work only on consequences and do not start to challenge the dynamics of globalisation including exclusion and exploitation that create social injustice, there is the risk of colluding with an unjust stumbling block as we apply projects as sticking plasters that ignore the true nature of the problem. It is possible to take action to contrast the dynamics of inequality and injustice caused by globalisation, and thereby to challenge those with power and to demand accountability. From a gender perspective, to be effective women have to be more policy literate with regard to the phenomenon of globalisation.

Governments have to re-examine their roles and responsibilities in the context of globalisation and its impacts on women if they are to make a positive contribution to world development. Women should be able to decide where they stand vis-à-vis globalisation and understand the impact it has in South Africa and on their work. Bridging the gender gap should be the benchmark for deciding to make globalisation work for women. This would require a grounded analysis of the real opportunities the process provides for women. It should involve a thorough analysis of the impact of international trade on women and the poor and embarking on programmes and processes that make international trade work for them.

On a continental level, seeking alternatives to globalisation would involve an in-depth understanding of the power relations between developed and poor economies and an analysis of the alternatives that have already evolved in response to it. To an extent whether it is seeking alternatives to globalisation, or by trying to make it work for women and the poor, countering the negative impact of globalisation can only be effective if it is grounded in a thorough analysis of the current form of globalisation (Kiff & Kandikirira 2002). Its origination, evolution and the thinking behind it must be understood.

Conclusion

For the majority of women, existing socio-economic rights as guaranteed by the constitution remain inaccessible. The result is the perpetuation and increase, as well as the feminisation of poverty. This situation is abominable for women in rural areas, as constitutional guarantees of equality and non-discrimination remain merely theoretical rights that lack implementation in light of globalisation.

Even though recent government policies appear to have opened the doors of work to women, there are quite a substantial number of constraints, which still cast a shadow on the opportunities hitherto created. The greatest underlying factor, though seldom openly admitted, is that the fulfilment of women's strategic needs to rescue them from the doldrums of poverty is seen as a threat, a destabilising agent to social order. Yet what ought to be recognised is the fact that the full measure of impacts of globalisation on women, and the development of progressive policy measures to counter these measures will not receive the attention it deserves until this dominant knowledge and attitudinal base is challenged and reconstructed.

Only the effectiveness of the translation from the theory of equality and non-discrimination into a real practice of empowerment and socio-economic upliftment of women and the poor should be a true criterion determining success or failure to counter the negative impact of the globalisation process. What has become apparent is that forms of inequality exist regardless of prevailing political ideology. Their manifestation may differ, but the reality is that women's subordination remains constant. Advancement in the interest of women is susceptible to being lost through political, economic and societal change that are deemed generally progressive and those that are destructive.

References

Amin, S., 1997, *Capitalism in the Age of Globalization*, London: Zed Books.

Bridge, 2001, 'Briefing Paper on the Feminization of Poverty', Report No 59. Institute for Development Studies, University of Sussex, UK.

Finnemore, M. & Cunningham, P., 1995, 'Women and the Workplace', in van der Merwe, A., ed., *Industrial Sociology: A South African Perspective*, Johannesburg: Lexicon Publishers.

Fairshare, 2001, *How the South African Economy Works: Understanding Globalization, Part 1*. School of Government, University of Cape Town.

Horgan, G., 2001, 'How does Globalization affect Women?', Issue 92 of *International Socialism Journal*.

Genge M., 2002, 'The New Partnership for Africa's Development in the Era of Globalization', Paper presented at the International Conference on 'Peace, Unity and People Centred Development: The Legacy of Mwalimu J. K. Nyerere', University of Venda, Thohoyandou, 8-9 August.

Guttal, S., 2000, 'Women and Globalization: Some Key Issues', Paper presented at the Conference on Strategies of the Thai Women's Movement in the 21st Century, Bangkok, March 28-29.

Hamelink, C. J., 1999, 'The Elusive Concept of Globalization', *Global Dialogue*, Vol. 1., No. 1.

IIED, 2000, 'Globalization and Sustainable Development', Globalization Issue Paper – Second Draft Report.

ILO, 1997–1998, *World Employment Report*, Geneva: ILO

Kehler, J., 2001, *Women and Poverty: The South African Experience*, Cape Town.

Kiff, F. & Kandirikirira, N., 2002, *The Implications of Globalization on Africa's Development*, Report of ACORD's Pan African Workshop on Global Programming, London.

Lebakeng, T. J. & Phalane, M.M, 2001, 'Globalisation and the Rising Structural and Social Inequalities: the African Search for Identity and Solutions', Paper presented at the South African Sociological Association Annual Congress, University of South Africa, Sunnyside Campus, Pretoria.

Lebakeng, T. J. & Phalane, M. M., 2001, 'Africanisation of the Social Sciences within the Context of Globalization', *CODESRIA Bulletin*, Nos 3&4.

Mehta, J., 1998, *Women and Globalization*, Oxford University Press.

Pape, J., 2000, *Gender and Globalization in South Africa: Some Preliminary Reflections on Working Women and Poverty*, Cape Town, ILRIG.

Phalane, M. M. & Lebakeng, T. J., 2002, 'Gender, Poverty and HIV/AIDS: Some Implications for Development', *Youth Work Journal*, Vol 2 pp 2-5 & 36.

Phalane, M. M., 2001, 'Sharing the Workplace with Men: The Reality of Gender-Based Development and Transformation', Paper presented at the Joint Centre for Political and Economic Studies Conference, Centurion Lake Hotel, Centurion.

Sandrasagra, M. J., 2000, *Globalization Heightening Gender Inequalities*, New York: Third World Network.

Schalkwyk, J. & Woroniuk, B., 1998, 'Globalization', Article Prepared for SIDA, Stockholm: Sweden.

10

Globalization and the Question of Gender-Justice: the Nigerian Experience

Chris Okechukwu Uroh

Introduction

The philosophy underlining neo-liberal economy, a major component of globalisation, is that state intervention in the economic life of the people, however well intentioned, is 'counter-productive' and therefore undesirable. The major elements of globalisation policy thus include trade liberalisation, devaluation of national currencies against 'major' currencies like the US dollar, and deregulation of the public sector or, simply, privatisation of public utilities. The social and economic consequences of these policies have been the retrenchment of workers and consequently, massive unemployment, reduction in government spending on social infrastructure, cut in government subsidies for social services wherever they are available and subsequent increase in the cost of these services.

For women, the impact of market liberalisation and the integration of the national economy 'into the global economy' have been 'complex and equally contradictory'. The failure of neo-liberal economic policies, especially the structural adjustment programme (SAP), to achieve the envisaged economic empowerment of the general populace in developing nations is a copiously documented and almost over-researched issue by scholars (Mbiliyi 1991; World Bank 1998; 1994; Adedeji 1994, etc). Instructively, not so much attention has been paid to the fact that SAP has been more disastrous for women than their men counterparts. In Nigeria, for example, women occupy the lowest rung of the societal ladder and are the least educated thereby usually employed at the lower grades. As the 'domestic gender' whose 'traditional' roles include domestic chores and reproductive activities, women are also the first to feel the direct impact of policies that adversely affect social services.

This paper is an attempt to fill-in this theoretical and empirical void in gender studies in the Third World, using Nigeria as a case. It interfaces the prevalent patriarchal ideology and its cultural inferiorisation of women with the deplorable socio-economic conditions of the Nigerian woman. Specifically, the paper argues that while men and women in the developing countries suffer economic dislocation as a result of neo-liberal economic policies, women suffer even more because of their culturally constructed position as 'domestic gender'. It also makes the case that the main source of women disadvantageous economic positioning which has been further worsened by structural adjustment policies is not, strictly speaking, economic. It is in fact rooted in the age-long cultural biases and practices which devalue womanhood through patriarchy and socially sidelines her by 'domestication'. However, in line with the general theme of the Cairo meeting, I shall preface this discussion with the examination of some of the issues that have engaged the attention of gender scholars in Africa in the past millennium.

The African Gender Discourse

In a sense, one would be right to say that the early major attempt to theorise the gender issue in Africa equated it with feminism. Gender scholarship was reduced to the interrogation of 'the woman question.' Its main concern was the examination of issues relating to women's marginalisation and/or oppression by their men counterparts and the society at large. The recurring themes on gender discourse in Africa then remained the economic disintegration of the African woman, the discrimination against her in the labour market and work places, her political disempowerment; the neglect and sometimes deliberate denial of women rights and so on.

The second rating of the woman is the issue here. Sometimes this is clumsily put as: Women are not given the chance (Mohammed 1985:50) which then raises the question, 'not given the chance' by who? From this stand-point, feminist literati in Africa, engaged in a more or less deconstructive scholarship dictated and sustained basically by the desire to answer a cluster of questions made imperative by the social positioning of the woman: How did male domination arise? Why was it so widely accepted in the past? Why does it still have a lot of potency in many societies in the world till today? What are its consequences? How and why, until recently, did men manage, with a semblance of legitimacy, to exclude women from formal politics, gainful economic ventures, social recognition and so on? (Mansbridge and Okin 1996:271).

Many factors were implicated in attempts to respond to these questions. Among these is the exaltation of 'the male subject by conversely obscuring the female,' in such a way that women became 'absent in human history' (Ahikire 1994:41). By denying women the status of *historical actors*, and portraying, 'men, their lives and their beliefs as the human norm', (Harding and Hintikka 1983:x), we are left with only the account of human development as a narrative dominated by men. The attempt to displace or deconstruct 'history' and properly situate the woman within what became known as *herstory* (an ideological enterprise whose goal is to 're-proach' *history* through the feminisation of accounts of human experience) was taken up by some scholars. The historicisation of womanity in this manner was aimed at centring as against the present *peripheralisation* of the woman. The end is to make the woman a *historical actor* rather a mere *passive spectator* in the crowded theatre of human history.

Another issue which dominated gender scholarship was the question of the *genderisation* of division of labour which assigns certain kinds of work to men and others to women (Mbiliyi 1994:4). As already mentioned, women are assigned more work in production and reproduction activities within household and small holder farming systems in agrarian societies and 'petty trading' and other *informal businesses*, in the cities. The idea that there are certain jobs men and women are tailor-made for has become crystallised in the psyche of the peoples, with the woman usually assigned the most debased and less profitable of these jobs. The woman thus experiences two kinds of marginalisation. First, certain jobs are formally reserved for men automatically knocking off the chance that any woman whatever her expertise would be employed to do them. Second, as a result of the feminisation of the domestics or the domestication of the feminine, women who work outside the mould end up suffering even more. For example, women are gainfully employed and perform full-time paid jobs work longer hours because tradition requires that they still perform unremunerated domestic chores such as cooking, washing and child caring from which men are excused. Therefore, beyond the possibility that they could be discriminated against in the labour market, even where they are gainfully employed, women are worse off considering the socially mandated domestic chores dubiously assigned to them.

The question of how this idea of domesticating the woman attained an al-most universal presence, if not acceptance, has also not escaped the curious mind of scholars, some of whom have attempted some scientific theorisation of the subject. Socio-biology is one of such theories. The thesis generally states that there is a correlation between *physiology* (or is it the anatomy) and *natural* capabili-ties of sexes and by implications, the socially assigned responsibilities for both men and women. In other words, *social organisation is here conceived of as nothing short of the behavioural outcome of the interaction of organisms having biologically fixed inclina-tions.* In a plain language the biological make up of the woman as well as that of the man is such that each sex has been programmed or predetermined to effec-tively perform specific roles. Any deviation from these naturally assigned roles is considered abnormal. This thesis makes the subordination of women appear *natural*, a kind of validation of male and female biological capacities (Imam 1985:16).

A study by Barbara and Schildrout (1986) among women in the predomi-nantly Muslim-Northern Nigeria underscores the extent to which childhood indoctrination can colour people's understanding of social phenomena, including their own oppression. According to the study most Muslim women in Northern Nigeria believed that God decreed that they should remain submissive to their husbands irrespective of their behaviours. Their research reveals that most women believed that the woman is only a *subject* of the law, and that the interpretation and use of the laws were the prerogative of the men. Aristotle (1952) does not see any leadership quality in women. 'The male is more fitted to rule than the female, unless conditions are quite abnormal,' he writes. And so, unless there are no men to hold positions of authority, it would be wrong to give it to a woman, which is why Aristotle was against democracy. Aristotle berates democracy because it gives everybody, especially women, equal opportunity to take part in the decision making process. 'Between male and female this relationship of superior and inferior is permanent', Aristotle says.

This idea of variations in the *abilities* of the two sexes, and the superiority of the man over the woman, was also shared by Hegel (1973). 'The natural determinancies of both sexes acquire through its reasonableness *intellectual* as well as *ethical* significance'. He writes further:

> Thus one sex is mind in its self-diremption into explicit self-subsistence and the knowledge and volition of free universality, i.e. the self-consciousness of conceptual thought and the volition of the objective final end. The other sex is mind maintaining itself in unity as knowledge and volition in the form of concrete individuality and feeling. In relation to externality, the former is powerful and active, the latter passive and subjective. It follows that man has his actual substantive life in the state, in learning and so forth, as well as in labour and struggle with the external world and with himself so that it is only out of his diremption that he fights his way to self-subsistent unity with himself. In the family he has a tranquil intuition of this unity, and there he lives a subjective ethical life on the plane of feeling. *The woman, on the other hand, has her substantive destiny in the family, and to be imbued with family piety is her ethical frame of mind* (Hegel 1973).

Modern political theorists have equally affirmed that society's 'sexual differentiation' of roles and assignment of different political meanings to *womanhood and manhood* are biologically programmed. In politics, women take precedence only after the children. Because this perception has been internalised by women themselves, even when they engage in politics, it is usually at the peripheral level, at the level of *women wing* of their parties or the *first ladies* of their states. Thus, 'the different attributes, capacities and characteristics ascribed to men and women by political theorists have become central to the way in which each has defined the political' (Pateman and Shanley 1991:9-10). As Pateman and Stanley further put it, '[M]anhood and politics go hand in hand, and everything that stands in contrast to and opposed to political life and the political virtues has been represented by women; their capacities and the tasks seen as natural to their sex, especially motherhood (1991:3).

This 'systematic exclusion of women from taking part in and as full member and citizen of the polity in political debate, deliberation and contest' remains the greatest wrong to womanhood. Consequently women are perceived and treated as *objects* or at most *minors*, who cannot take decisions on their own and so, have to be decided for by men.

There have also been some attempts to implicate the colonial experience of African societies in the condition of the African woman. The argument here is that the 'colonial imposition of European systems in Africa undermined the traditional empowering structures of African women's socio-cultural systems,' (Amadiume 1995:37). Thus, by imposing and reinforcing 'patriarchal systems' colonial rule 'compounded the woes of African women by (further) augmenting their ordinary burdens with those of their Western sisters' (Oduyoye 1995:80). This was made possible, according to Lebeuf-Anne, 'by a habit of thought deeply rooted in Western mind (in which) women are neglected to the sphere of domestic tasks and private life, and men alone are considered equal to the task of shouldering the burden of public affairs (Lebeuf-Anne 1962: 93).

Implicit in the above is that colonialism 'corroded the privileged life of the African women' (Acholonu 1995:3). Since 'the question of *choice* is very central to the issue of women's status in traditional Africa,' (Ibid: 54) 'the presentation of the African woman as oppressed, suppressed by a male dominated culture, and with a status subordinate to that of the man, is a dangerous misinterpretation of the true state of affairs....' (Ibid: 2-3).

Let us pause for a while and examine some of the issues raised above and ask, to what extent they represent what should be our concern as pursuants of gender equity. One of the major flaws of the compensatory history or *herstory* project, like many other *African discourses*, is that of overgeneralization. The impression is usually created that there is a *uniform* cultural practice among pre-colonial African societies. We must acknowledge that 'there are many and not one African community. There are numerous communities on the vast continent of Africa which have lived in self-contained isolation, under varying conditions of life and experience' (Bussia 1975:147). Consequently, one can expect almost different status for women in different African communities. For instance, it would be totally incorrect to expect that the status of women in matrilineal societies was the same in patriarchal societies. I am not saying that these cultural practices were good in themselves. All I am saying is that some of them had been with us before we were colonised and so attributing them to colonialism would be a falsification of historical facts. Yet many such misrepresentations of the traditional African settings have occurred, in the name of *re-writing* women history.

Furthermore, while the idea of *herstory* to point out some of the *achievements* of women in history, may help to rouse consciousness and reveal past errors and oversights, such 'compensatory histories' have not shown any paradigmatic shift or alternative to the dominant discourse. In fact, what it has done is to further legitimise the already existing historiography; a historiography accused of male-domination or male-centred. In other words, the *herstory* project, with all its claim to *correct* a suppose prejudiced history, still remains within the paradigm of the traditional conventional history. Whenever women appeared in those stories, it was only the names of women whom great men loved or those who could enter fields customarily reserved for upper class men (Ahikire 1994:7) like Cleopatra of Egypt, Amina of Zaria, Efusetan of Ibadan, and so on.

By implication, what such historiography tells is simply that *women are capable of doing those things men have done*. Or as it has almost become customary to put it: *what a man can do, a woman can (also) do*. Funmilayo Ransome-Kuti, is the first Nigerian woman to ride a motor car', is an example of this kind of history.' By taking this rather *defeatist* position, feminist scholars and activists unconsciously (perhaps) submitted themselves to the same masculinist standard of measuring achievements. And in that case, they are left with little than search for parallels in the activities of a handful of women and their men counterparts, which leaves them with one conclusion: 'we can also do it' usually punctuated with 'if given the chance'. If the *herstory* project must achieve its ambitious goals (assuming this is desirable) it must transcend the existing paradigm and give us an alternative historiography.

There is also the danger that the methodology of gender discourse in the last millennium had the tendency of abstracting women or womanhood as 'a cat-egory, frozen in time and isolated from general historical developments' (Ahikire 1994:10). Yet, the 'women question' in Africa, as elsewhere, can hardly be 'di-vorced from the realities of local and international economic relations' (CLO 1991:24) which affect both men and women one way or the other. The impres-sion that 'women as women, have been oppressed throughout history' (Bello, 1985:24) has further raised the question of whether or not 'history is not in fact a succession of class oppression and revolution'. Are women not an integral part of these classes? Has there been no qualitative change in the position of classes in general and women (as members of classes) in particular?' (Bello 1985:24)

Furthermore, a separate woman's history will only 'stress stereotypes. One of such stereotypes is the conception of women as victims of this or that system' (Ahikire 1994:6) giving the erroneous impression that *women have never fought back and have never been effective social agents on behalf of themselves* (Harding 1987). This implicitly presents women as a docile group marked out in every society for op-pression. Not even the attempts to acknowledge the role of women in liberation struggles have helped matters in this respect. This is because in such accounts, 'women are defined as having 'contributed' to this or that movements - as if they are contributing to something that exists/existed independent of them ... as though they are contributing to a project to which they do not have an intrinsic stake' (Ahikire 1994:89). Conceptualising women as 'contributing, participating or being manipulated' denotes a kind of separation between women and society, and this itself is grounded within the premise that primarily defines women as the 'other' (Ahikire 1994:89).

It is therefore doubtful if the *herstory* project has not in fact worsened 'the woman quest' in more ways than one. At the level of theory for instance, it has led to the continuous 'marginalisation' of women studies from the 'main-stream' social science. At the level of policy and practice, there has equally been the marginalisation of women's interests as represented in the so called 'women projects', isolated from the rest of development planning, poorly funded and, in the words of Ayesha Imam (1990:243), scarcely taken seriously.

Globalisation, Neo-liberalism and the Nigerian Woman

The concept, globalisation, is slippery and multi-vocal; 'used in so many different contexts, by so many different people, for so many different purposes, that it is difficult to ascertain what is at stake in the globalisation problematics, what function the term serves, and what effects it has for contemporary theory and politics' (Kellner 1998:23). In the economic sense, globalisation could mean the creation of a 'world market' where commodities in one part of the *globe* can easily get to other parts. It is thus a 'social process in which constraints of geography on social and cultural arrangements recede and in which people become aware that they are receding' (Waters 1995:3). In this context, globalisation implies 'that there has occurred an increase in the density of contacts between locations worldwide; that our life is structured in such a way that social interactions are embedded in global networks' (Axtmann 1998:2). It means, in other words, the absence of local as distinct from the universal or the national from the international. There is interface of everything with every other thing, of values against values, of distance in context of distances, of histories in context of histories, of *their* worlds against *ours*.

This *reconfiguration of space and temporal shrinking of the world,* 'has made the identification of boundaries and associated notions of 'here' and 'there', 'far' and 'near', 'outside' and 'inside', home' and 'away', 'them' and 'us'-more problematic than ever' (Scholte 1996:49). Whichever way one views it however, one thing that remains obvious is that globalisation 'is strengthening the dominance of a world capitalist economic system, supplanting the primacy of the nation-state by transnational corporations and organisations, and eroding local cultures and traditions through global culture' (Kellner 1998:23). To put the matter another way, *globalisation* is only an intellectual distraction, the displacement of the earlier focus by scholars of the South, especially in the *cold war* eras, on 'the domination of the developing countries by the developed ones, or of national and local economies by transnational corporations'. Globalisation is a cover up for 'part of a discourse of neo-imperialism that serves to obscure the continuing exploitation of much of the world by a few super powers and giant transnational corporations, thus cloaking some of the more barbaric and destructive aspects of contemporary development' (Kellner 1998:25). One instrument that has sustained this domination is the neo-liberal economic policies forced on the less developed nations by the North-dominated International Monetary Fund (IMF) and World Bank among other international finance institutions (IFIs). That unequal exchange sustained by globalisation has led to social dislocation in Nigeria, and more importantly, that it has further worsened the economic conditions of women, is the concern of this paper. It is to this that I shall now turn.

Though Nigeria formally introduced the structural adjustment programme (SAP) in 1986, it has always pursued dependent-capitalist or neo-liberal economic policies. The four 'National Development Plans' as well as the 'rolling plans' preceding SAP placed high premium on 'market and private initiatives' rather than public investments. By the time SAP was introduced, the Nigerian economy was in a bad shape and the expectation was that SAP would ensure 'national economic stabilisation and recovery through the simultaneous liberalisation of the market and the retrenchment of the state (Olukoshi and Agbu 1996:80). Nigeria's 'plummeting oil revenue was jeopardising the country's economic stability'. Thus devaluation was expected to boost 'government's Naira revenue in the short term'. Given Nigeria's precarious relationship with its creditors, it was felt that 'debt rescheduling would be acceptable to its creditors only under conditions defined clearly in an adjustment program'. Persuaded 'that the state intervention approach was not an effective development strategy', Nigerian policy makers concluded that a new development strategy that would turn 'away from government-led growth-was now most desirable' (Faruqee 1994:244). However, experience showed that the magic did not work and that SAP was destined to fail. The indices that could make it succeed do not exist in Nigeria.

Nigeria's economy falls short of the conditions that could make a country benefit from either the devaluation of its currency or liberalisation of its economy, the two major components of SAP. In the first place, the *demand* and *supply* of Nigeria's export produce are not *elastic*. The country's export goods cannot respond spontaneously to increase in demand. Secondly, Nigerian economy could not locally meet the domestic demands for some basic capital goods and services needed by the country. If it did, it would have ensured that whatever gains were made through the economies of large scale production were not 'recaptured', to borrow from Samir Amin, by the international market in the form of importation of needed capitals and services by Nigerians.

The sharp decline in Nigeria's economic fortune as well as the quality of life after SAP was introduced, was such that even the World Bank's acknowledged its failure. In its impact assessment of SAP in Nigeria, the Bank notes for instance that:

> Based on the World Bank Atlas Methodology GNP per capita (in Nigeria) in 1985 was estimated at some US$760... about twice the average for sub-Saharan Africa. However, with the drop in oil prices and the sharp devaluation of the Naira in 1986 to correct for its previous overvaluation, per capita GNP fell to US$370 in 1987 and it is expected to be about US$280 in 1988 and US$230 in 1989, as the effect of the exchange rate depreciation is more fully reflected in the factor for converting the Naira value of GNP into U.S. dollars (World Bank 1988:2)

Of course the obvious implication of the above is that within two years of the introduction of SAP, Nigeria's GNP had gone down by half of the pre-SAP period. SAP thus failed to 'stem decline in the country's fortunes and restore the economy to the path of growth'. It probably could not have been otherwise, especially since massive and repeated devaluation of the naira, the liberalisation of prices, interest rates and trade, and spirited efforts by the State, to curb public expenditures and recover costs, aided further decimation of the national manu-facturing capacity (International IDEA 2000:93).

It was at this stage that women became perhaps, not the intended but the first target of the adverse effects of SAP in Nigeria. Certain underlining assumptions which have informed the general positioning of the woman in the Nigerian soci-ety have been responsible for the fate women suffered under SAP and it would be necessary to highlight them in the course of this paper. First, there is the traditionally held view that 'women's role was domiciliary and procreative' (Alele-Williams 1988). Second, the custom of most Nigerian communities, privilege the male child over his female counterparts, and so, when the choice is to be made between for instance, educating the male child and the female, the boy child gets it. Third, because, formal education has become the major determinant of ones placement in the employment ladder, women, being the least educated, (though not the least intelligent) are mostly 'found at the lowest rung of occupational ladder' (Mbanefoh 1995). Therefore, 'in spite of the fact that women are found in virtually all professions in Nigeria, they remain underrepresented at the top management level' (Ibid.).

The implications of the foregoing for women under a liberal economy, where 'rolling back the state' is a major policy guideline, are many. First, when there is any need for retrenchment, the first targeted groups are usually the junior level workers who are mostly women. Second, the withdrawal of subsidies from kero-sene, the main cooking gas in the cities, forced many low-income families to resort to charcoal as alternative to kerosene. Coal cooking is not only tedious, it is equally hazardous for the coal has to be worked throughout the cooking. Several women and children were reportedly killed in the several fire outbreaks at filling stations where they had gone in search of the commodity that became scarce.

Perhaps, the most profound of these impacts which has not been given adequate attention is in the way the number of female candidates admitted into higher institutions dropped immediately after the introduction of SAP. For instance in the 1982/83 academic session, the enrolment figure for female students was 42 per cent, 35 per cent, and 26 per cent for University of Ife and University of Benin, respectively. However, by the 1986/87 session, the percentage dropped to 23 per cent and 28 per cent, respectively. In fact, while the total female enrolment into 21 Federal Government-owned universities in the 1982/83 academic session was 23,855 representing 24 per cent, the percentage went down to 23 per cent in the 1986/87 session. The gap is higher when one considers the figure at the postgraduate level. The implication of this to the question of gender justice is quite obvious and, I think, one issue that must be covered by gender scholarship in this millennium.

The African woman has been a victim of a rather anti-feminist belief system that places more premium on the proper upbringing of the male child, at the expense of his female counterpart. The male child is seen in many African societies as the bearer of the 'family name', the heir apparent. He is the one who will carry forth the name of the family to subsequent generations and so immortalise the lineage. The female child, on the other hand, is more or less a temporary member of the family, who, soon becomes a member of her would-be husband's family. Whatever resources expended on training her is thus seen as a waste. The consequence of this is that less attention is paid to the education of the female child compared to the male counterpart. One implication of this for the question of gender equality, is that with literacy increasingly becoming 'a requirement for jobs, illiterate women who were denied educational opportunities in early life are' almost automatically, 'being displaced from employment opportunities' (Rathgeber 1992:18).

The African Regional Studies Program (1994:18) observed that 'men and women play different roles and face different constraints in responding to economic policy changes and to shifts in relative prices and incentives'. This point, said to be overlooked by scholars and anti-feminist literature, was equally elaborated on by the 1990 Report of a Commonwealth Expert Group on Women and Structural Adjustment. The Report highlighted women's disproportionate suffering from the debt crisis and adjustment policies, not only as producers and workers in formal sector employment, but also as reproducers who have been forced to provide private and individual basic health and other social services formerly provided by the State (Commonwealth Secretariat 1990).

The aftermath of these is that women have less time to engage in profitable ventures. With women's reduced access to regular formal employment, 'the gender division of labour in household economy' is further 'strengthened ' (Ibid.).

Consequently, women and girls are forced 'to work harder in unpaid household work, casual employment and highly exploitative forms of self employed cottage industry' (Ibid.).

Another remarkable development from this is the way 'sexual works' have become one of the major sources of higher income for many women. Thus, prostitution among girls has been increasing. At the same time even many married 'women prostitute themselves on a part-time basis to bosses, teachers and other 'big' men in exchange for gifts of food, clothing, or an outing at one of the night clubs which flourish in all urban cities' (Ibid.). It could be that bad. Rathgeber has almost an exhaustive and graphic presentation of *what have become the lots* of the African woman in the face of the deepening crisis of economic adjustment in Africa:

> Women in developing countries (now) work longer hours, earn less money, have greater responsibilities, are less literate and numerate and have lower caloric intake in proportion to body weight than do men. In countries and among social groups where there are few opportunities to escape from poverty women usually have none. In situations where everyone must work long hours to secure sufficient income to provide basic needs, women must work even longer for they are faced not only with the necessity to contribute to household income but also must undertake all or most of the reproductive labour, including bearing and caring for children, preparation of food, looking after the elderly, nursing the sick and the multitude of other tasks that are labeled 'women work' in most parts of the world (Rathgeber 1992:11).

When Tomorrow Comes

Let me conclude by suggesting that in the new millennium, our quest for gender-equity should acknowledge that while women-men relations are important, our research should focus more on the girl-boy relationship. In other words, it is not just women and men, but girls and boys who participate and are affected by economic adjustment policies differently. It is needless concentrating our researches on the effects of the globalisation of the neo-liberal economic values on adults at the expense of children. The girl child should be accorded equal status as the woman in our studies if gender-justice research must achieve one of its major goals of bringing sex-based injustices to the realm of public discourse. Therefore as the *state is painfully being rolled back in Africa, our policy makers should remember the most vulnerable of the vulnerable group in our society, the GIRL CHILD.*

References

Acholonu, C., 1995, *Motherism: The Afrocentric Alternative to Feminism*, Alfa Publications, Owerri.

African Regional Studies Program of the World Bank, 1994, 'Gender and Economic Adjustment in Sub-Saharan Africa: Findings', *Africa Technical Development*, No. 19, June.

Ahikire, J., 1994, 'Bringing Women Bank In: A Search for Alternative Historiographies', *Quest: Philosophical Discussions*, Vol. VIII, No. 2, December.

Akumadu, T., 1985, 'Patterns of Abuse of Women's Rights in Employment and Police Custody in Nigeria', *Liberty*, Lagos: Civil Liberty Organisation.

Allen, J., 1976, 'Aba Riots or the Igbo Women's War? Ideology, Stratification and the Invisibility of Women', in Hafkin & Bay, eds., *Women in Africa*, Stanford: Stanford University Press.

Amadiume, I., 1995, 'Gender, Political Systems and Social Movements: West African Experience' in Mamdani, M. and Wamba-dia-Wamba, E.,eds., *African Studies in Social Movements and Democracy*, Dakar: CODESRIA.

Aristotle, 1952, *Politics*, London: Penguin Books Ltd.

Barbara, C. and Schildrout, E., 1986, 'Law, Education and Social Change: Implications for Hausa Muslim Women in Nigeria' in Iglitzin, L. & Ross, R., eds., *Women in the World, 1975–1985*, Santa Barbara: ABC CLIO Inc.

Bay, E., ed., 1982, *Women and Work in Africa*, Colorado: Westview Press.

Bello, S., 1985, 'Problems of Theory and Practice in Women's Liberation Movements' in *Women in Nigeria Today*, London: Zed Books Ltd.

Beneria, L., 1981, 'Conceptualising the Labour Force: The under-estimation of women's economic activities' in Nelson, N., ed., *African Women in Development Process*, London:Frank Cass.

Bussia, K., 1975, 'The African World-View' in Drachler, J., ed., *African Heritage: An Anthology of Black African Personality and Culture*, London: Collier Macmillan Publishers.

CLO, 1991, 'State of Africa's Women', *Liberty*, Civil Liberties Organisation, Lagos, June-August.

Commonwealth Secretariat, 1990, *Report of a Commonwealth Expert Group on Women and Structural Adjustment*. London: Commonwealth Secretariat.

Harding, S. and Hintikka, M., eds., 1983, 'Introduction', *Discovering Reality: Feminist Perspectives on Epistemology, Metaphysics, Methodology, and Philosophy of Science*, Dordrecht: Reidel Publishing Company.

Harding S., ed., 1987, 'Introduction: Is There a Feminist Method?' in *Feminism and Methodology*, Bloomington: Indiana University Press.

Hirschmann, N., 1989, 'Freedom, Recognition and Obligation: A Feminist Approach to Political Theory', *American Political Science Review*, Vol. 83, No. 4., December.

Ihimodu, I., 1996, *The Impact of the Better Life Programme on the Economic Status of Women*, Ibadan: IFRA/African Book Builders,

Imam, A., 1985, 'Towards an Adequate Analysis of the Position of Women in Society', in *Women in Nigeria Today*, London: Zed Books Ltd.

Imam, A., 1990, 'Gender Analysis and Social Sciences in the 1990s', *Africa Development*, Vol. XV, No. 3-4.

Kelly, J., 1984, *Women History and Theory*, Chicago: The University of Chicago Press.

Lebeuf, A., 1953, 'The Role of Women in Political Organisation of African Societies' in Denise, P., ed., *Women of Tropical Africa*, Berkeley: University of California Press.

Lerner, A., 1979, *The Majority Finds its Past: Placing Women in History*, Oxford: Oxford University Press.

Mansbridge, J. and Okin, S., 1996, 'Feminism' in Goodin, R. & Pettit, S., eds., *A Companion to Political Philosophy*, Oxford: Blackwell Publishers.

Mbanefoh, N., 1995, 'Women Participation in Higher Education in Nigeria, in *Women in Higher Education in Africa*, Dakar: UNESCO.

Mbiliyi, M., 1994, 'Gender and Structural Adjustment', *Paper for the Symposium on Gender and Structural Adjustment: Empowerment and Disempowerment*, Dar es Salaam, February 26.

Millet, K., 1969, *Sexual Politics*, London: Virago.

Mohammed, H., 1980, 'Women in Nigerian History: Examples from Borno Empire, Nupeland and Igboland', in *Women in Nigeria Today*, London: Zed Books Ltd.

Oduyoye, M., 1990, *Daughters of Anowa: African Woman & Patriarchy*, New York: Orbis Books.

Palmer, H., 1926, *Sudanese Memoirs, vol.1*, Lagos: Government Printer.

Pateman, C. and Shanley, M., eds., 1991, *Feminist Interpretations and Political Theory*, Oxford: Polity Press.

Pietela, M. *et al*, 1990, *Making Women Matter: The Role of the United Nations*, London: Zed Books.

Rathgeber, E., 1992, 'Integrating Gender into Development Research and Action: Agenda for the 1990s' *Journal of Development Studies*, Vol. viii.

Uroh, C., 1998, *Africa and the Challenge of Development*, Ibadan: Hope Publications.

Uroh, C., 2000, 'Myth and Gender Question in Africa', In Nkwi, P., ed., *The Anthropology of Africa: Challenges for 21st Century*, Yaounde: APA.

Uthman, I., 1992, *Infaq al-Maisuri*, cited in Mohammed, H., 1980, 'Women in Nigerian History: Examples from Borno Empire, Nupeland and Igboland', in *Women in Nigeria Today*, London: Zed Books Ltd.

The Publisher

The **Council for the Development of Social Science Research in Africa** (CODESRIA) is an independent organisation whose principal objectives are facilitating research, promoting research-based publishing and creating multiple forums geared towards the exchange of views and information among African researchers. It challenges the fragmentation of research through the creation of thematic research networks that cut across linguistic and regional boundaries.

CODESRIA publishes a quarterly journal, *Africa Development*, the longest standing Africa-based social science journal; *Afrika Zamani*, a journal of history; the *African Sociological Review, African Journal of International Affairs (AJIA), Africa Review of Books* and *Identity, Culture and Politics: An Afro-Asian Dialogue.* It co-publishes the *Journal of Higher Education in Africa* and *Africa Media Review.* Research results and other activities of the institution are disseminated through 'Working Papers', 'Monograph Series', 'CODESRIA Book Series', and the *CODESRIA Bulletin.*

www.ingramcontent.com/pod-product-compliance
Lightning Source LLC
Chambersburg PA
CBHW020000290326
41935CB00007B/249